PETER PANZERFAUST
VOLUME IV: THE HUNT

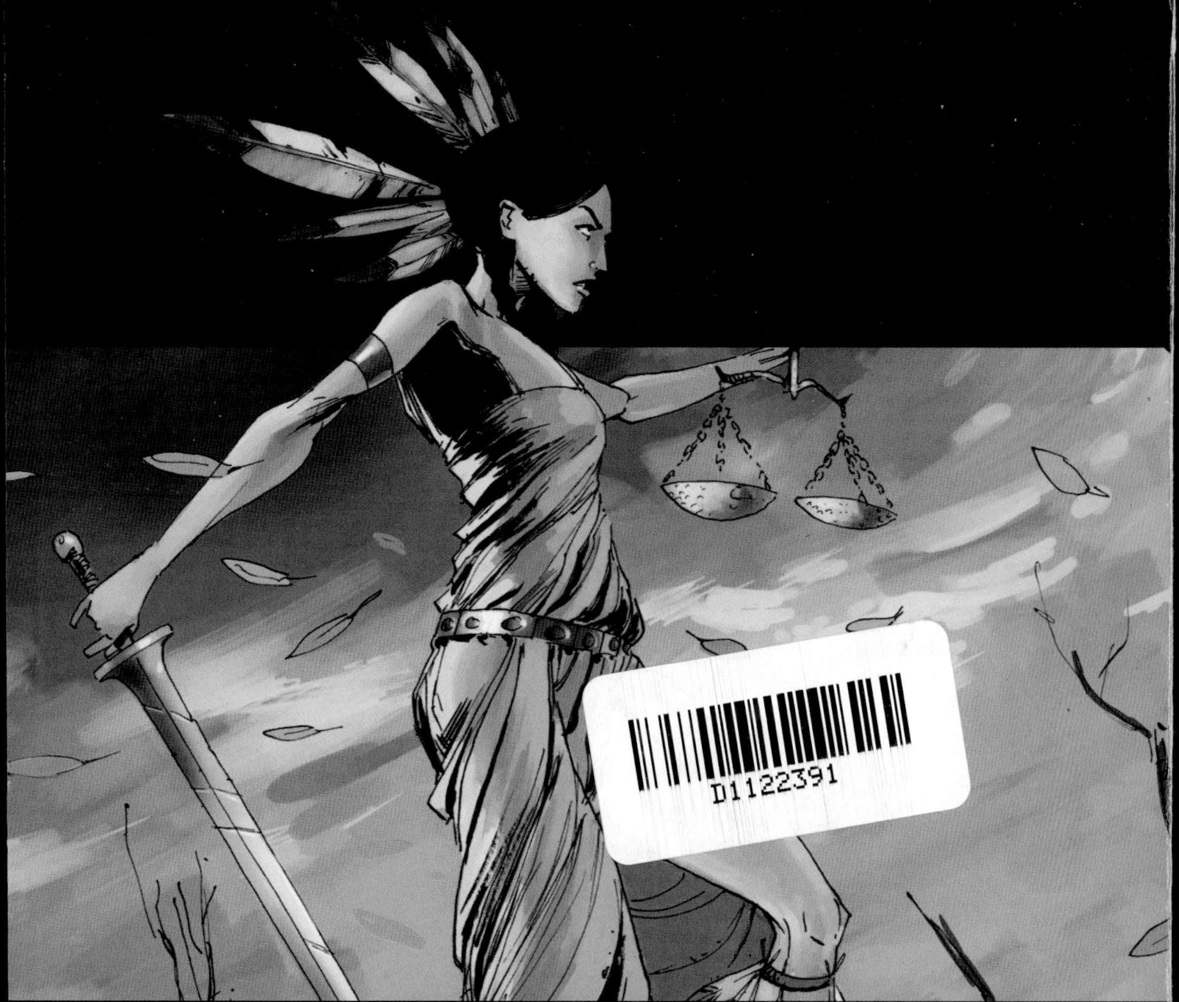

Shadowline™
image®
www.ShadowlineOnline.com

PETER PANZERFAUST VOLUME FOUR: THE HUNT

First Printing September, 2014   ISBN: 978-1-63215-062

Published by Image Comics, Inc. Office of publication: 2001 Center Street, Sixth Floor, Berkeley, California 94704. Copyright © 2014 KURTIS J. WIEBE and TYLER JENKINS. Originally published in single magazine form as PETER PANZERFAUST #16-20. All rights reserved. PETER PANZERFAUST™ (including all prominent characters featured herein), its logo and all character likenesses are trademarks of KURTIS J. WIEBE and TYLER JENKINS, unless otherwise noted. Image Comics® and its logos are registered trademarks of Image Comics, Inc. Shadowline and its logos are registered trademarks ® of Jim Valentino. No part of this publication may be reproduced or transmitted, in any form or by any means (except for short excerpts for review purposes) without the express written permission of Mr. Wiebe and/or Jenkins. All names, characters, events and locales in this publication are entirely fictional. Any resemblance to actual persons (living or dead), events or places, without satiric intent, is coincidental. Printed in the USA. For information regarding the CPSIA on this printed material call: 203-595-3636 and provide reference #RICH–572490. For international rights, contact: foreignlicensing@imagecomics.com.

image COMICS PRESENTS

CO-CREATORS

KURTIS J. WIEBE · TYLER JENKINS
WRITER   ILLUSTRATOR

KELLY FITZPATRICK
COLORS

ED BRISSON
LETTERS

LAURA TAVISHATI   MARC LOMBARDI
EDITS   COMMUNICATIONS

JIM VALENTINO
PUBLISHER
BOOK DESIGN

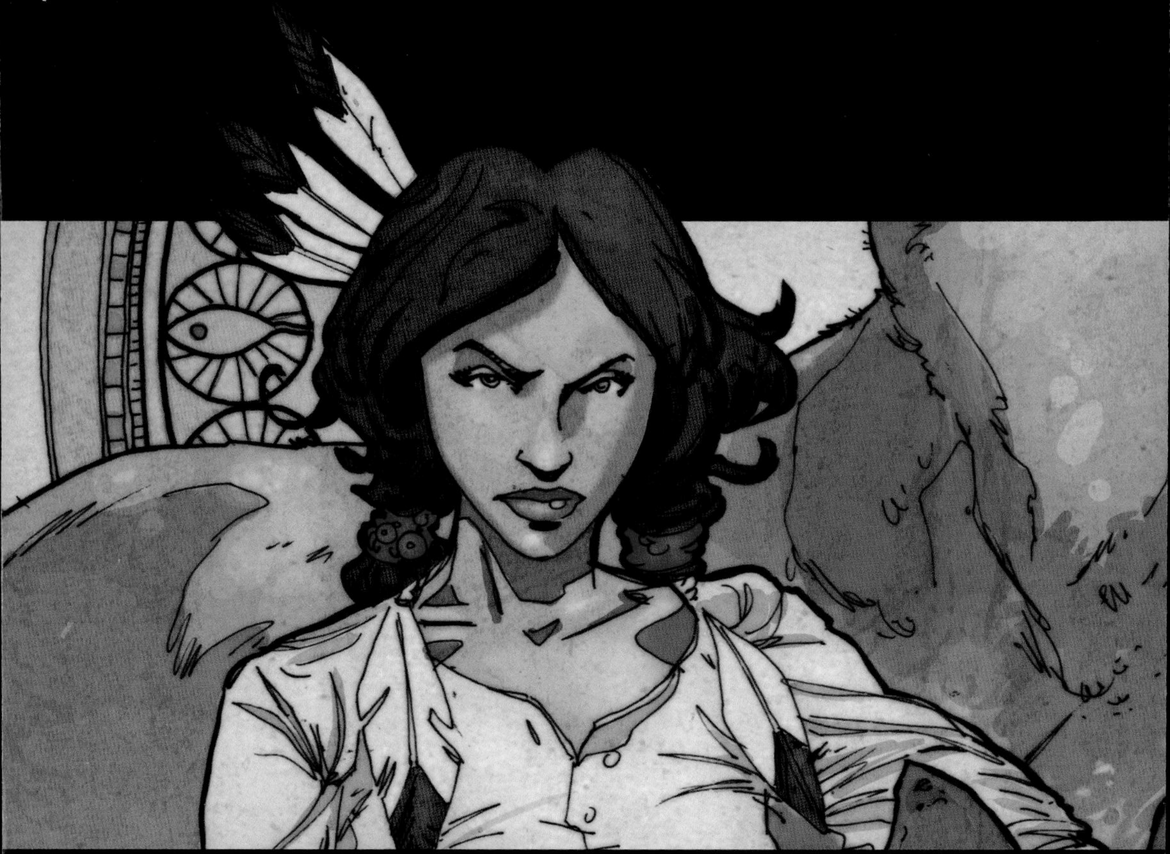

IMAGE COMICS, INC.
Robert Kirkman – Chief Operating Officer
Erik Larsen – Chief Financial Officer
Todd McFarlane – President
Marc Silvestri – Chief Executive Officer
Jim Valentino – Vice-President

Eric Stephenson – Publisher
Ron Richards – Director of Business Development
Jennifer de Guzman – Director of Trade Book Sales
Kat Salazar – Director of PR & Marketing
Jeremy Sullivan – Director of Digital Sales
Emilio Bautista – Sales Assistant
Branwyn Bigglestone – Senior Accounts Manager
Emily Miller – Accounts Manager
Jessica Ambriz – Administrative Assistant
Tyler Shainline – Events Coordinator
David Brothers – Content Manager
Jonathan Chan – Production Manager
Drew Gill – Art Director
Meredith Wallace – Print Manager
Monica Garcia – Senior Production Artist
Jenna Savage – Production Artist
Addison Duke – Production Artist
Tricia Ramos – Production Assistant
IMAGECOMICS.COM

A Shadowline™ PRODUCTION

www.ShadowlineOnline.co

Follow SHADOWLINECOMICS on FACEBOOK and TWIT

CHAPTER SIXTEEN

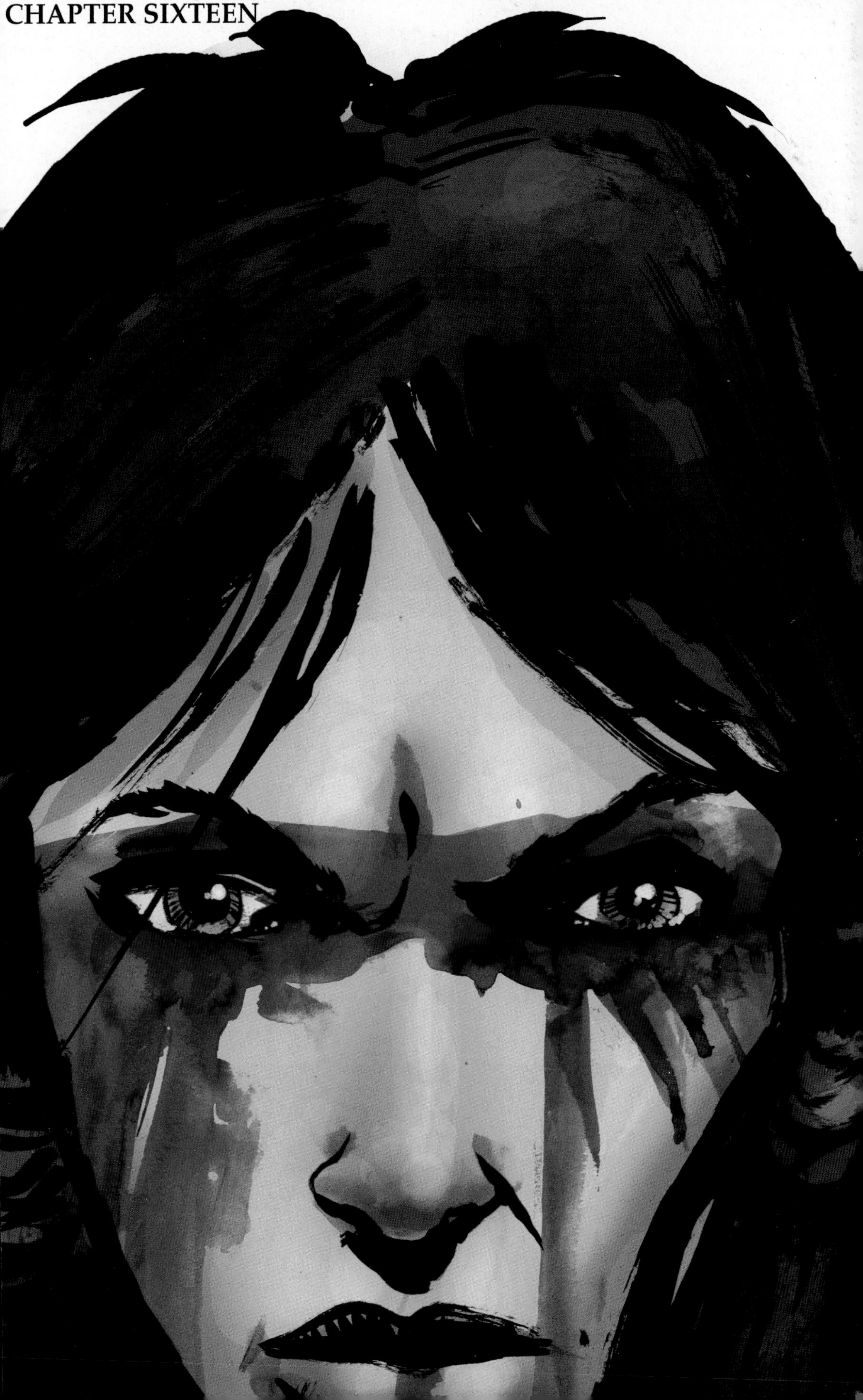

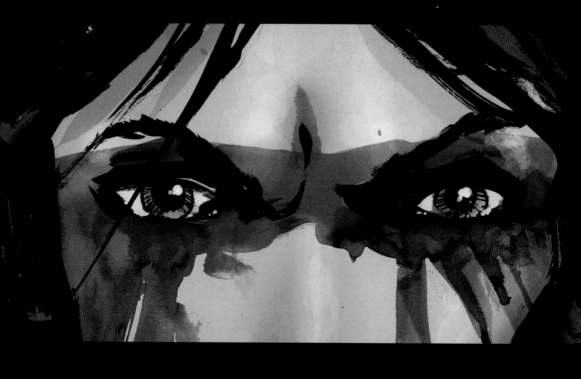

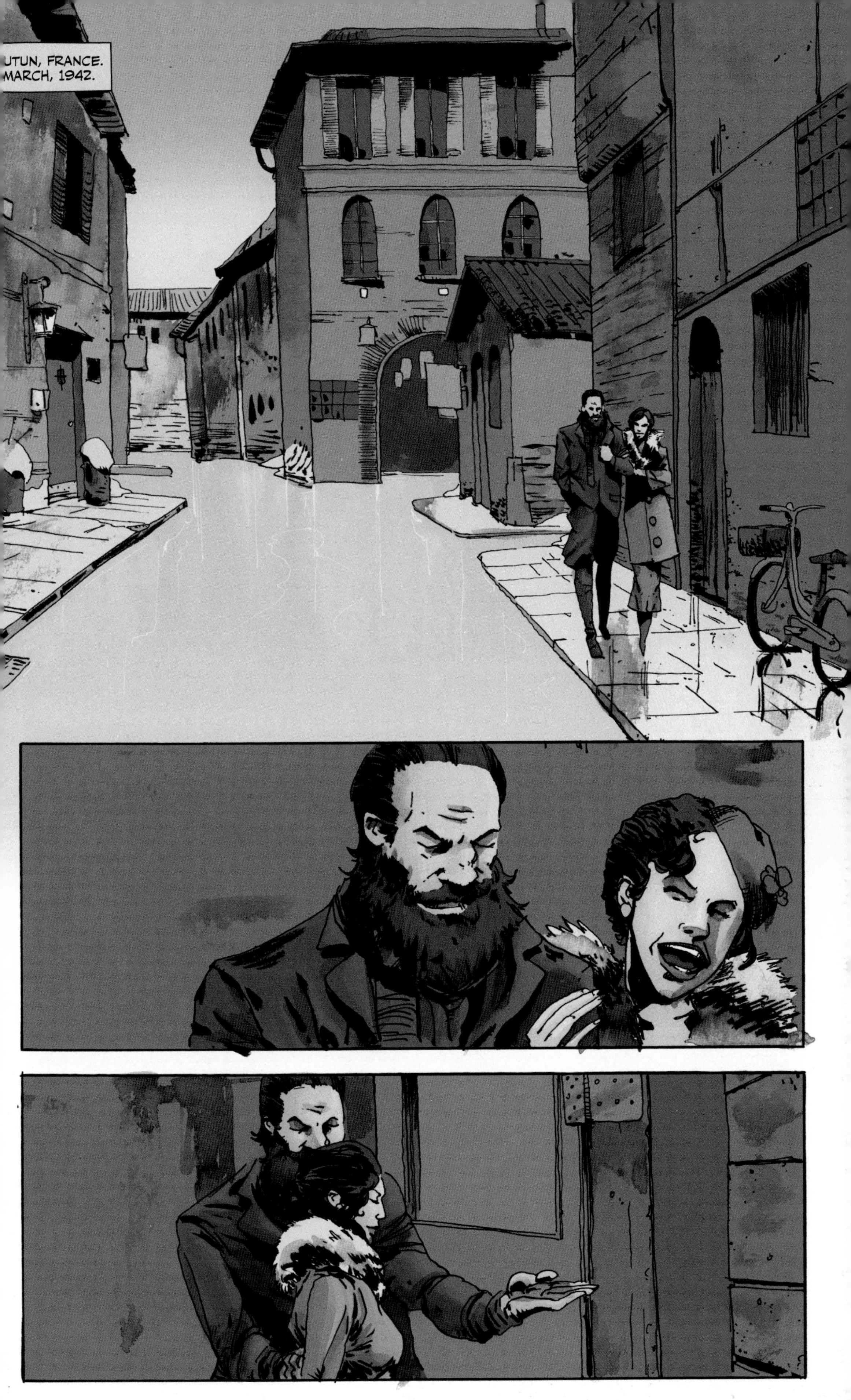
UTUN, FRANCE.
MARCH, 1942.

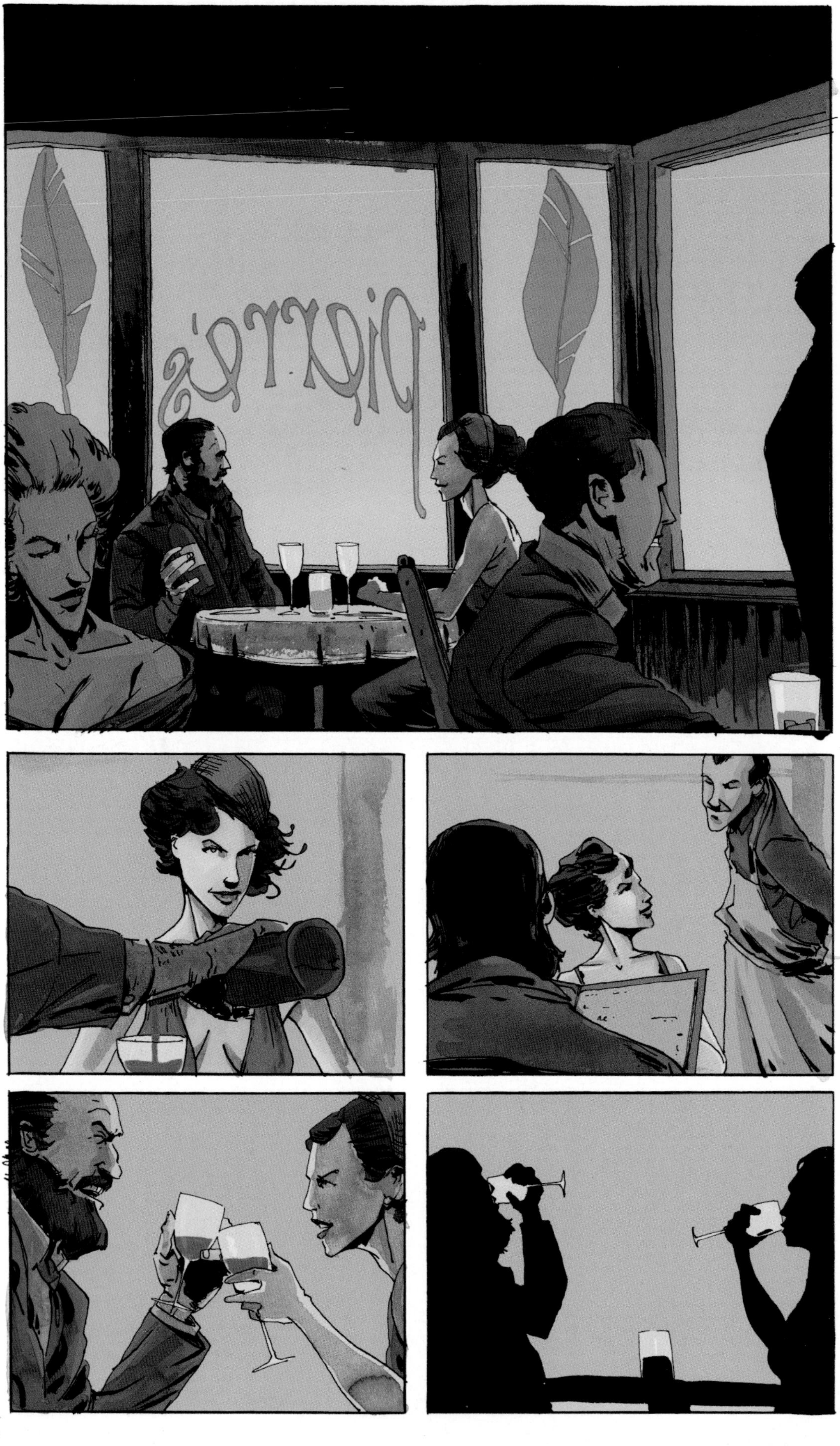
Pierre's

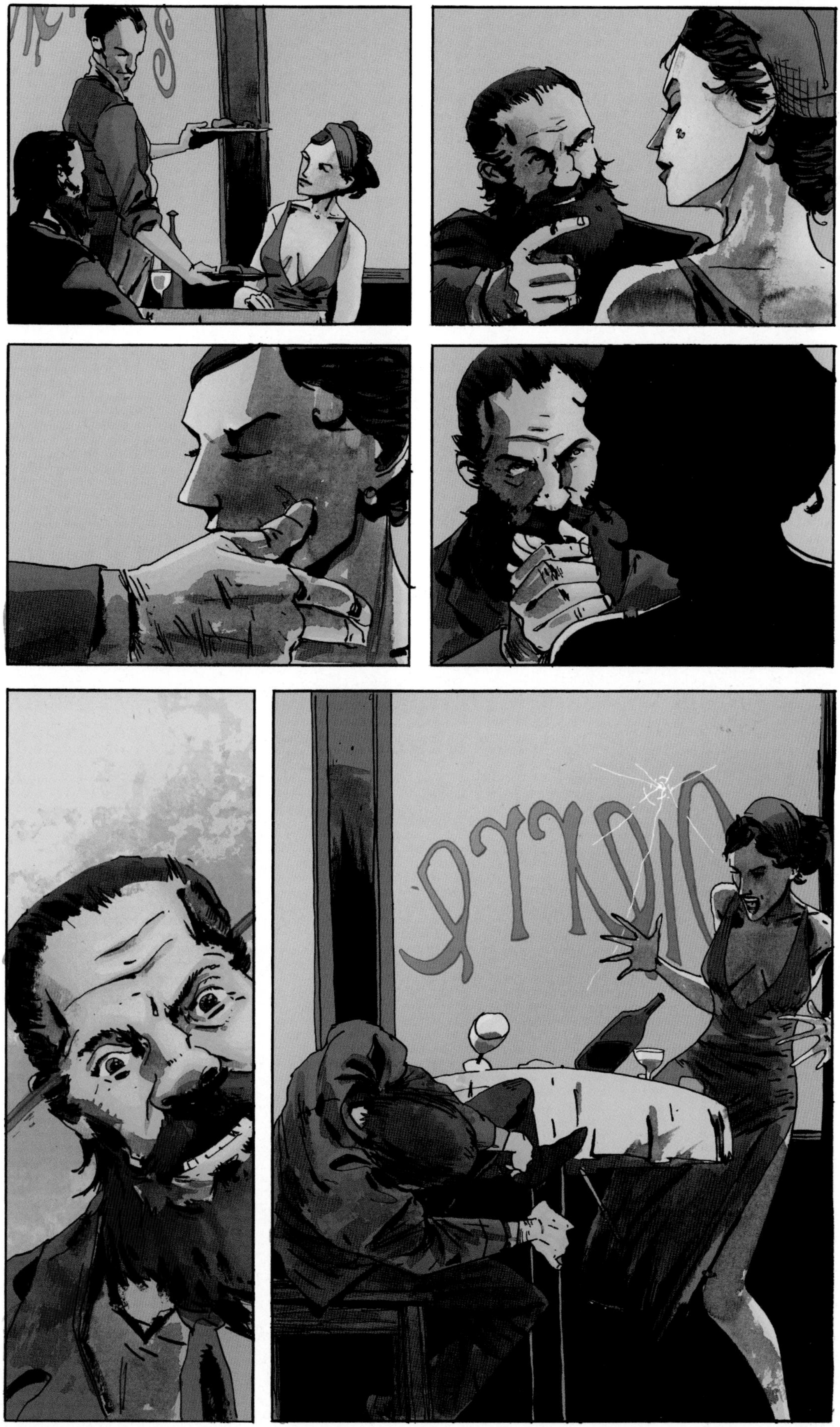

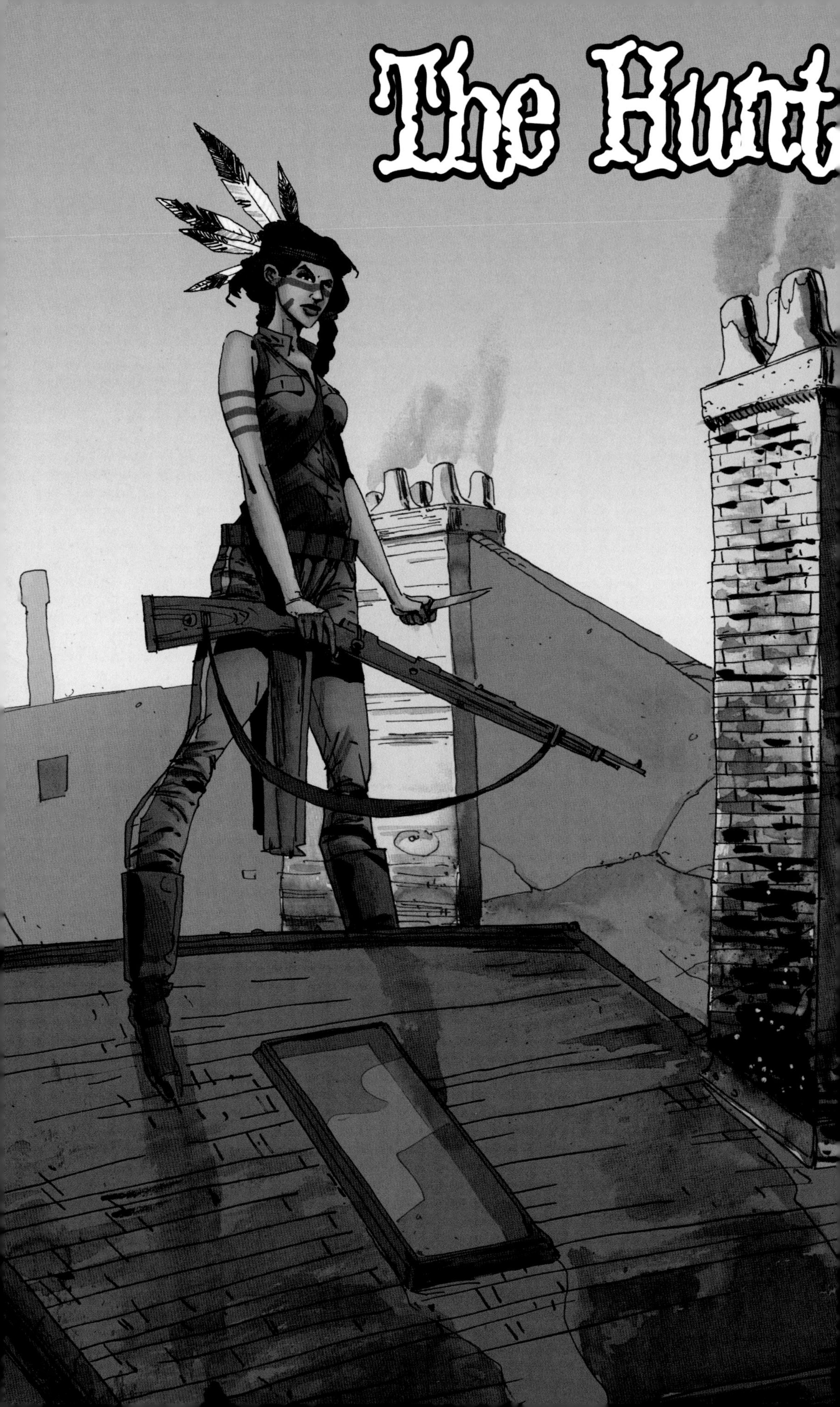
The Hunt

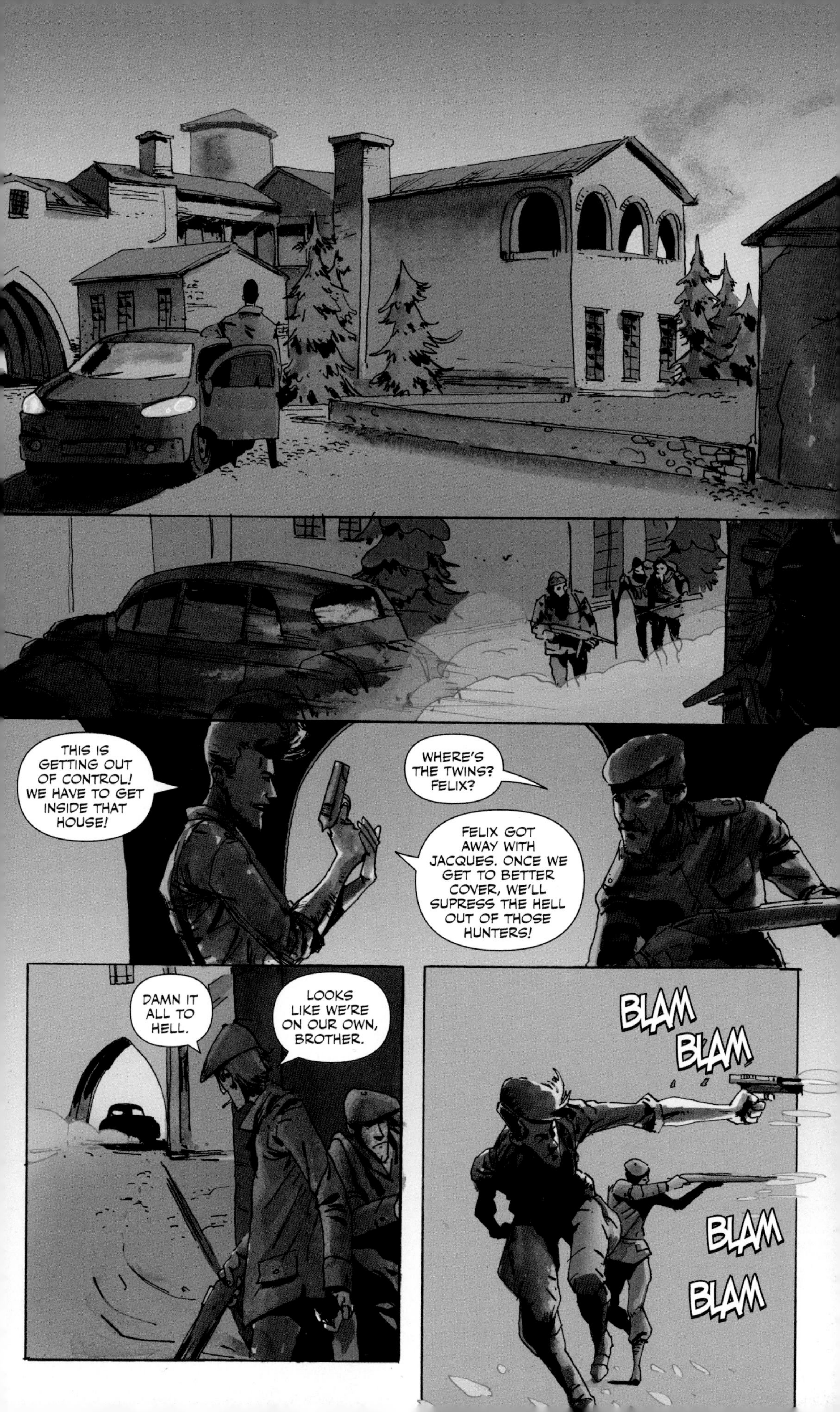

THIS IS GETTING OUT OF CONTROL! WE HAVE TO GET INSIDE THAT HOUSE!
WHERE'S THE TWINS? FELIX?
FELIX GOT AWAY WITH JACQUES. ONCE WE GET TO BETTER COVER, WE'LL SUPRESS THE HELL OUT OF THOSE HUNTERS!
DAMN IT ALL TO HELL.
LOOKS LIKE WE'RE ON OUR OWN, BROTHER.
BLAM
BLAM
BLAM
BLAM

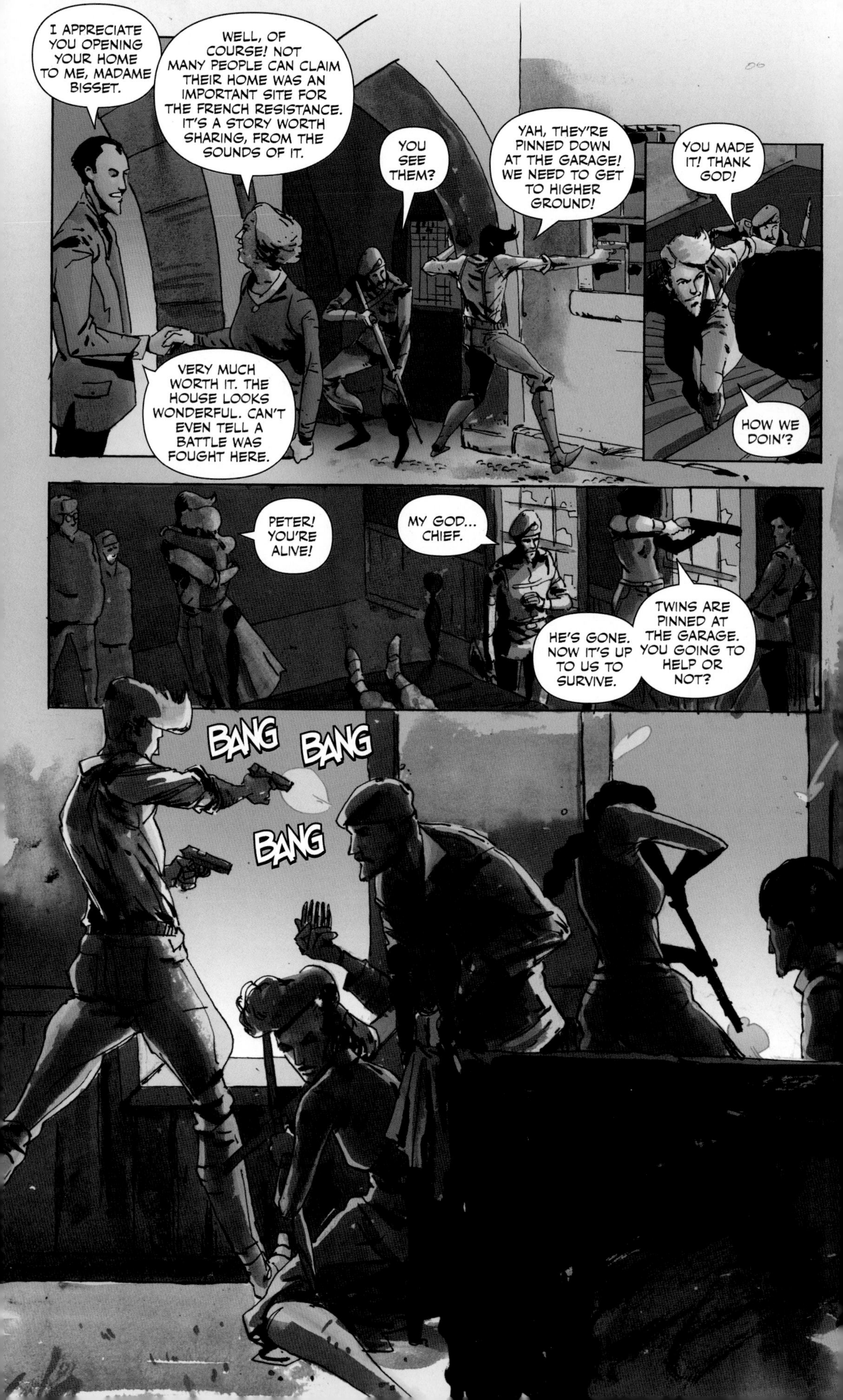
I APPRECIATE YOU OPENING YOUR HOME TO ME, MADAME BISSET.
WELL, OF COURSE! NOT MANY PEOPLE CAN CLAIM THEIR HOME WAS AN IMPORTANT SITE FOR THE FRENCH RESISTANCE. IT'S A STORY WORTH SHARING, FROM THE SOUNDS OF IT.
VERY MUCH WORTH IT. THE HOUSE LOOKS WONDERFUL. CAN'T EVEN TELL A BATTLE WAS FOUGHT HERE.
YOU SEE THEM?
YAH, THEY'RE PINNED DOWN AT THE GARAGE! WE NEED TO GET TO HIGHER GROUND!
YOU MADE IT! THANK GOD!
HOW WE DOIN'?
PETER! YOU'RE ALIVE!
MY GOD... CHIEF.
HE'S GONE. NOW IT'S UP TO US TO SURVIVE.
TWINS ARE PINNED AT THE GARAGE. YOU GOING TO HELP OR NOT?
BANG
BANG
BANG

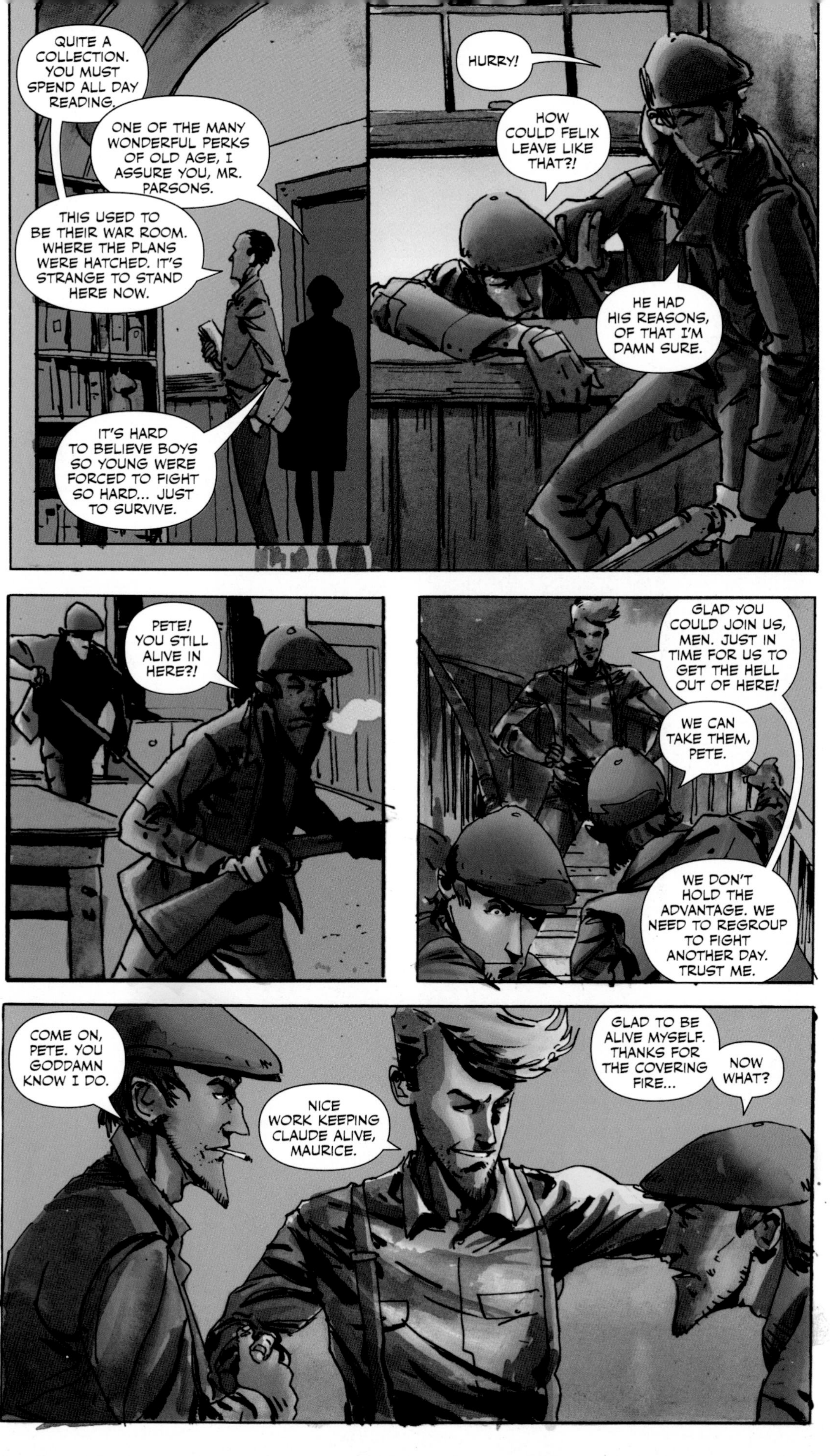
QUITE A COLLECTION. YOU MUST SPEND ALL DAY READING.
ONE OF THE MANY WONDERFUL PERKS OF OLD AGE, I ASSURE YOU, MR. PARSONS.
THIS USED TO BE THEIR WAR ROOM. WHERE THE PLANS WERE HATCHED. IT'S STRANGE TO STAND HERE NOW.
IT'S HARD TO BELIEVE BOYS SO YOUNG WERE FORCED TO FIGHT SO HARD... JUST TO SURVIVE.
HURRY!
HOW COULD FELIX LEAVE LIKE THAT?!
HE HAD HIS REASONS, OF THAT I'M DAMN SURE.
PETE! YOU STILL ALIVE IN HERE?!
GLAD YOU COULD JOIN US, MEN. JUST IN TIME FOR US TO GET THE HELL OUT OF HERE!
WE CAN TAKE THEM, PETE.
WE DON'T HOLD THE ADVANTAGE. WE NEED TO REGROUP TO FIGHT ANOTHER DAY. TRUST ME.
COME ON, PETE. YOU GODDAMN KNOW I DO.
NICE WORK KEEPING CLAUDE ALIVE, MAURICE.
GLAD TO BE ALIVE MYSELF. THANKS FOR THE COVERING FIRE...
NOW WHAT?

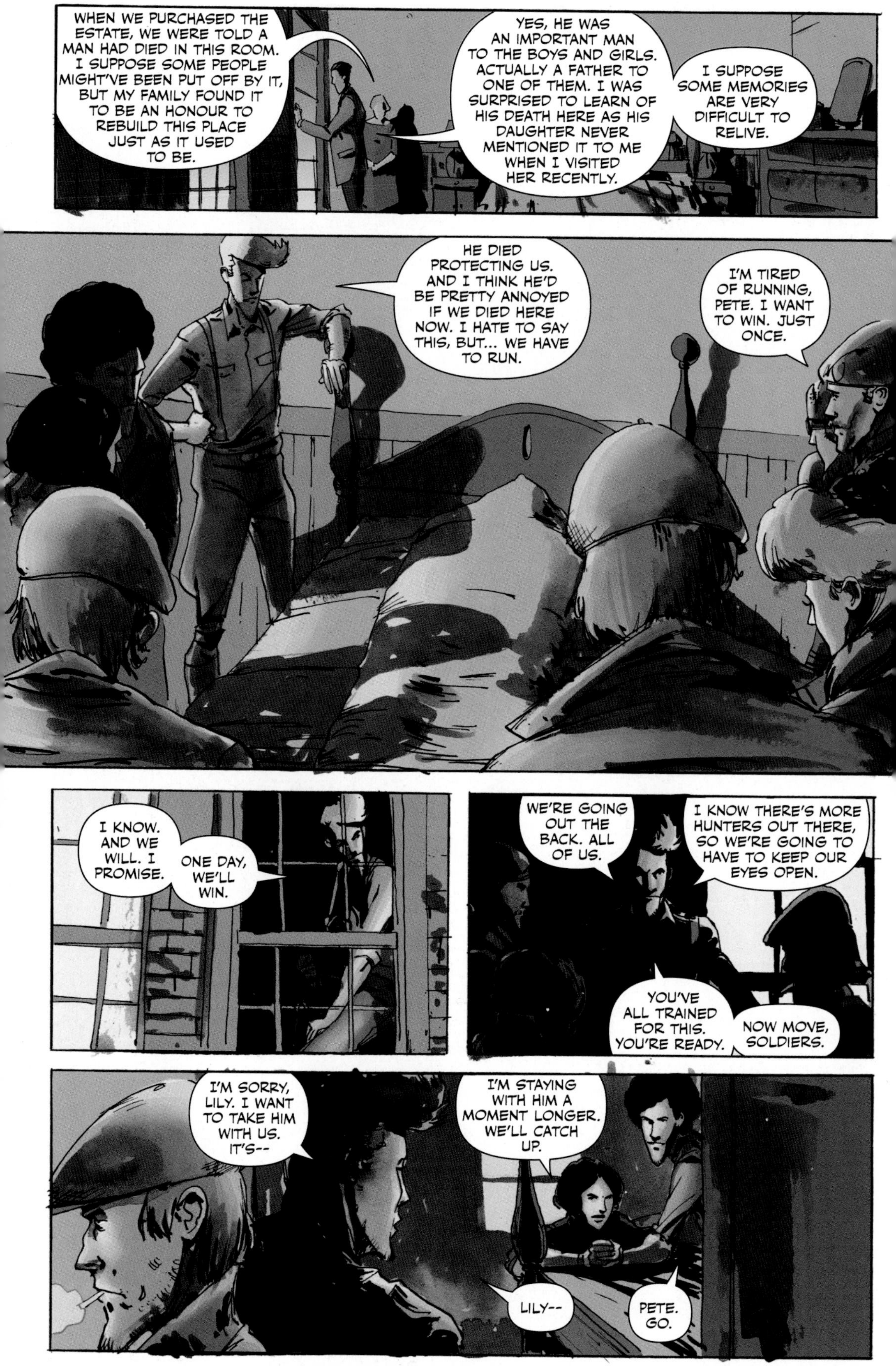
WHEN WE PURCHASED THE ESTATE, WE WERE TOLD A MAN HAD DIED IN THIS ROOM. I SUPPOSE SOME PEOPLE MIGHT'VE BEEN PUT OFF BY IT, BUT MY FAMILY FOUND IT TO BE AN HONOUR TO REBUILD THIS PLACE JUST AS IT USED TO BE.
YES, HE WAS AN IMPORTANT MAN TO THE BOYS AND GIRLS. ACTUALLY A FATHER TO ONE OF THEM. I WAS SURPRISED TO LEARN OF HIS DEATH HERE AS HIS DAUGHTER NEVER MENTIONED IT TO ME WHEN I VISITED HER RECENTLY.
I SUPPOSE SOME MEMORIES ARE VERY DIFFICULT TO RELIVE.
HE DIED PROTECTING US. AND I THINK HE'D BE PRETTY ANNOYED IF WE DIED HERE NOW. I HATE TO SAY THIS, BUT... WE HAVE TO RUN.
I'M TIRED OF RUNNING, PETE. I WANT TO WIN. JUST ONCE.
I KNOW. AND WE WILL. I PROMISE.
ONE DAY, WE'LL WIN.
WE'RE GOING OUT THE BACK. ALL OF US.
I KNOW THERE'S MORE HUNTERS OUT THERE, SO WE'RE GOING TO HAVE TO KEEP OUR EYES OPEN.
YOU'VE ALL TRAINED FOR THIS. YOU'RE READY.
NOW MOVE, SOLDIERS.
I'M SORRY, LILY. I WANT TO TAKE HIM WITH US. IT'S--
I'M STAYING WITH HIM A MOMENT LONGER. WE'LL CATCH UP.
LILY--
PETE. GO.

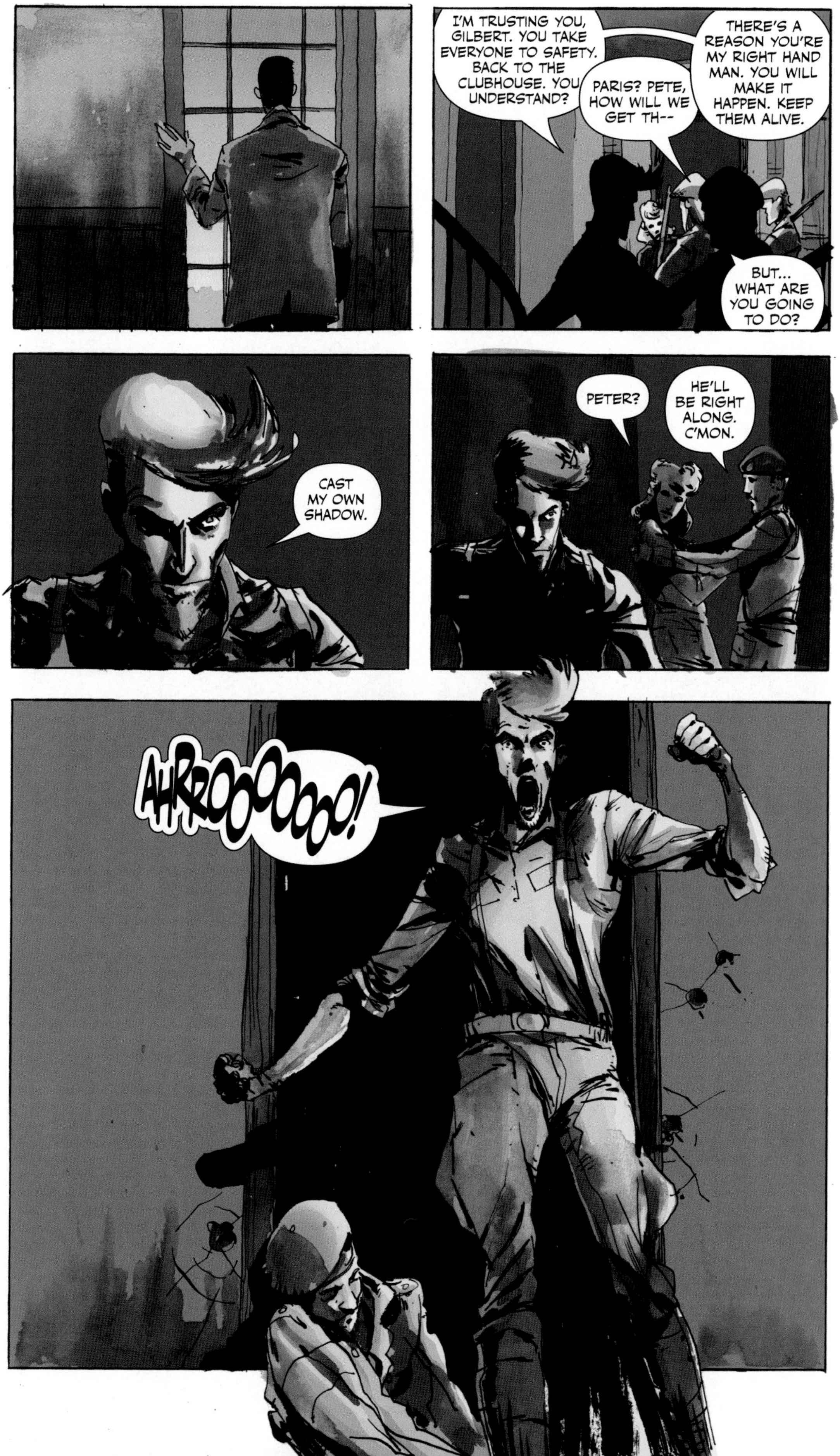
I'M TRUSTING YOU, GILBERT. YOU TAKE EVERYONE TO SAFETY. BACK TO THE CLUBHOUSE. YOU UNDERSTAND?
PARIS? PETE, HOW WILL WE GET TH--
THERE'S A REASON YOU'RE MY RIGHT HAND MAN. YOU WILL MAKE IT HAPPEN. KEEP THEM ALIVE.
BUT... WHAT ARE YOU GOING TO DO?
CAST MY OWN SHADOW.
PETER?
HE'LL BE RIGHT ALONG. C'MON.
AHRROOOOOOO!

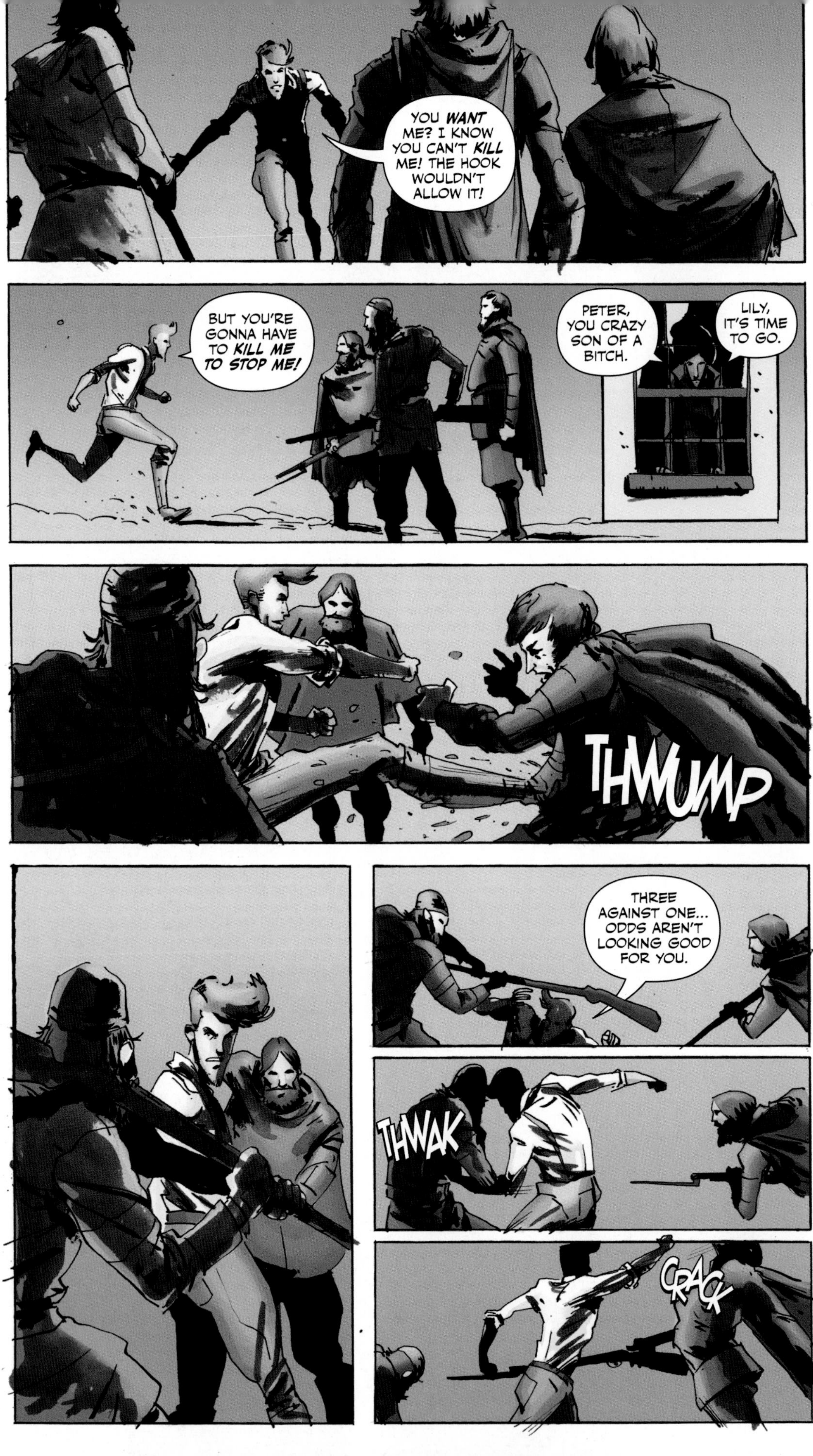
YOU *WANT* ME? I KNOW YOU CAN'T *KILL* ME! THE HOOK WOULDN'T ALLOW IT!
BUT YOU'RE GONNA HAVE TO *KILL ME TO STOP ME!*
PETER, YOU CRAZY SON OF A BITCH.
LILY, IT'S TIME TO GO.
THWUMP
THREE AGAINST ONE... ODDS AREN'T LOOKING GOOD FOR YOU.
THWAK
CRACK

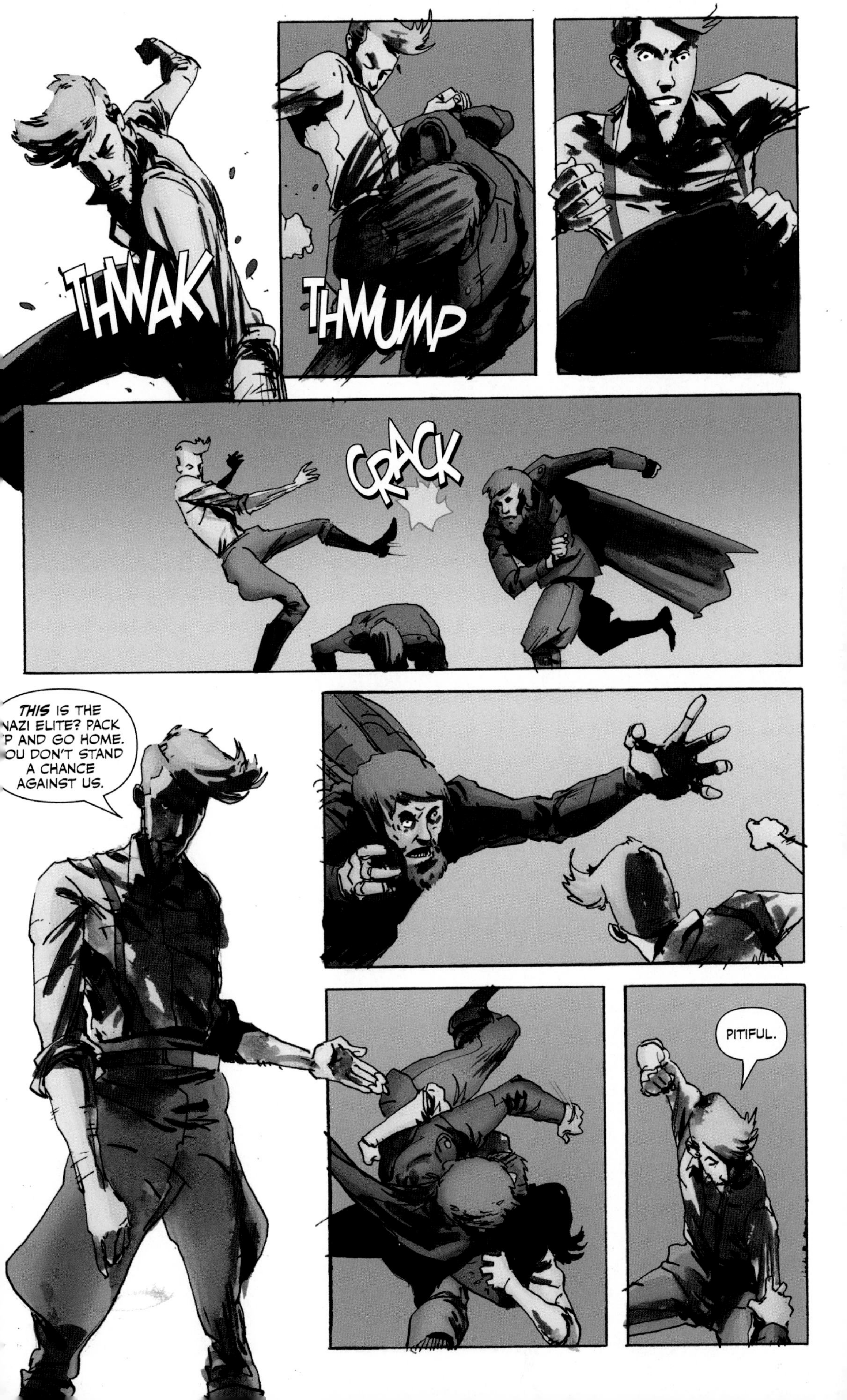
THWAK
THWUMP
CRACK
THIS IS THE NAZI ELITE? PACK UP AND GO HOME. YOU DON'T STAND A CHANCE AGAINST US.
PITIFUL.

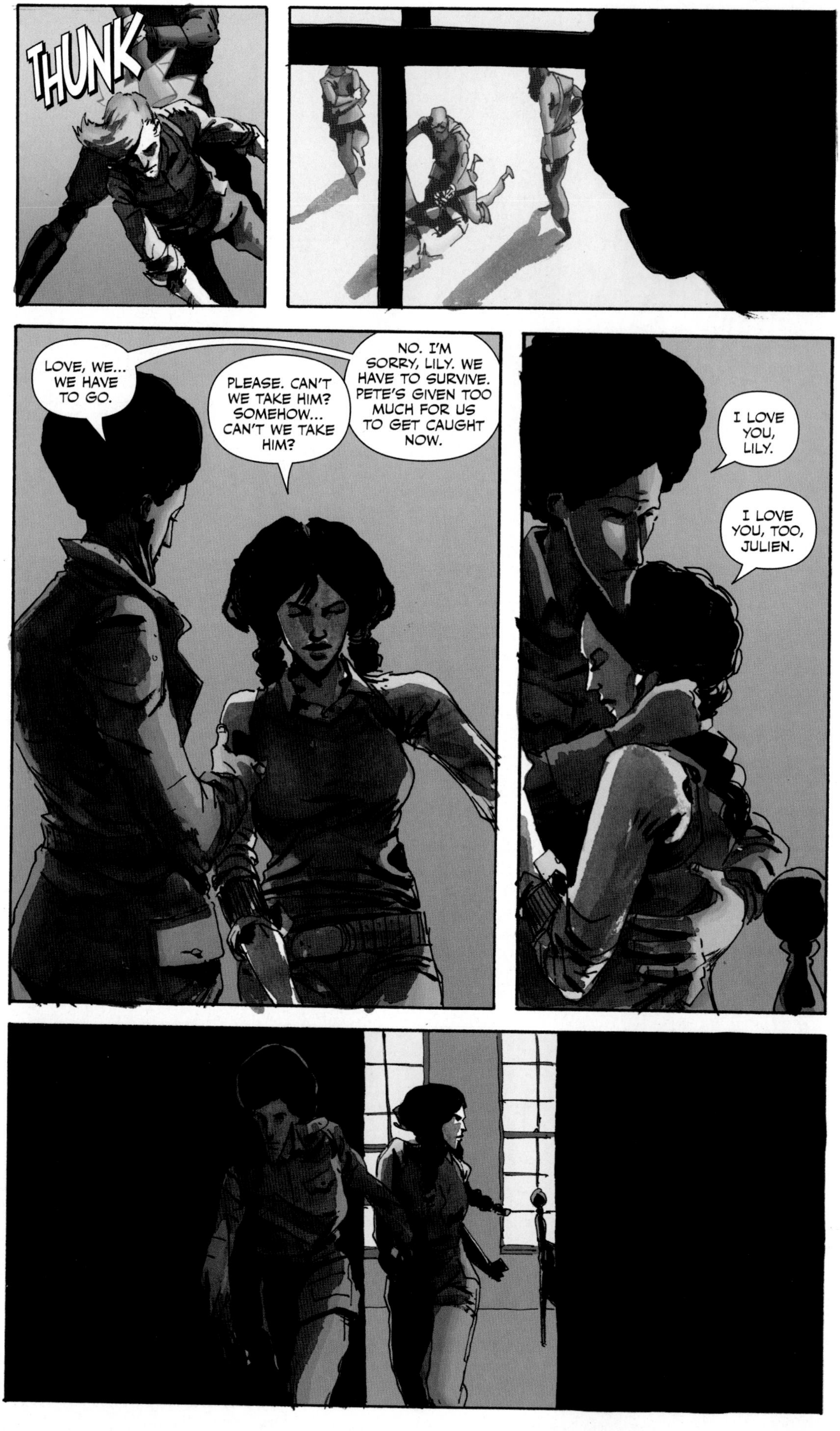
THUNK
LOVE, WE... WE HAVE TO GO.
PLEASE. CAN'T WE TAKE HIM? SOMEHOW... CAN'T WE TAKE HIM?
NO. I'M SORRY, LILY. WE HAVE TO SURVIVE. PETE'S GIVEN TOO MUCH FOR US TO GET CAUGHT NOW.
I LOVE YOU, LILY.
I LOVE YOU, TOO, JULIEN.

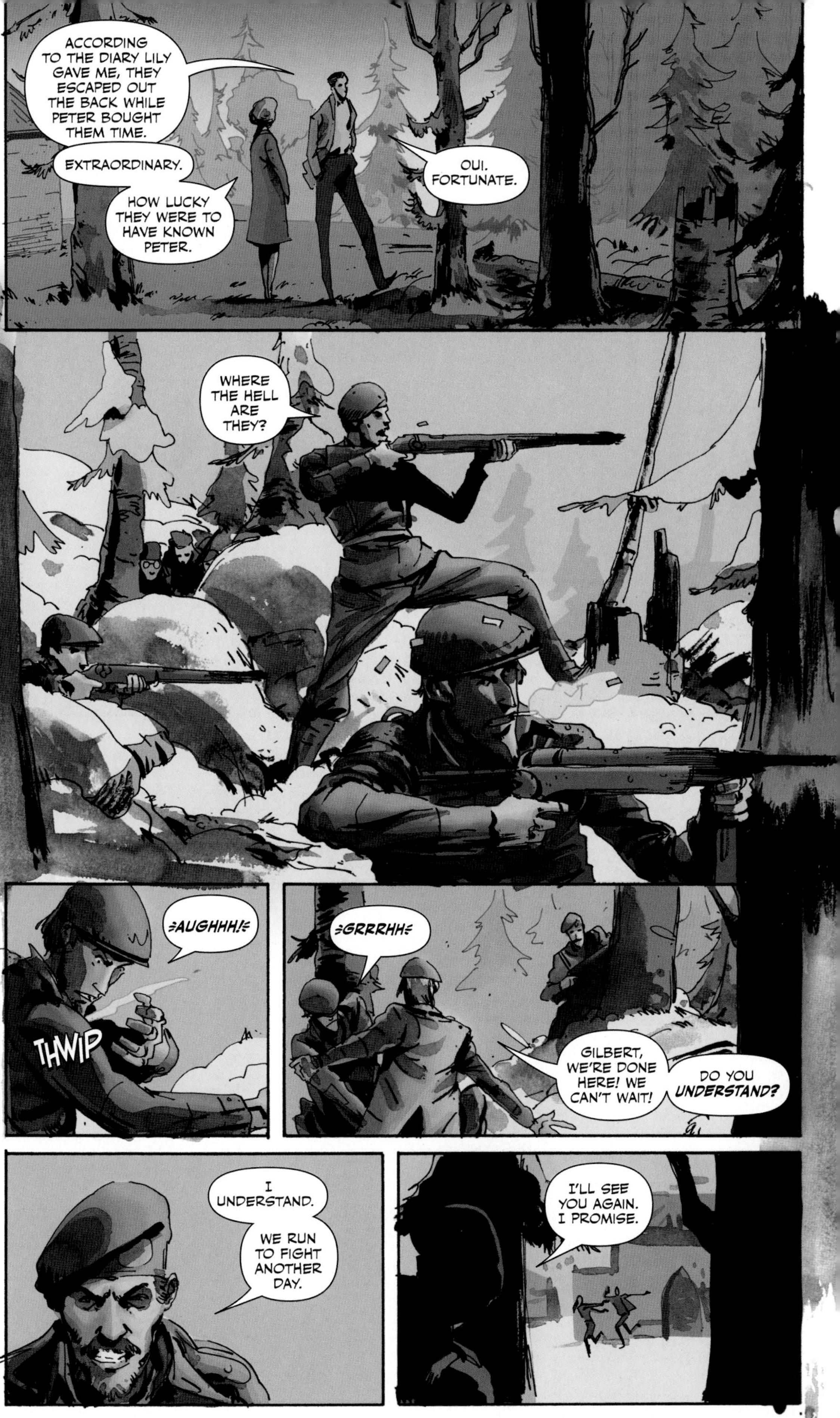

ACCORDING TO THE DIARY LILY GAVE ME, THEY ESCAPED OUT THE BACK WHILE PETER BOUGHT THEM TIME.
EXTRAORDINARY.
HOW LUCKY THEY WERE TO HAVE KNOWN PETER.
OUI. FORTUNATE.
WHERE THE HELL ARE THEY?
AUGHHH!
THWIP
GRRRHH
GILBERT, WE'RE DONE HERE! WE CAN'T WAIT!
DO YOU *UNDERSTAND?*
I UNDERSTAND.
WE RUN TO FIGHT ANOTHER DAY.
I'LL SEE YOU AGAIN. I PROMISE.

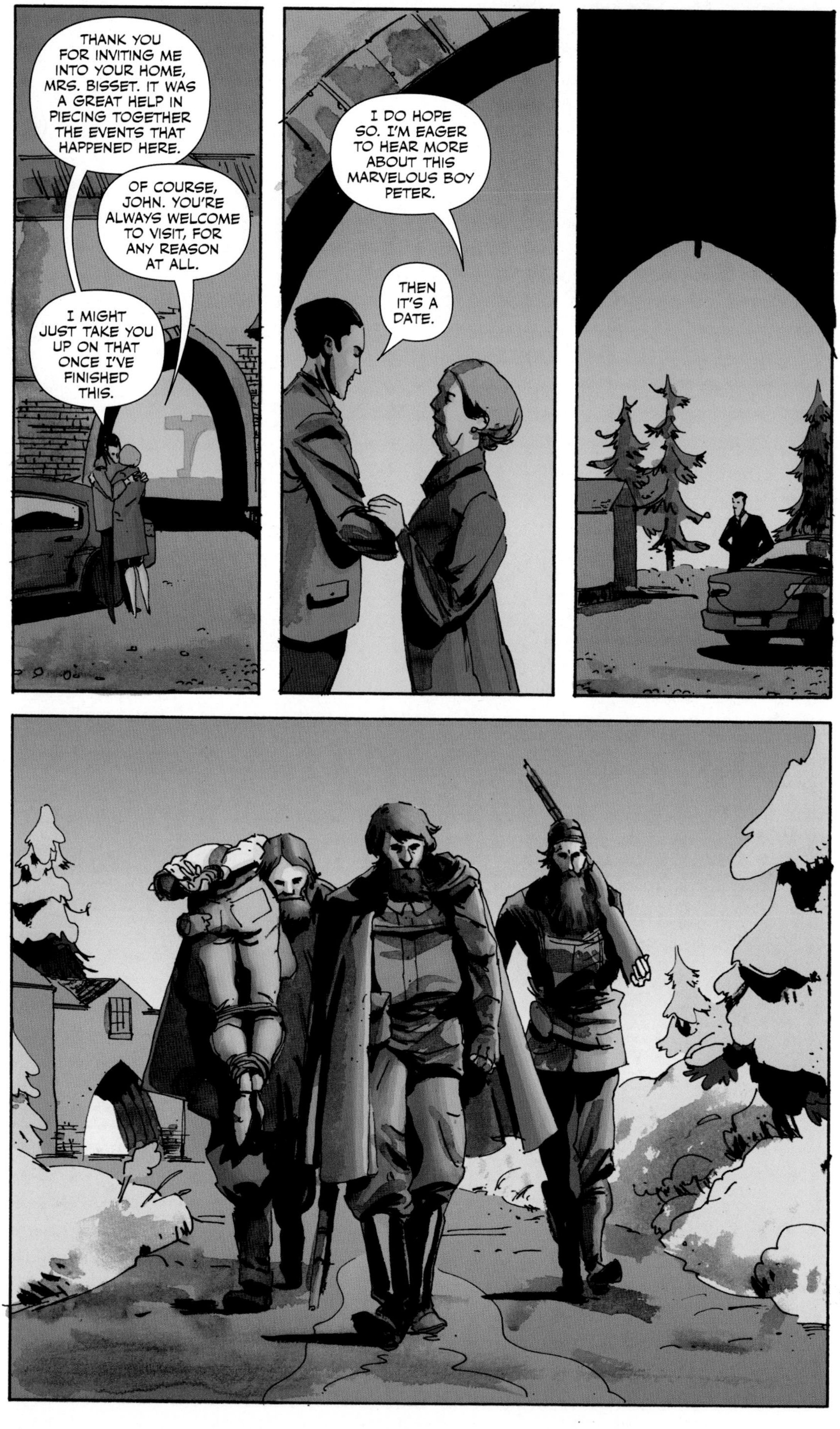
THANK YOU FOR INVITING ME INTO YOUR HOME, MRS. BISSET. IT WAS A GREAT HELP IN PIECING TOGETHER THE EVENTS THAT HAPPENED HERE.
OF COURSE, JOHN. YOU'RE ALWAYS WELCOME TO VISIT, FOR ANY REASON AT ALL.
I MIGHT JUST TAKE YOU UP ON THAT ONCE I'VE FINISHED THIS.
I DO HOPE SO. I'M EAGER TO HEAR MORE ABOUT THIS MARVELOUS BOY PETER.
THEN IT'S A DATE.

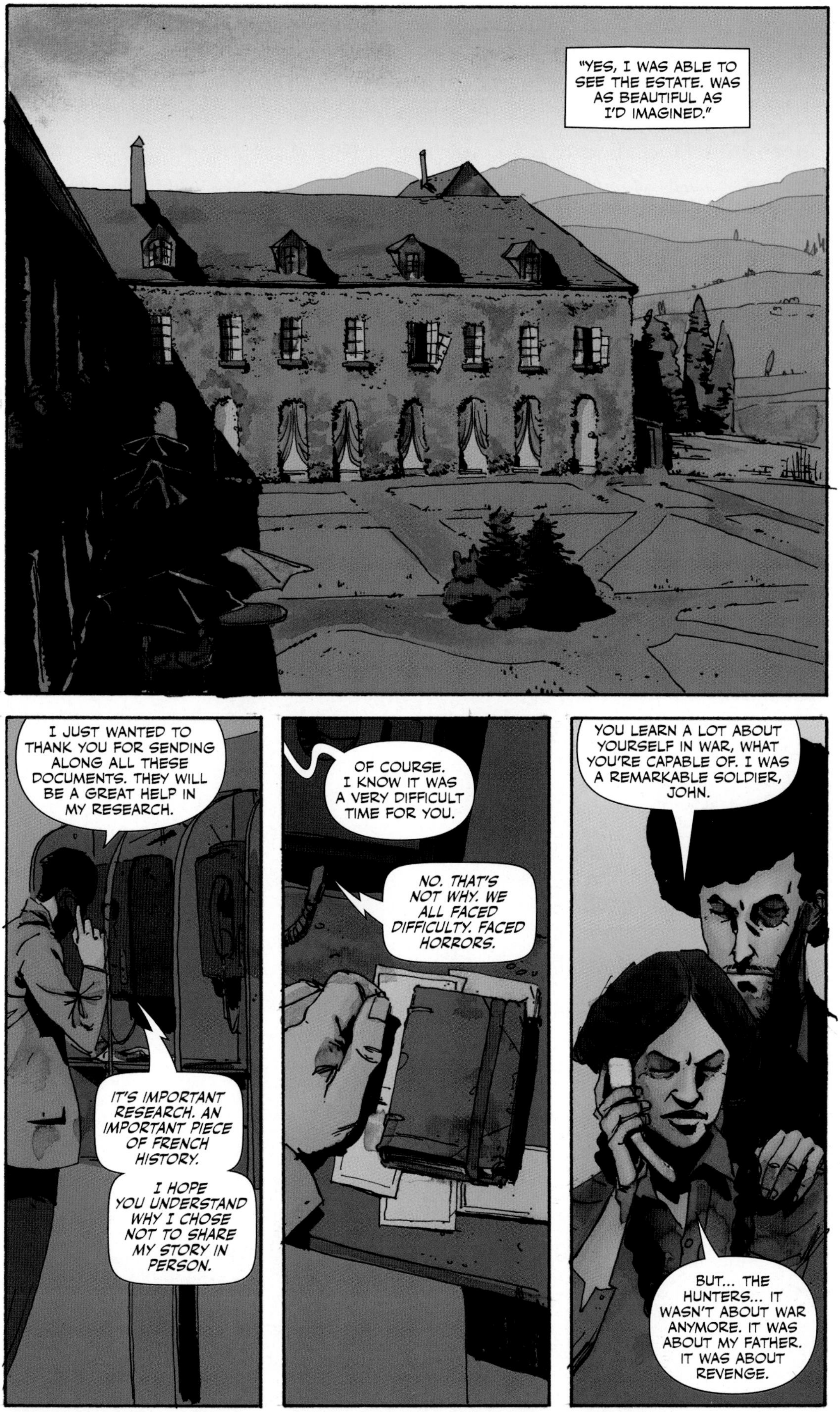
"YES, I WAS ABLE TO SEE THE ESTATE. WAS AS BEAUTIFUL AS I'D IMAGINED."
I JUST WANTED TO THANK YOU FOR SENDING ALONG ALL THESE DOCUMENTS. THEY WILL BE A GREAT HELP IN MY RESEARCH.
IT'S IMPORTANT RESEARCH. AN IMPORTANT PIECE OF FRENCH HISTORY.
I HOPE YOU UNDERSTAND WHY I CHOSE NOT TO SHARE MY STORY IN PERSON.
OF COURSE. I KNOW IT WAS A VERY DIFFICULT TIME FOR YOU.
NO. THAT'S NOT WHY. WE ALL FACED DIFFICULTY. FACED HORRORS.
YOU LEARN A LOT ABOUT YOURSELF IN WAR, WHAT YOU'RE CAPABLE OF. I WAS A REMARKABLE SOLDIER, JOHN.
BUT... THE HUNTERS... IT WASN'T ABOUT WAR ANYMORE. IT WAS ABOUT MY FATHER. IT WAS ABOUT REVENGE.

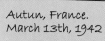

Autun, France.
March 13th, 1942

Katherine Cole has come through for us. Maybe these embedded Brits aren't so bad after all. It's been four long months of waiting but I've not lost focus. I've found the trail again. The hunt continues.

HURRY UP, YOU TWO!

EXCITING TIMES!

BLOOMIN' RIGHT EXCITING TIMES. C'MON THEN, INTO THE KITCHEN WITH THE BOTH OF YA.

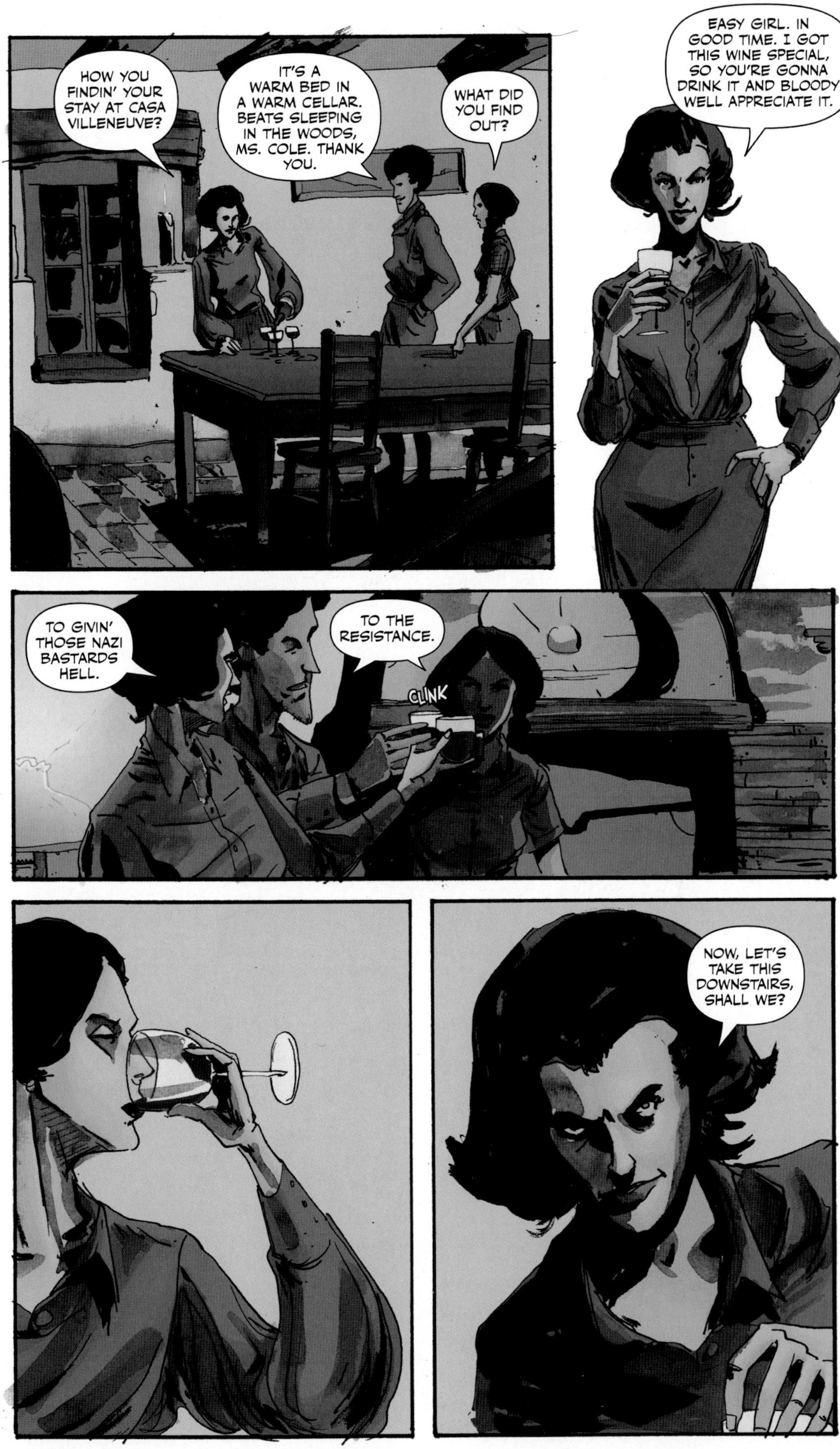
HOW YOU FINDIN' YOUR STAY AT CASA VILLENEUVE?
IT'S A WARM BED IN A WARM CELLAR. BEATS SLEEPING IN THE WOODS, MS. COLE. THANK YOU.
WHAT DID YOU FIND OUT?
EASY GIRL. IN GOOD TIME. I GOT THIS WINE SPECIAL, SO YOU'RE GONNA DRINK IT AND BLOODY WELL APPRECIATE IT.
TO GIVIN' THOSE NAZI BASTARDS HELL.
TO THE RESISTANCE.
CLINK
NOW, LET'S TAKE THIS DOWNSTAIRS, SHALL WE?

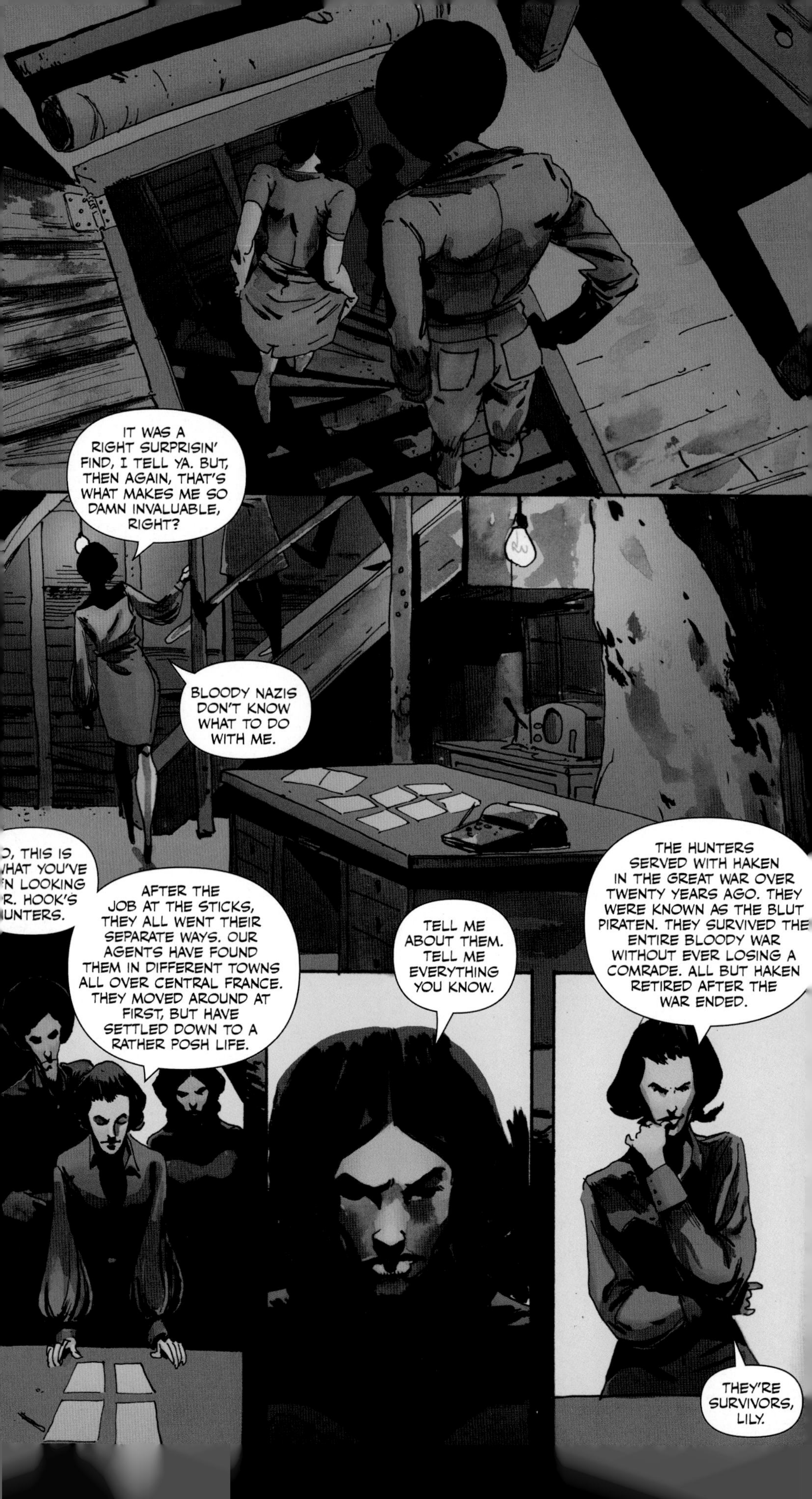
IT WAS A RIGHT SURPRISIN' FIND, I TELL YA. BUT, THEN AGAIN, THAT'S WHAT MAKES ME SO DAMN INVALUABLE, RIGHT?
BLOODY NAZIS DON'T KNOW WHAT TO DO WITH ME.
AFTER THE JOB AT THE STICKS, THEY ALL WENT THEIR SEPARATE WAYS. OUR AGENTS HAVE FOUND THEM IN DIFFERENT TOWNS ALL OVER CENTRAL FRANCE. THEY MOVED AROUND AT FIRST, BUT HAVE SETTLED DOWN TO A RATHER POSH LIFE.
TELL ME ABOUT THEM. TELL ME EVERYTHING YOU KNOW.
THE HUNTERS SERVED WITH HAKEN IN THE GREAT WAR OVER TWENTY YEARS AGO. THEY WERE KNOWN AS THE BLUT PIRATEN. THEY SURVIVED THE ENTIRE BLOODY WAR WITHOUT EVER LOSING A COMRADE. ALL BUT HAKEN RETIRED AFTER THE WAR ENDED.
THEY'RE SURVIVORS, LILY.

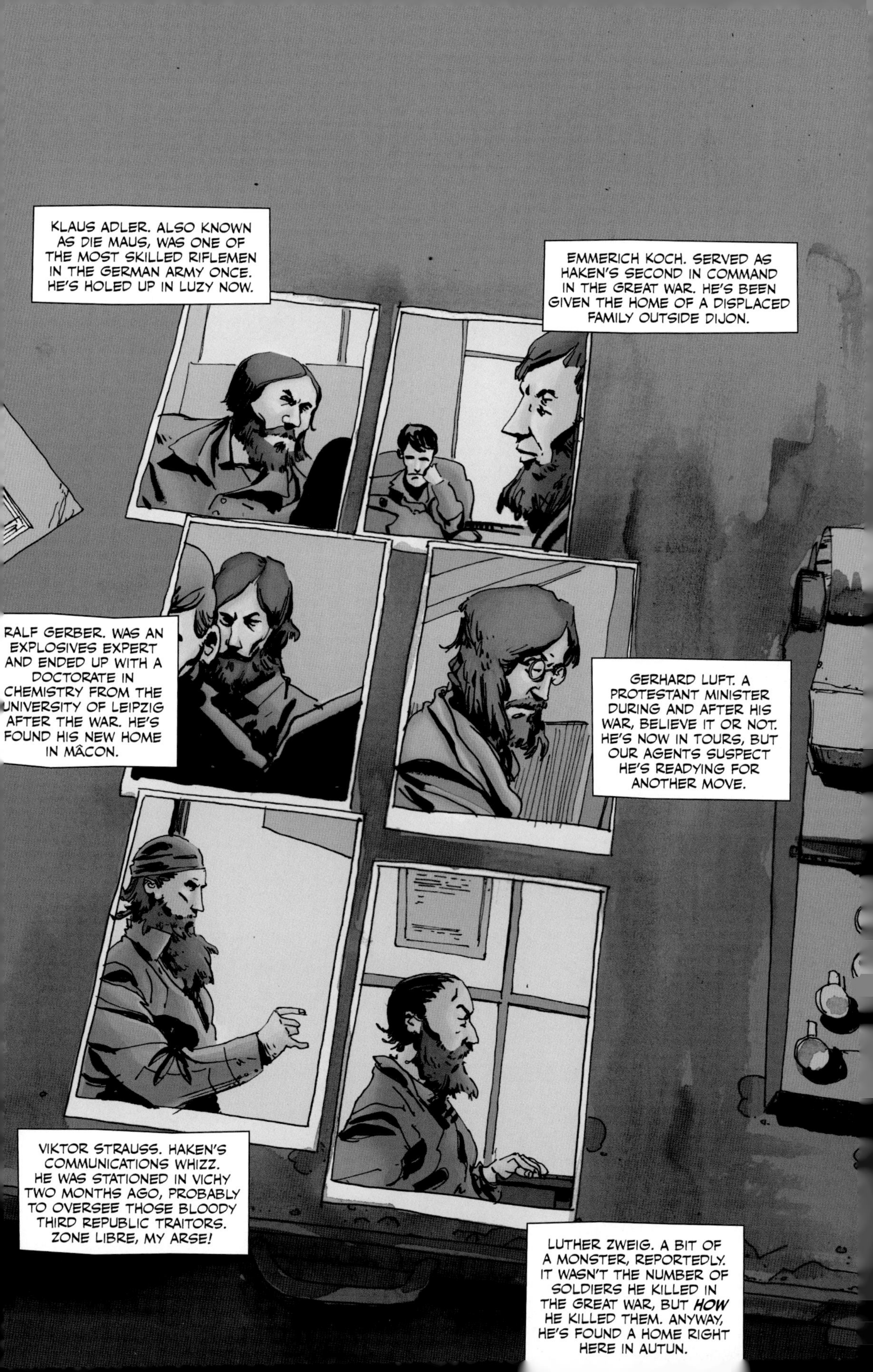

KLAUS ADLER. ALSO KNOWN AS DIE MAUS, WAS ONE OF THE MOST SKILLED RIFLEMEN IN THE GERMAN ARMY ONCE. HE'S HOLED UP IN LUZY NOW.
EMMERICH KOCH. SERVED AS HAKEN'S SECOND IN COMMAND IN THE GREAT WAR. HE'S BEEN GIVEN THE HOME OF A DISPLACED FAMILY OUTSIDE DIJON.
RALF GERBER. WAS AN EXPLOSIVES EXPERT AND ENDED UP WITH A DOCTORATE IN CHEMISTRY FROM THE UNIVERSITY OF LEIPZIG AFTER THE WAR. HE'S FOUND HIS NEW HOME IN MÂCON.
GERHARD LUFT. A PROTESTANT MINISTER DURING AND AFTER HIS WAR, BELIEVE IT OR NOT. HE'S NOW IN TOURS, BUT OUR AGENTS SUSPECT HE'S READYING FOR ANOTHER MOVE.
VIKTOR STRAUSS. HAKEN'S COMMUNICATIONS WHIZZ. HE WAS STATIONED IN VICHY TWO MONTHS AGO, PROBABLY TO OVERSEE THOSE BLOODY THIRD REPUBLIC TRAITORS. ZONE LIBRE, MY ARSE!
LUTHER ZWEIG. A BIT OF A MONSTER, REPORTEDLY. IT WASN'T THE NUMBER OF SOLDIERS HE KILLED IN THE GREAT WAR, BUT *HOW* HE KILLED THEM. ANYWAY, HE'S FOUND A HOME RIGHT HERE IN AUTUN.

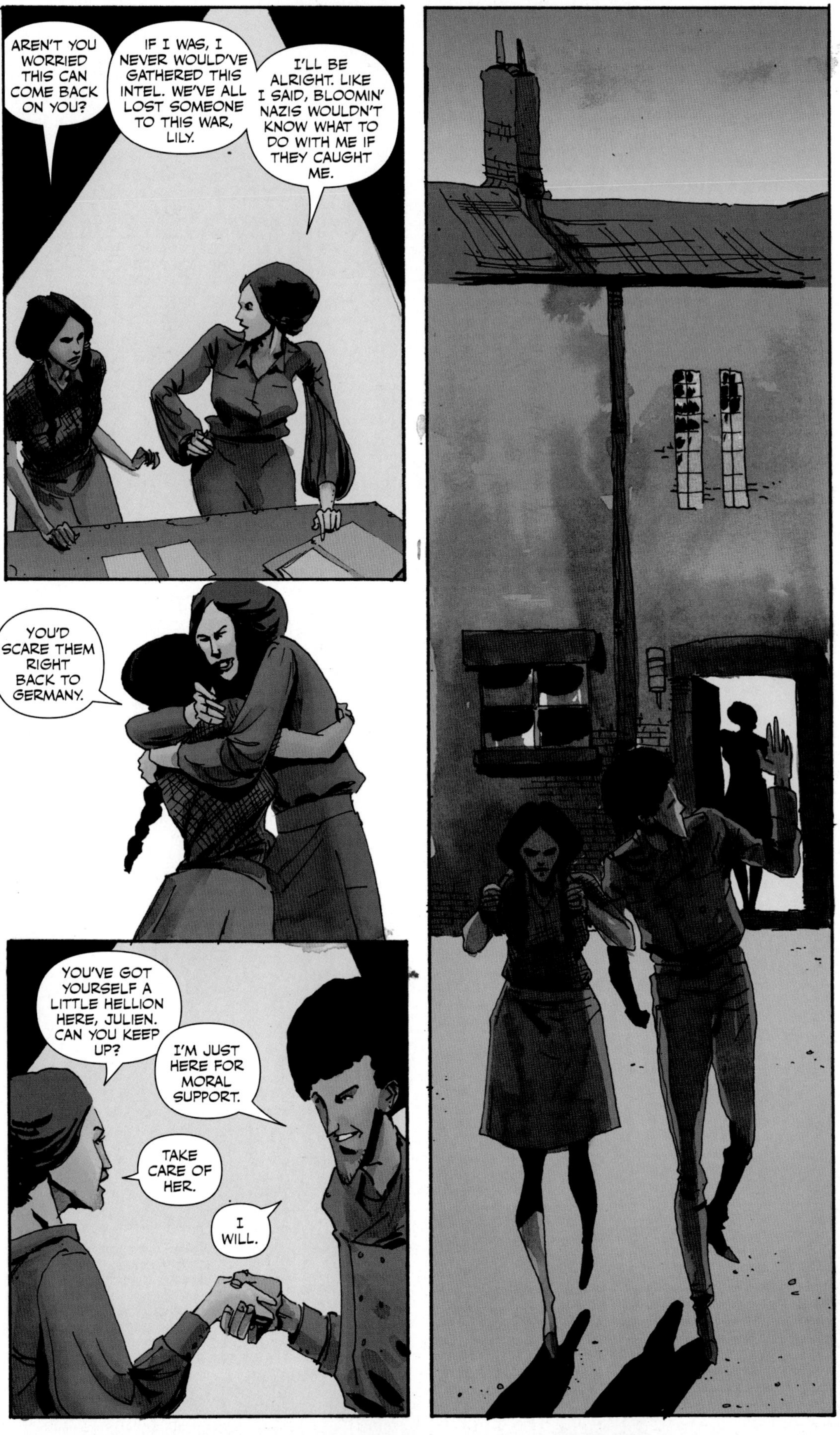
AREN'T YOU WORRIED THIS CAN COME BACK ON YOU?
IF I WAS, I NEVER WOULD'VE GATHERED THIS INTEL. WE'VE ALL LOST SOMEONE TO THIS WAR, LILY.
I'LL BE ALRIGHT. LIKE I SAID, BLOOMIN' NAZIS WOULDN'T KNOW WHAT TO DO WITH ME IF THEY CAUGHT ME.
YOU'D SCARE THEM RIGHT BACK TO GERMANY.
YOU'VE GOT YOURSELF A LITTLE HELLION HERE, JULIEN. CAN YOU KEEP UP?
I'M JUST HERE FOR MORAL SUPPORT.
TAKE CARE OF HER.
I WILL.

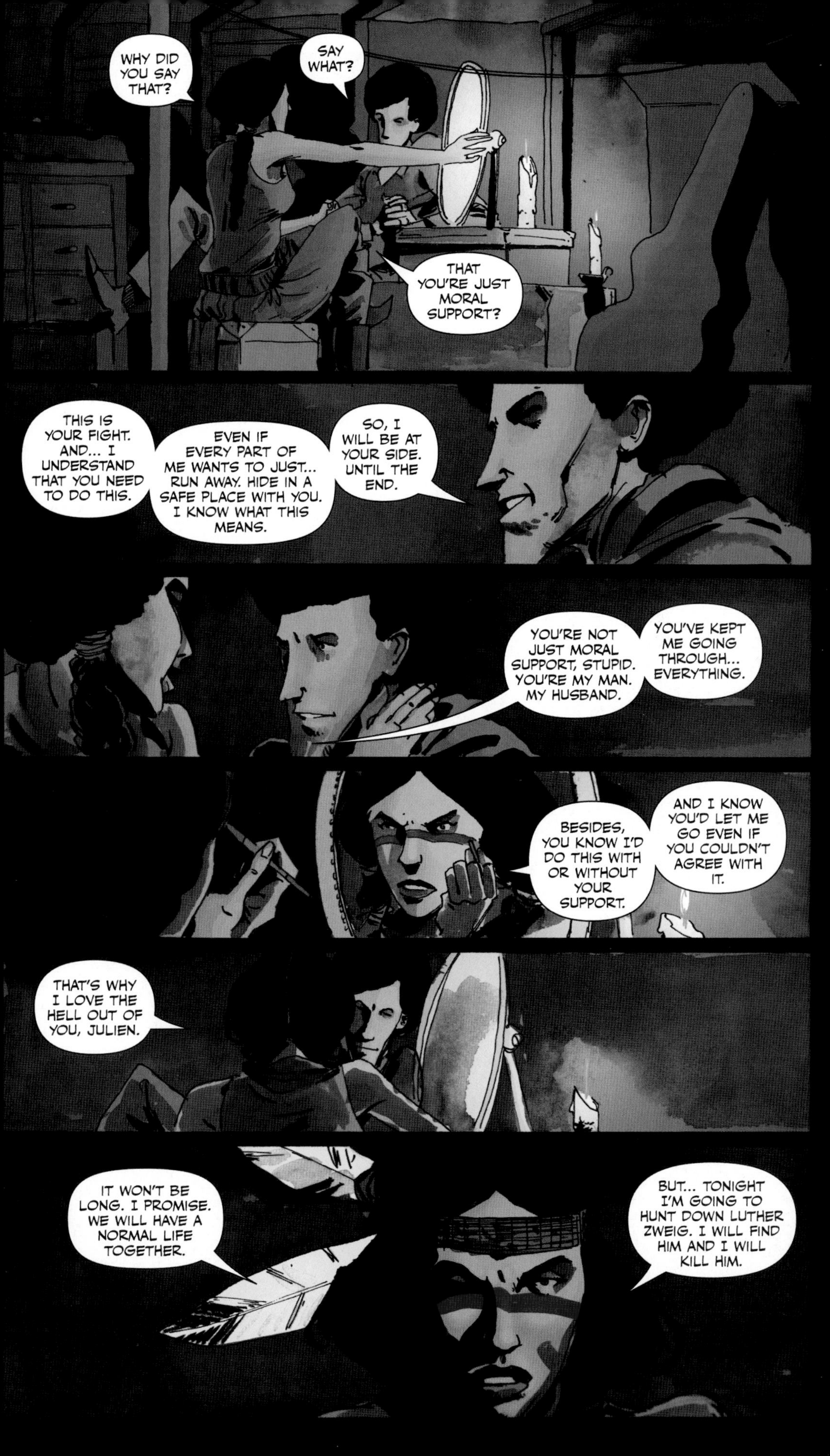
WHY DID YOU SAY THAT?
SAY WHAT?
THAT YOU'RE JUST MORAL SUPPORT?
THIS IS YOUR FIGHT. AND... I UNDERSTAND THAT YOU NEED TO DO THIS.
EVEN IF EVERY PART OF ME WANTS TO JUST... RUN AWAY. HIDE IN A SAFE PLACE WITH YOU. I KNOW WHAT THIS MEANS.
SO, I WILL BE AT YOUR SIDE. UNTIL THE END.
YOU'RE NOT JUST MORAL SUPPORT, STUPID. YOU'RE MY MAN. MY HUSBAND.
YOU'VE KEPT ME GOING THROUGH... EVERYTHING.
BESIDES, YOU KNOW I'D DO THIS WITH OR WITHOUT YOUR SUPPORT.
AND I KNOW YOU'D LET ME GO EVEN IF YOU COULDN'T AGREE WITH IT.
THAT'S WHY I LOVE THE HELL OUT OF YOU, JULIEN.
IT WON'T BE LONG. I PROMISE. WE WILL HAVE A NORMAL LIFE TOGETHER.
BUT... TONIGHT I'M GOING TO HUNT DOWN LUTHER ZWEIG. I WILL FIND HIM AND I WILL KILL HIM.

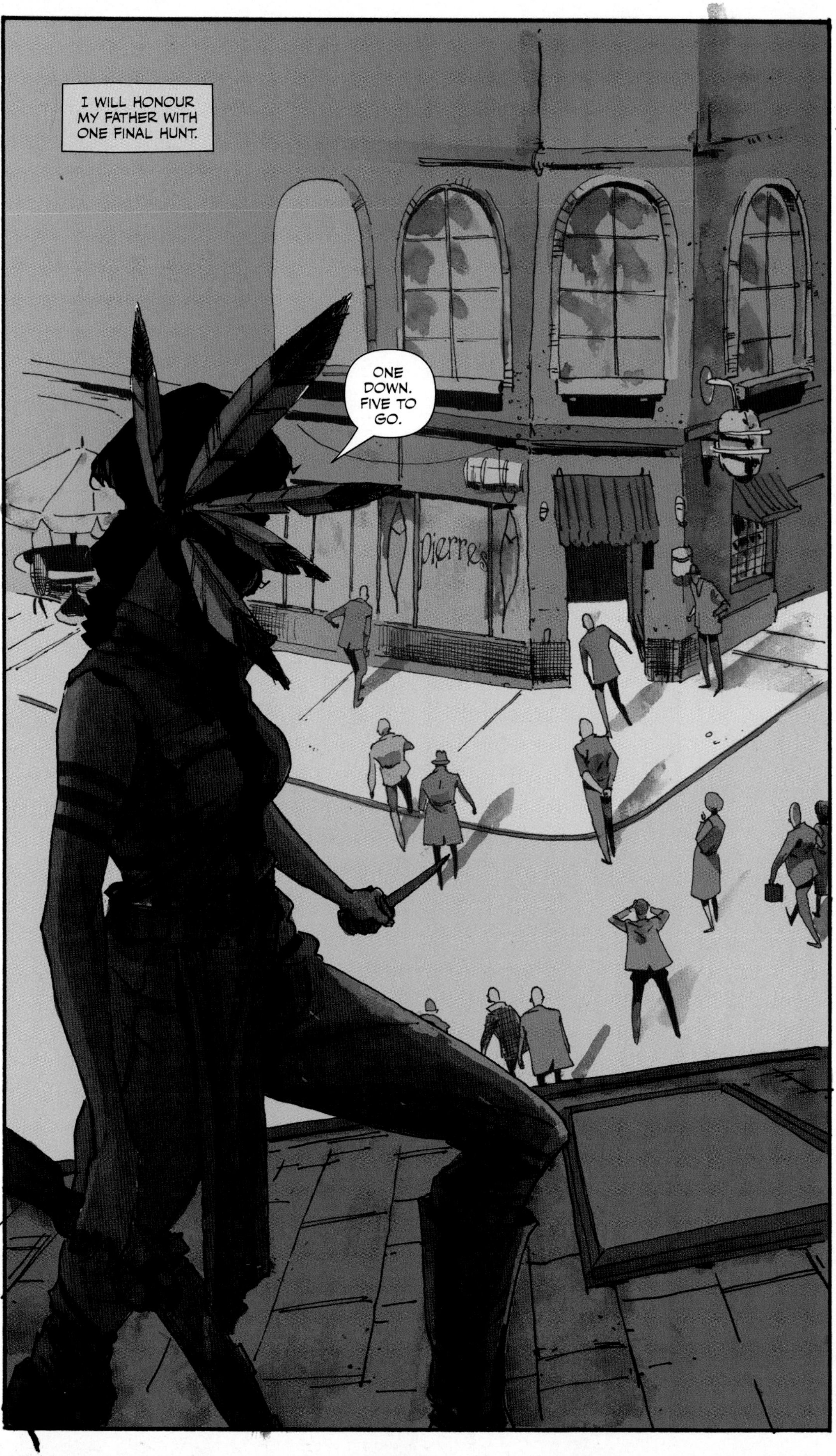
I WILL HONOUR MY FATHER WITH ONE FINAL HUNT.
ONE DOWN. FIVE TO GO.
Pierre's

CHAPTER SEVENTEEN

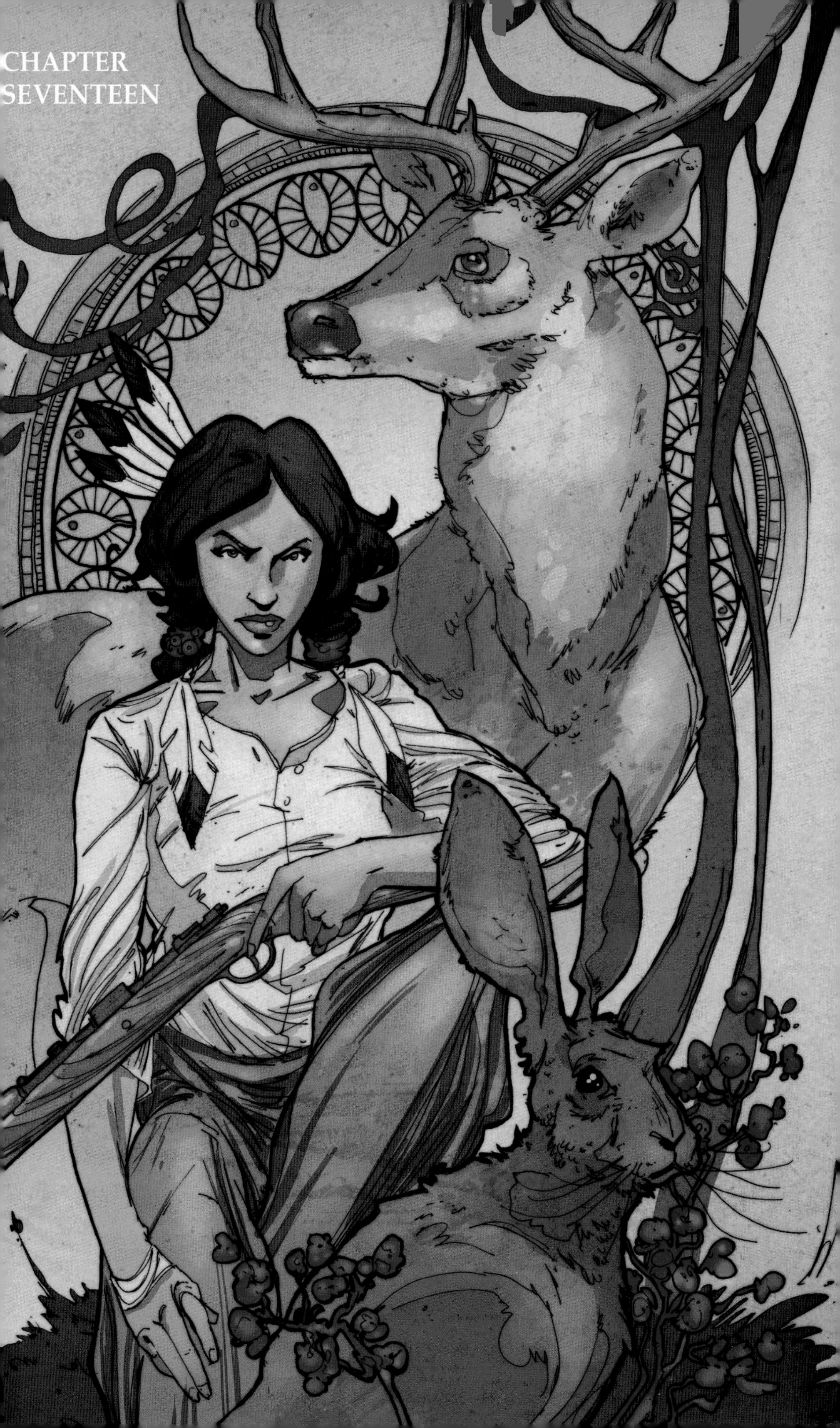

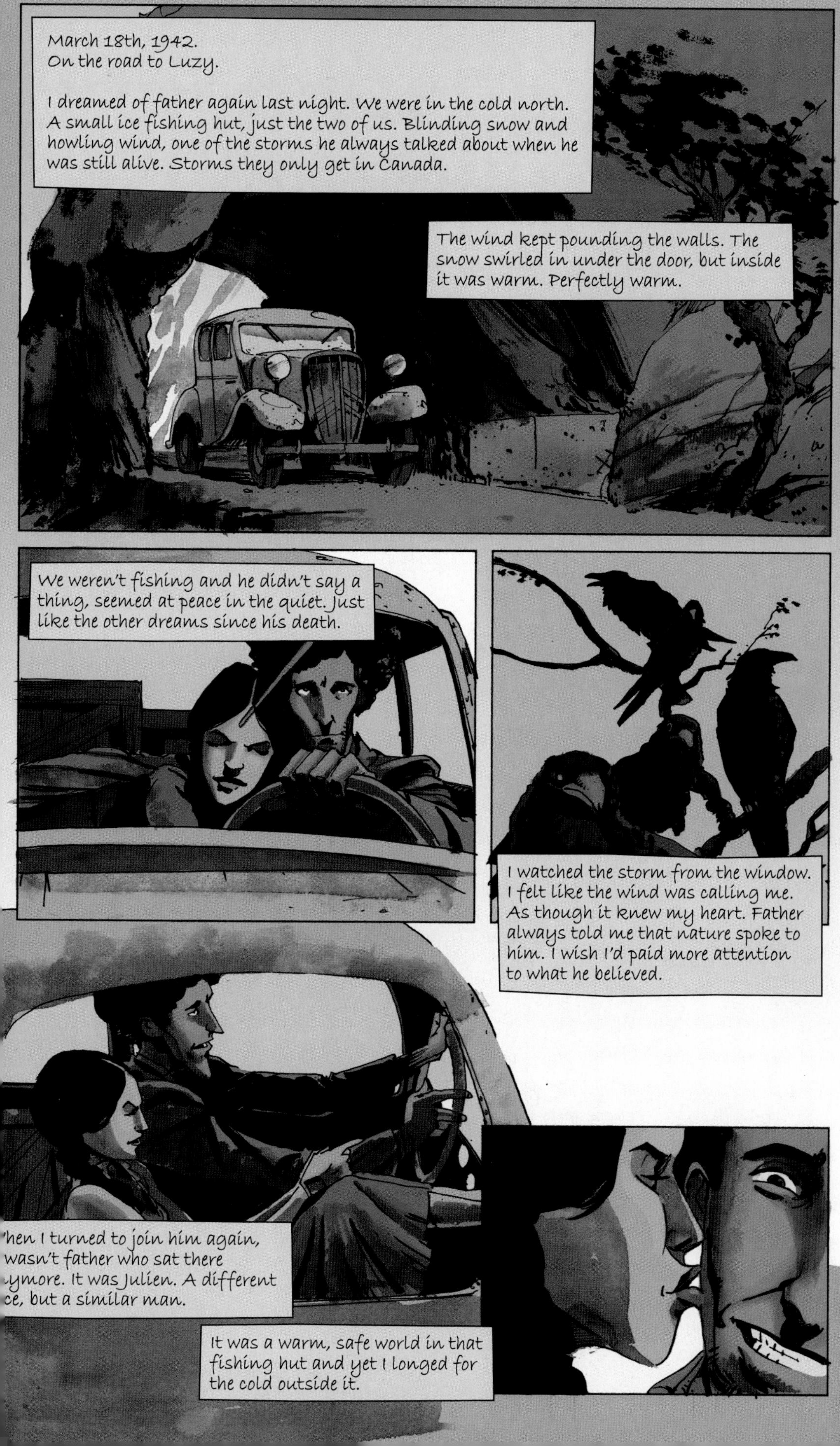
March 18th, 1942.
On the road to Luzy.
I dreamed of father again last night. We were in the cold north. A small ice fishing hut, just the two of us. Blinding snow and howling wind, one of the storms he always talked about when he was still alive. Storms they only get in Canada.
The wind kept pounding the walls. The snow swirled in under the door, but inside it was warm. Perfectly warm.
We weren't fishing and he didn't say a thing, seemed at peace in the quiet. Just like the other dreams since his death.
I watched the storm from the window. I felt like the wind was calling me. As though it knew my heart. Father always told me that nature spoke to him. I wish I'd paid more attention to what he believed.
hen I turned to join him again, wasn't father who sat there ymore. It was Julien. A different ce, but a similar man.
It was a warm, safe world in that fishing hut and yet I longed for the cold outside it.

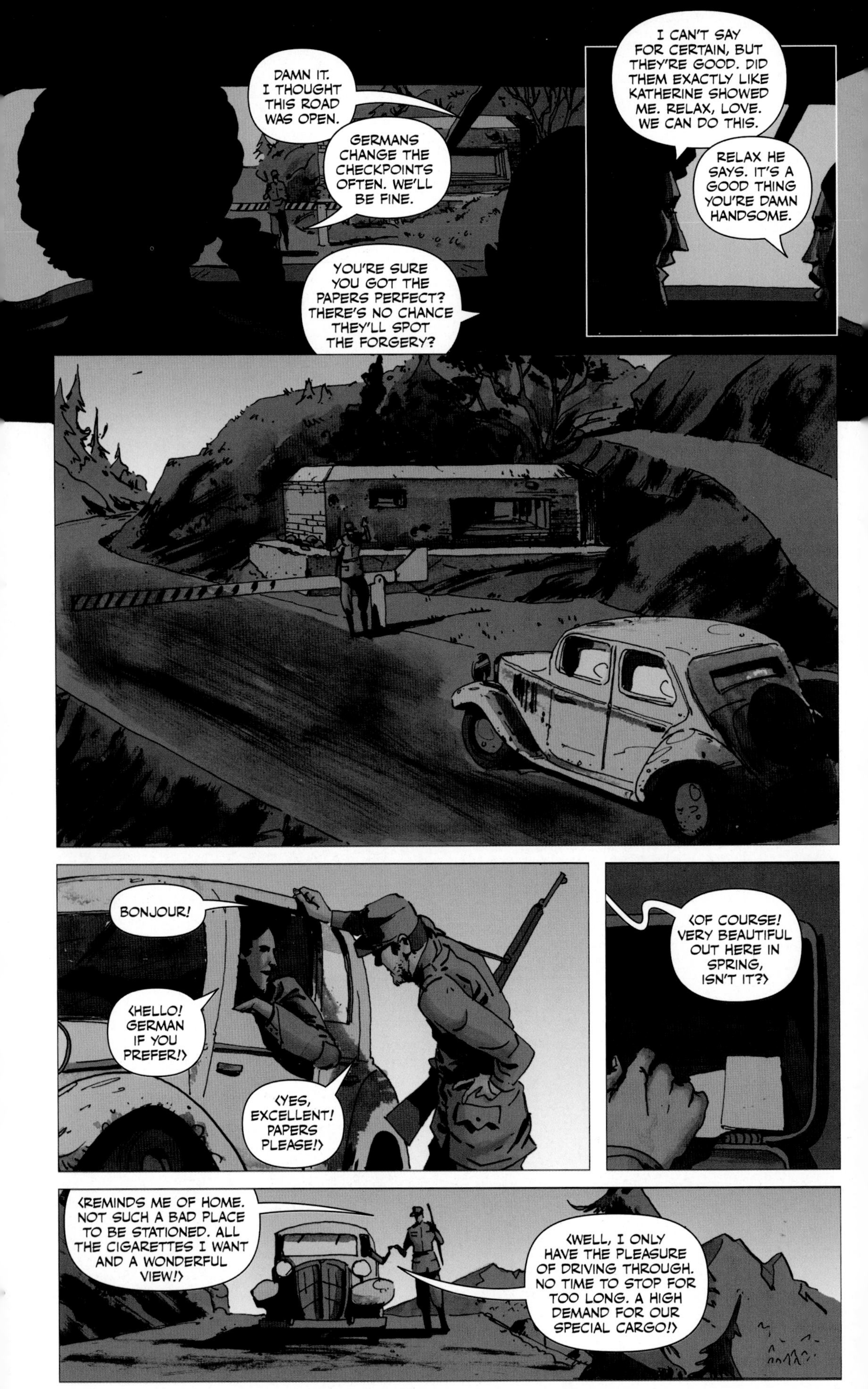
DAMN IT. I THOUGHT THIS ROAD WAS OPEN.
GERMANS CHANGE THE CHECKPOINTS OFTEN. WE'LL BE FINE.
YOU'RE SURE YOU GOT THE PAPERS PERFECT? THERE'S NO CHANCE THEY'LL SPOT THE FORGERY?
I CAN'T SAY FOR CERTAIN, BUT THEY'RE GOOD. DID THEM EXACTLY LIKE KATHERINE SHOWED ME. RELAX, LOVE. WE CAN DO THIS.
RELAX HE SAYS. IT'S A GOOD THING YOU'RE DAMN HANDSOME.
BONJOUR!
‹HELLO! GERMAN IF YOU PREFER!›
‹YES, EXCELLENT! PAPERS PLEASE!›
‹OF COURSE! VERY BEAUTIFUL OUT HERE IN SPRING, ISN'T IT?›
‹REMINDS ME OF HOME. NOT SUCH A BAD PLACE TO BE STATIONED. ALL THE CIGARETTES I WANT AND A WONDERFUL VIEW!›
‹WELL, I ONLY HAVE THE PLEASURE OF DRIVING THROUGH. NO TIME TO STOP FOR TOO LONG. A HIGH DEMAND FOR OUR SPECIAL CARGO!›

⟨WHAT'S THE CARGO, MR. DUPUIS?⟩

⟨YOU'RE THE YOUNGEST WINE CONNOISSEUR I'VE MET.⟩

⟨BURGUNDY REGION WINE. HAUTES-CÔTES DE NUITS, ACTUALLY. 1914.⟩

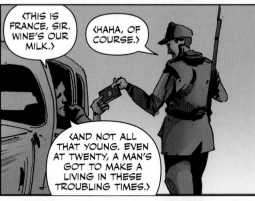

⟨THIS IS FRANCE, SIR. WINE'S OUR MILK.⟩

⟨HAHA, OF COURSE.⟩

⟨AND NOT ALL THAT YOUNG. EVEN AT TWENTY, A MAN'S GOT TO MAKE A LIVING IN THESE TROUBLING TIMES.⟩

⟨WHERE'S THE SHIPMENT GOING?⟩

⟨PARIS. THERE'S A HUGE DEMAND FOR IT IN THE FINE DINING ESTABLISHMENTS. LIFE GOES ON, RIGHT?⟩

⟨YOUR BUSINESS PARTNER. SHE'S VERY QUIET. BEAUTIFUL, BUT QUIET.⟩

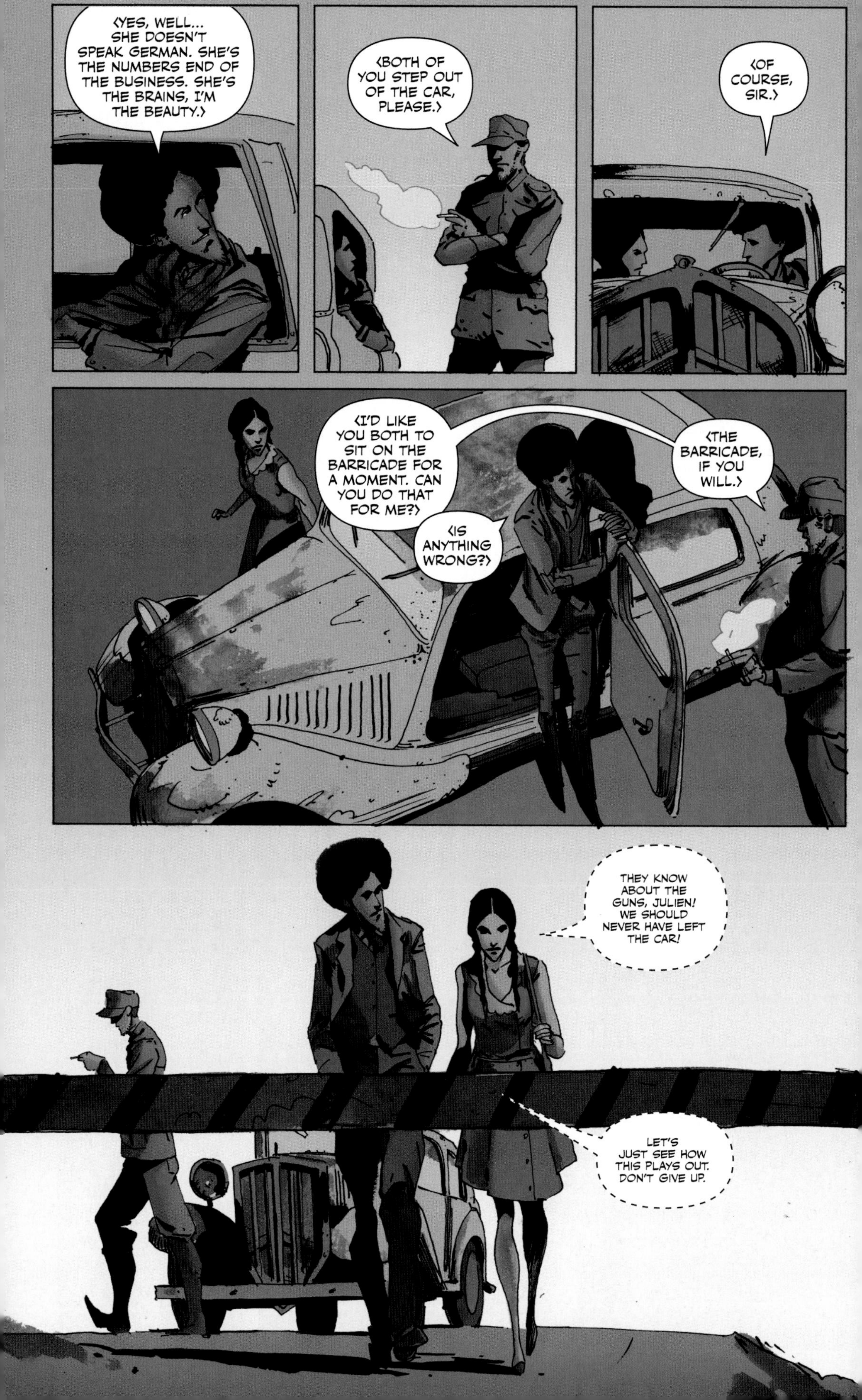
<YES, WELL... SHE DOESN'T SPEAK GERMAN. SHE'S THE NUMBERS END OF THE BUSINESS. SHE'S THE BRAINS, I'M THE BEAUTY.>
<BOTH OF YOU STEP OUT OF THE CAR, PLEASE.>
<OF COURSE, SIR.>
<I'D LIKE YOU BOTH TO SIT ON THE BARRICADE FOR A MOMENT. CAN YOU DO THAT FOR ME?>
<THE BARRICADE, IF YOU WILL.>
<IS ANYTHING WRONG?>
THEY KNOW ABOUT THE GUNS, JULIEN! WE SHOULD NEVER HAVE LEFT THE CAR!
LET'S JUST SEE HOW THIS PLAYS OUT. DON'T GIVE UP.

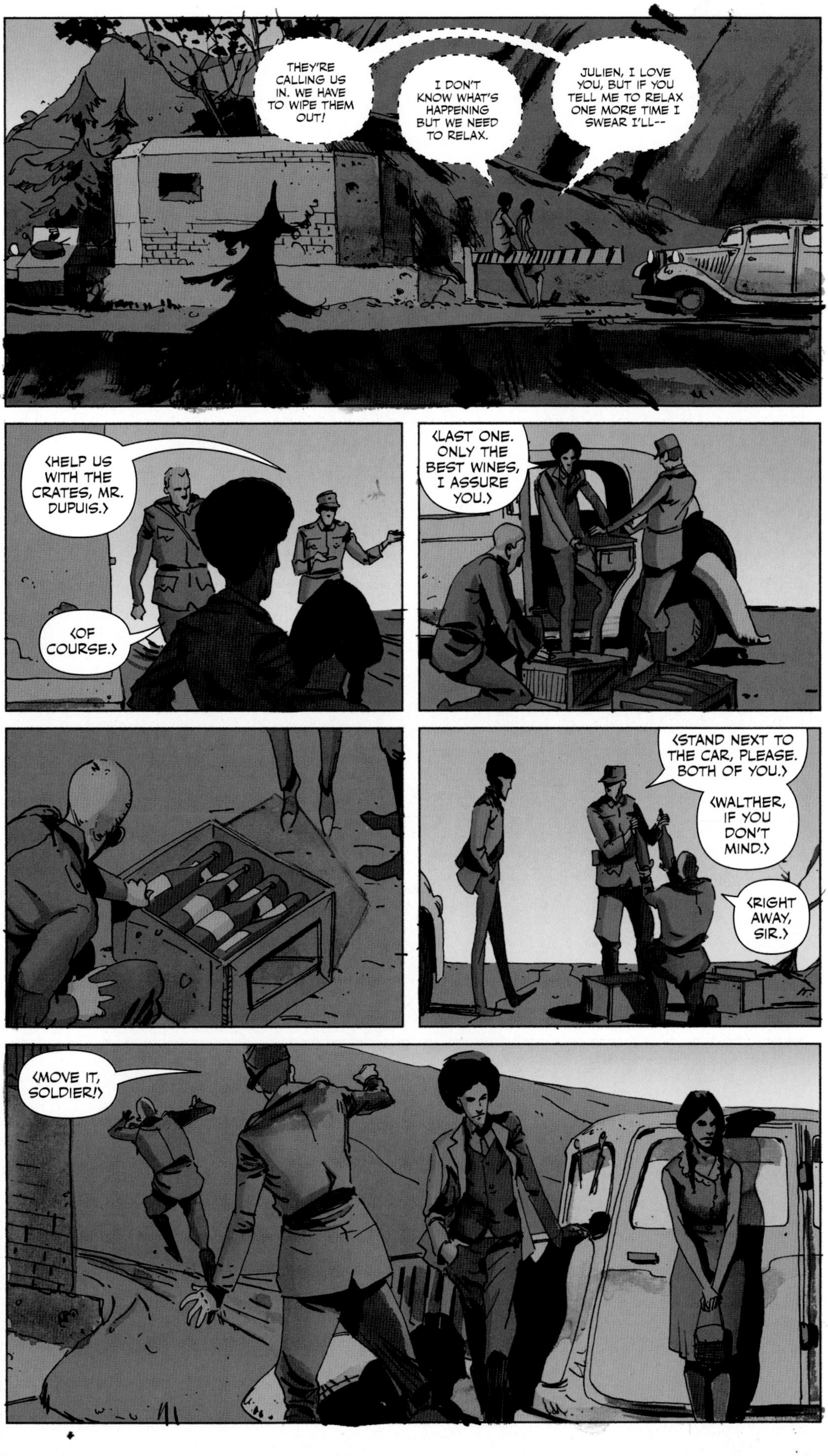
THEY'RE CALLING US IN. WE HAVE TO WIPE THEM OUT!
I DON'T KNOW WHAT'S HAPPENING BUT WE NEED TO RELAX.
JULIEN, I LOVE YOU, BUT IF YOU TELL ME TO RELAX ONE MORE TIME I SWEAR I'LL--
<HELP US WITH THE CRATES, MR. DUPUIS.>
<OF COURSE.>
<LAST ONE. ONLY THE BEST WINES, I ASSURE YOU.>
<STAND NEXT TO THE CAR, PLEASE. BOTH OF YOU.>
<WALTHER, IF YOU DON'T MIND.>
<RIGHT AWAY, SIR.>
<MOVE IT, SOLDIER!>

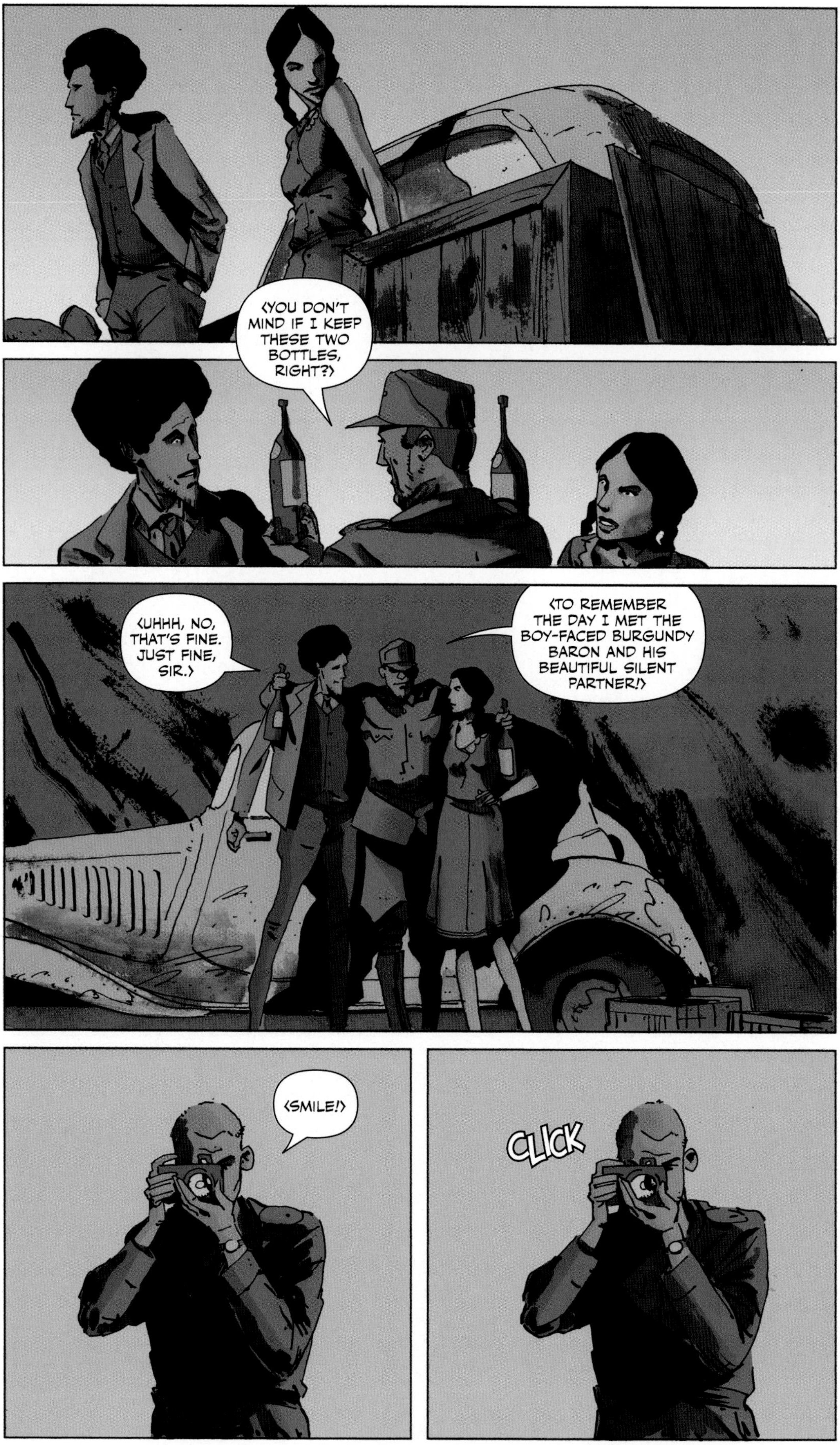
‹YOU DON'T MIND IF I KEEP THESE TWO BOTTLES, RIGHT?›
‹UHHH, NO, THAT'S FINE. JUST FINE, SIR.›
‹TO REMEMBER THE DAY I MET THE BOY-FACED BURGUNDY BARON AND HIS BEAUTIFUL SILENT PARTNER!›
‹SMILE!›
CLICK

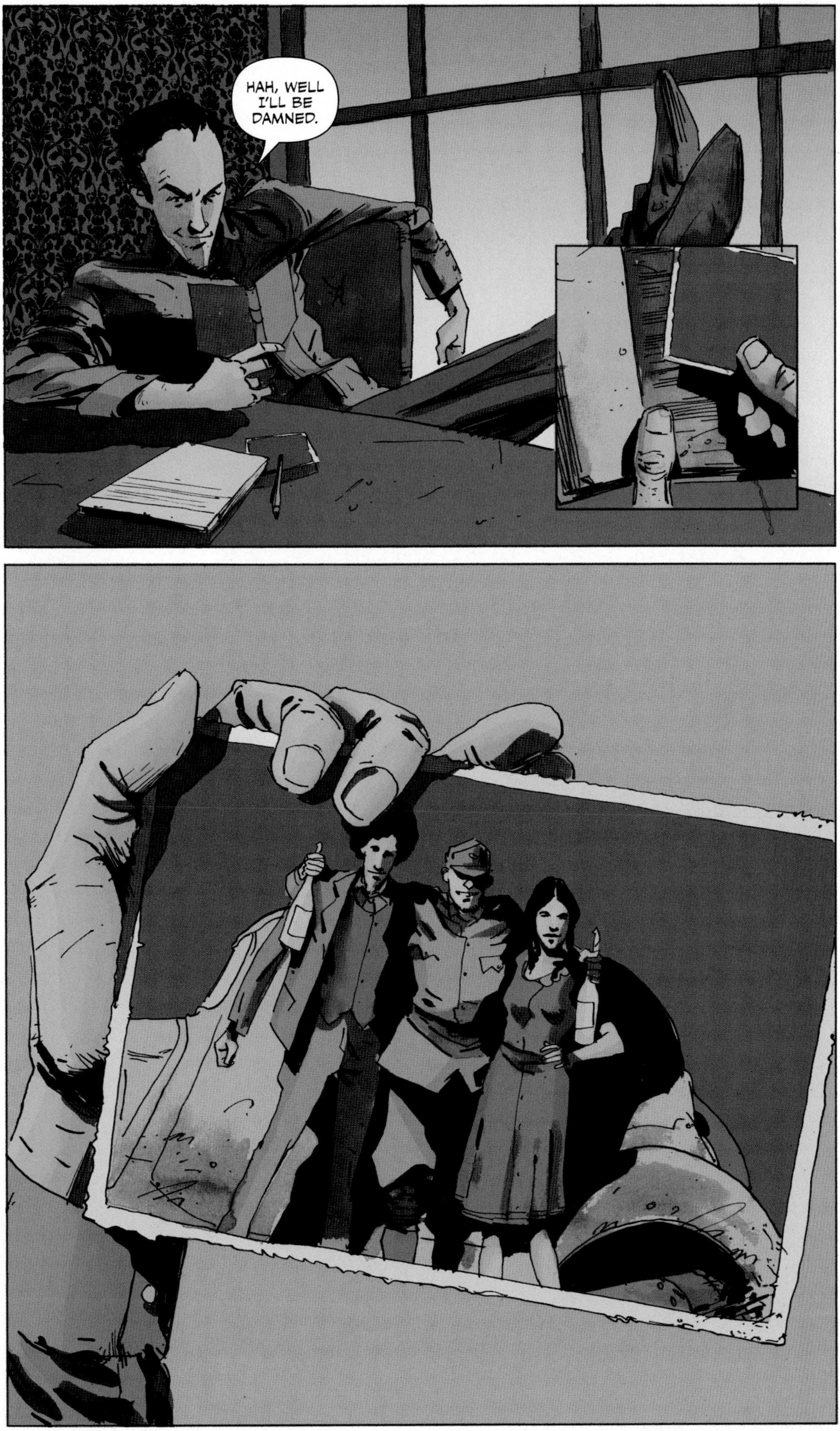
HAH, WELL I'LL BE DAMNED.

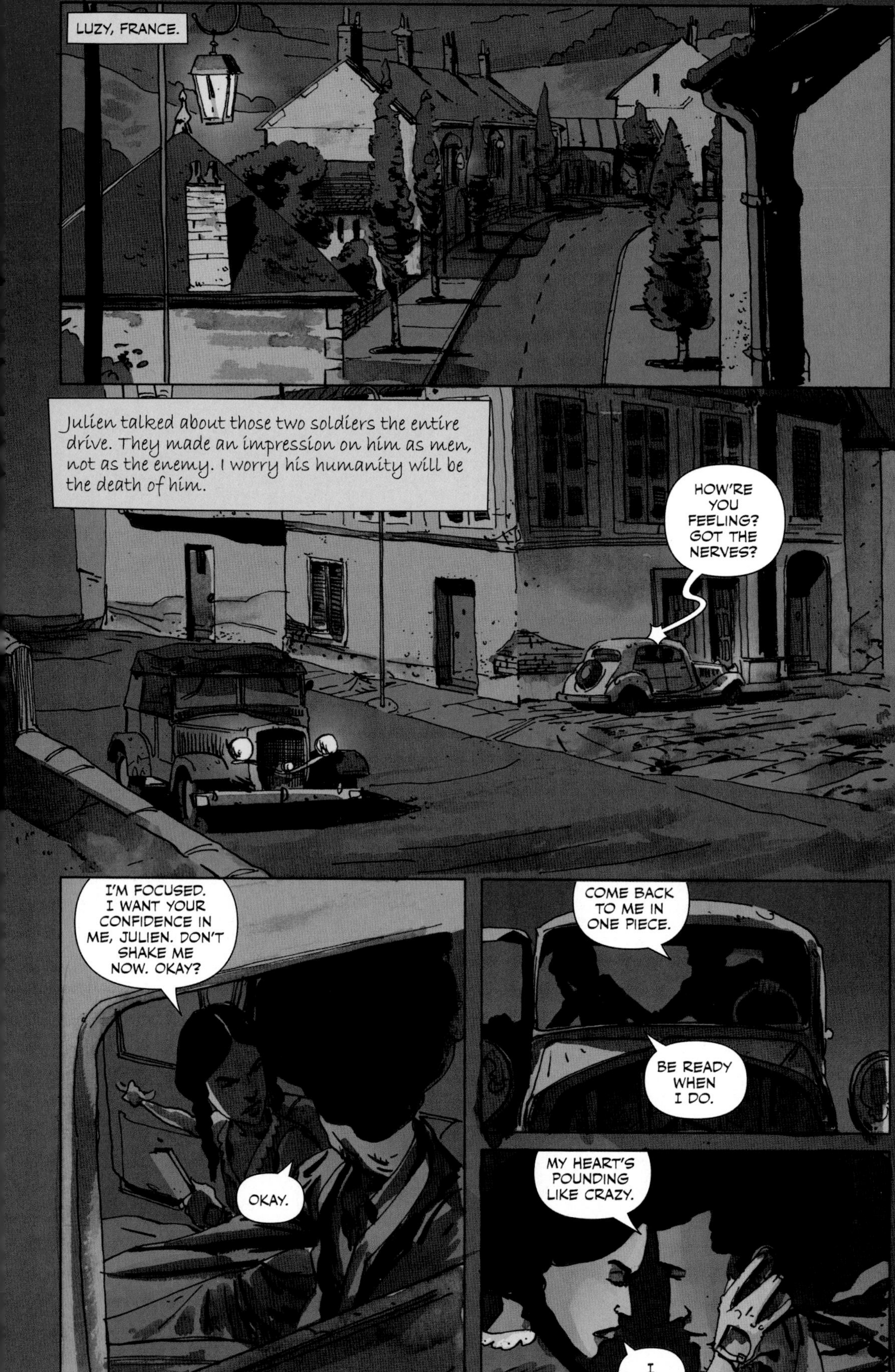
LUZY, FRANCE.
Julien talked about those two soldiers the entire drive. They made an impression on him as men, not as the enemy. I worry his humanity will be the death of him.
HOW'RE YOU FEELING? GOT THE NERVES?
I'M FOCUSED. I WANT YOUR CONFIDENCE IN ME, JULIEN. DON'T SHAKE ME NOW. OKAY?
OKAY.
COME BACK TO ME IN ONE PIECE.
BE READY WHEN I DO.
MY HEART'S POUNDING LIKE CRAZY.
I KNOW.

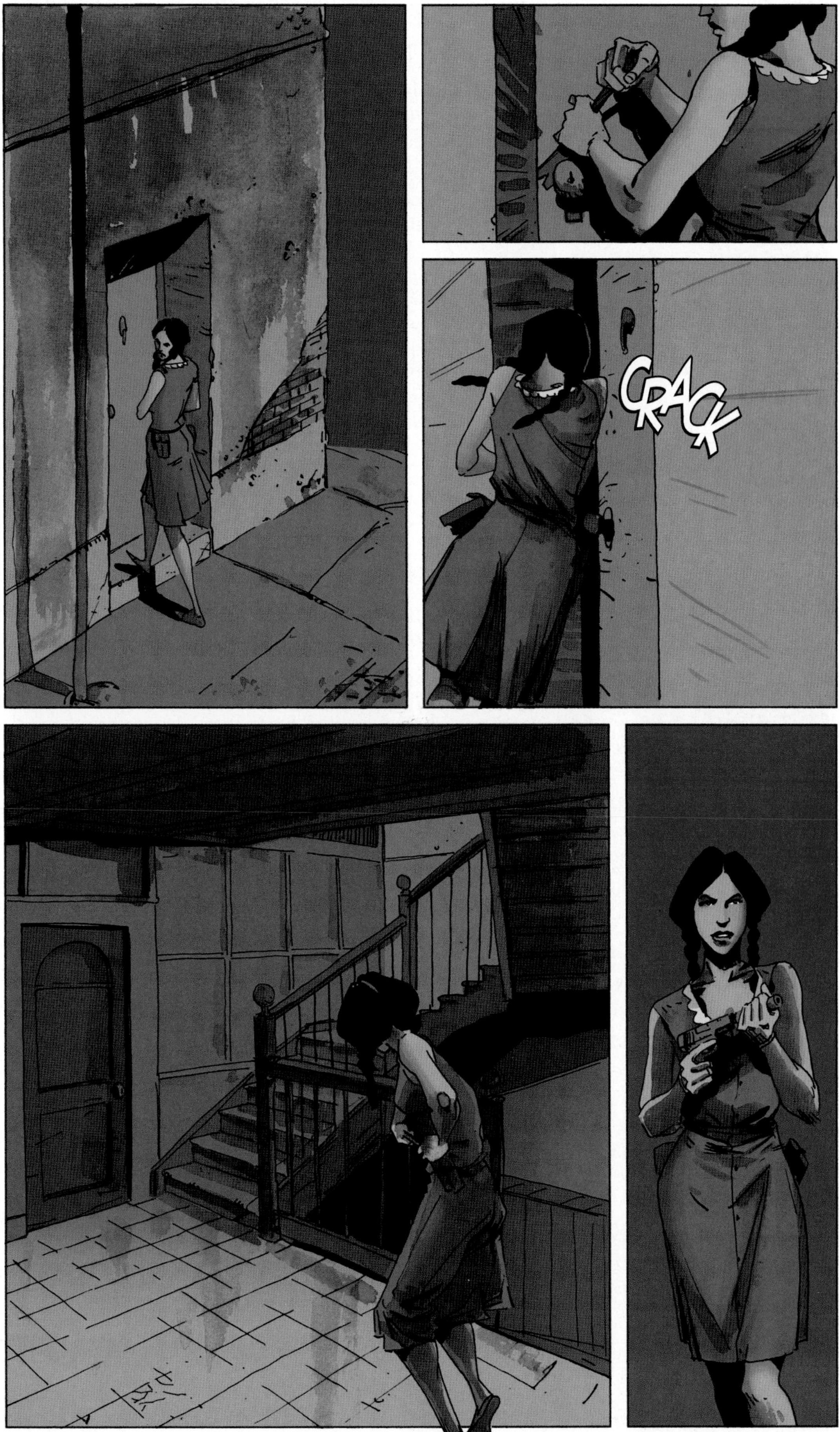
CRACK

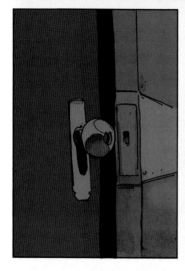

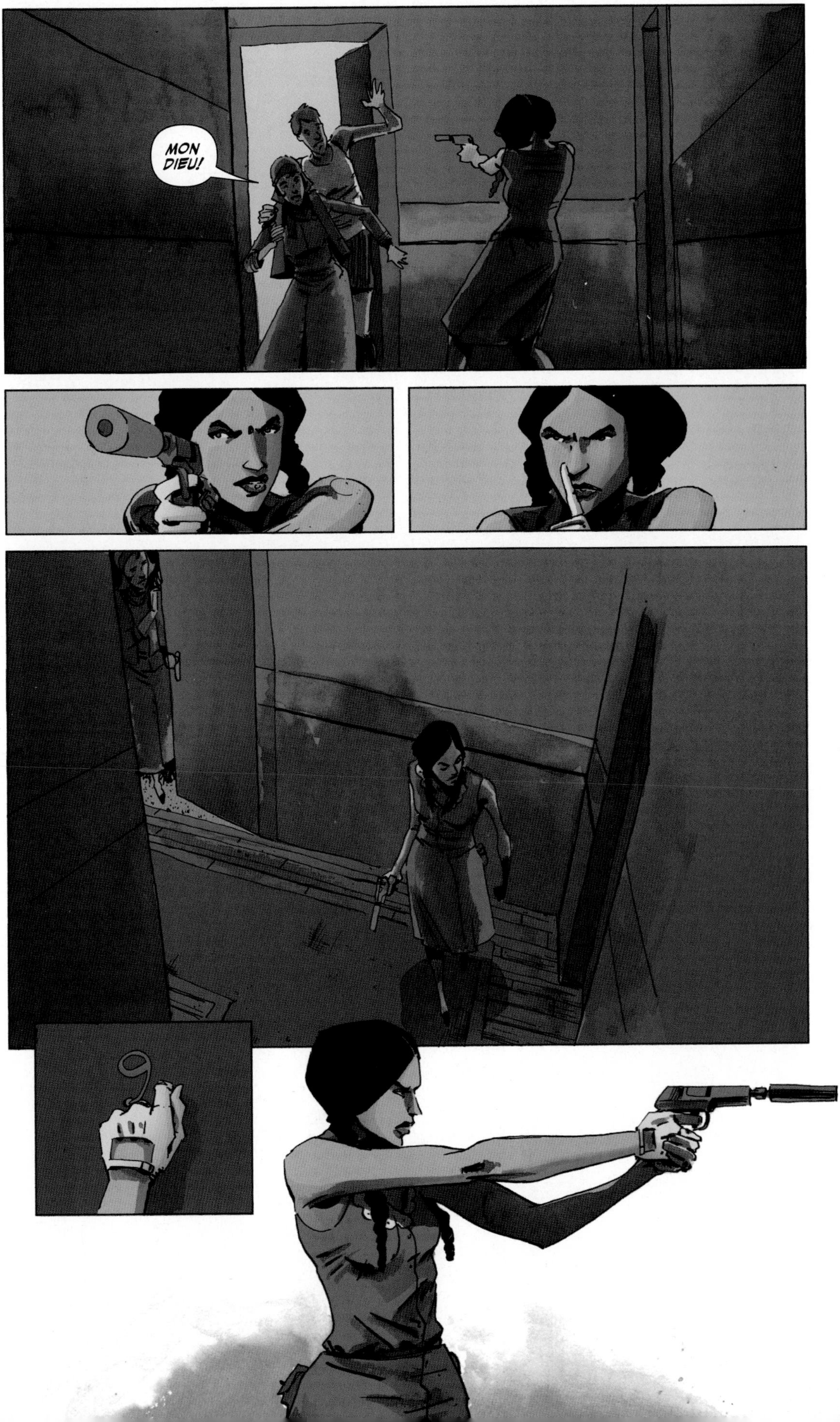
MON DIEU!

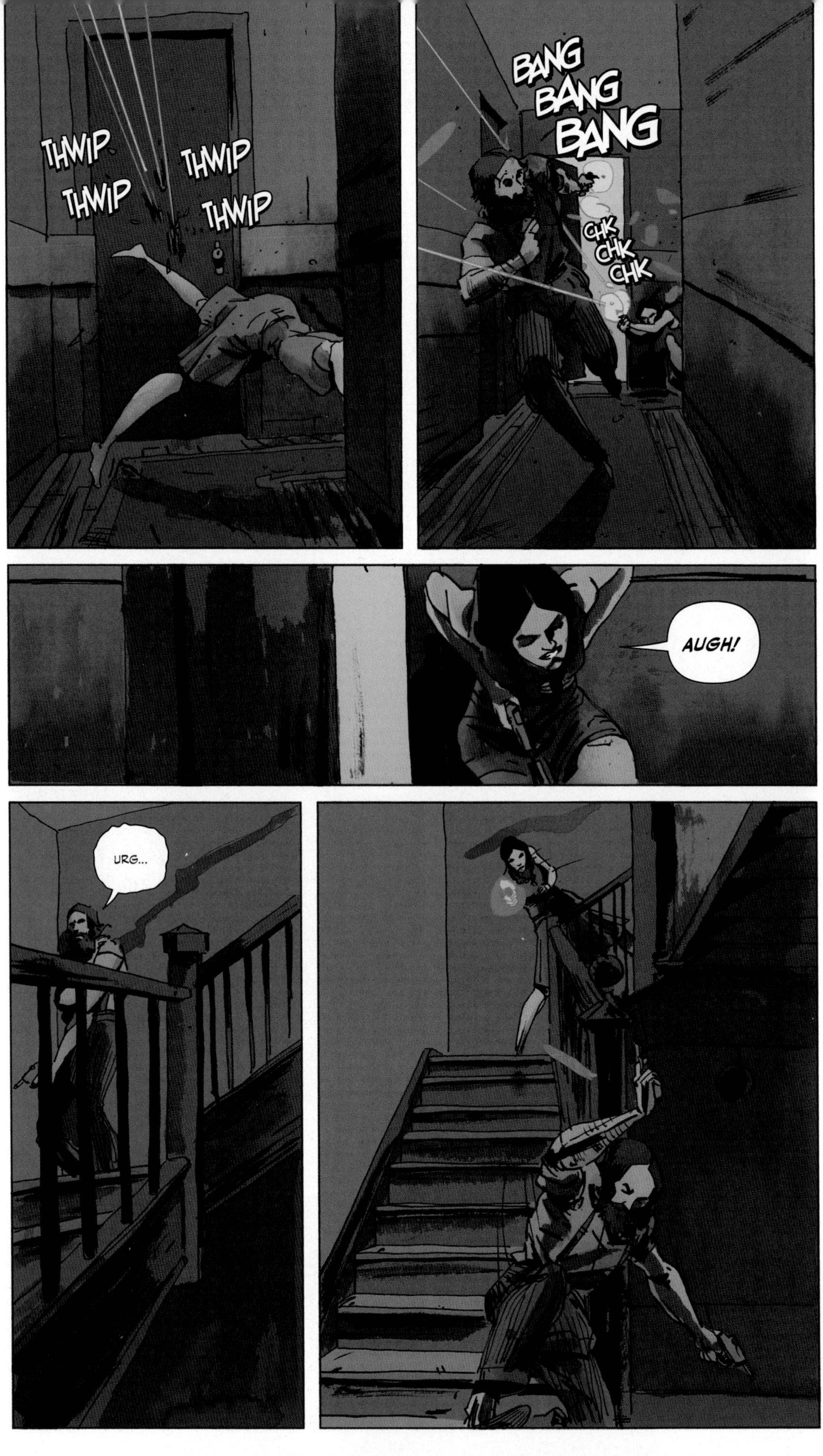
THWIP
THWIP
THWIP
THWIP
BANG
BANG
BANG
CHK
CHK
CHK
AUGH!
URG...

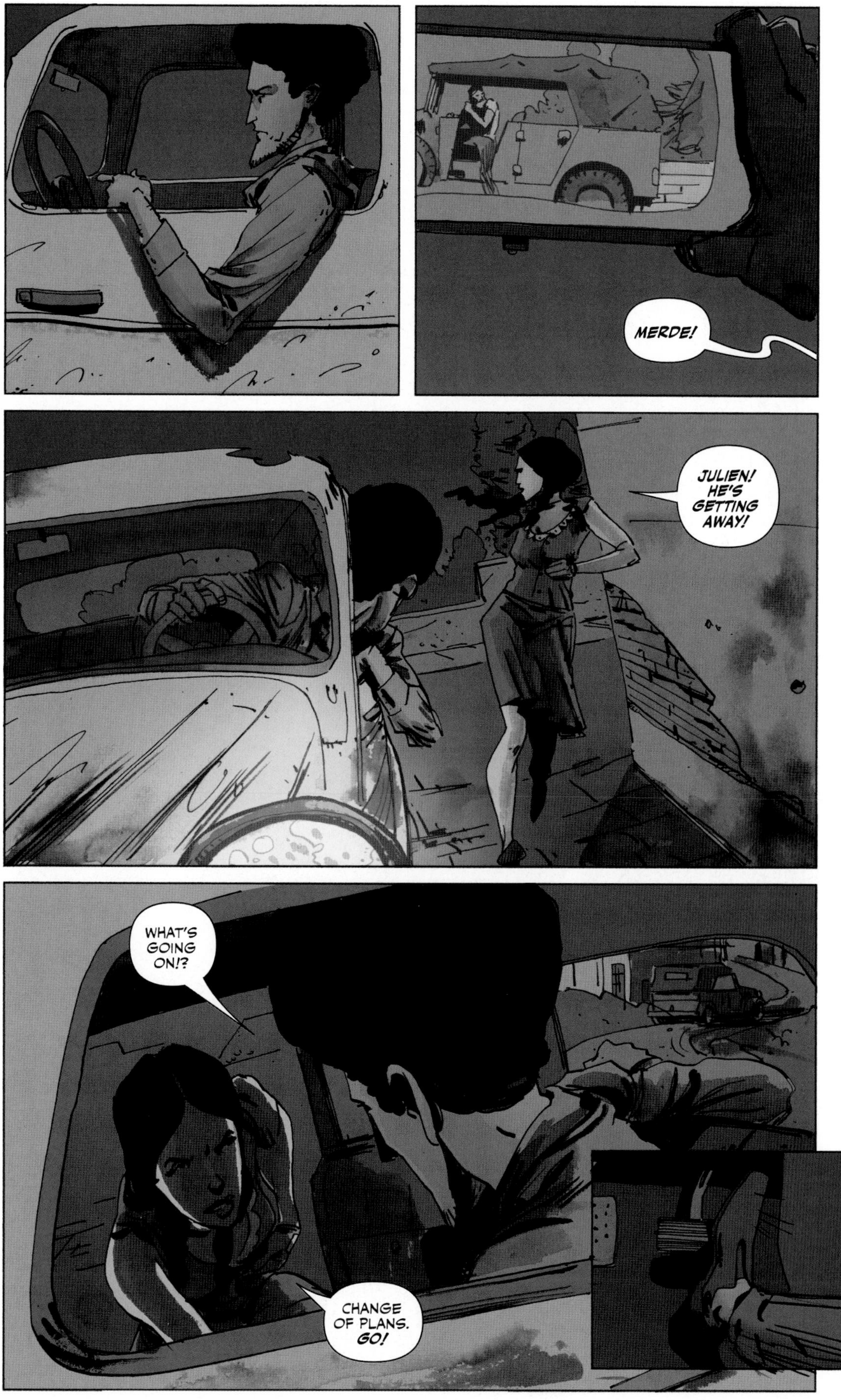

MERDE!
JULIEN! HE'S GETTING AWAY!
WHAT'S GOING ON!?
CHANGE OF PLANS. GO!

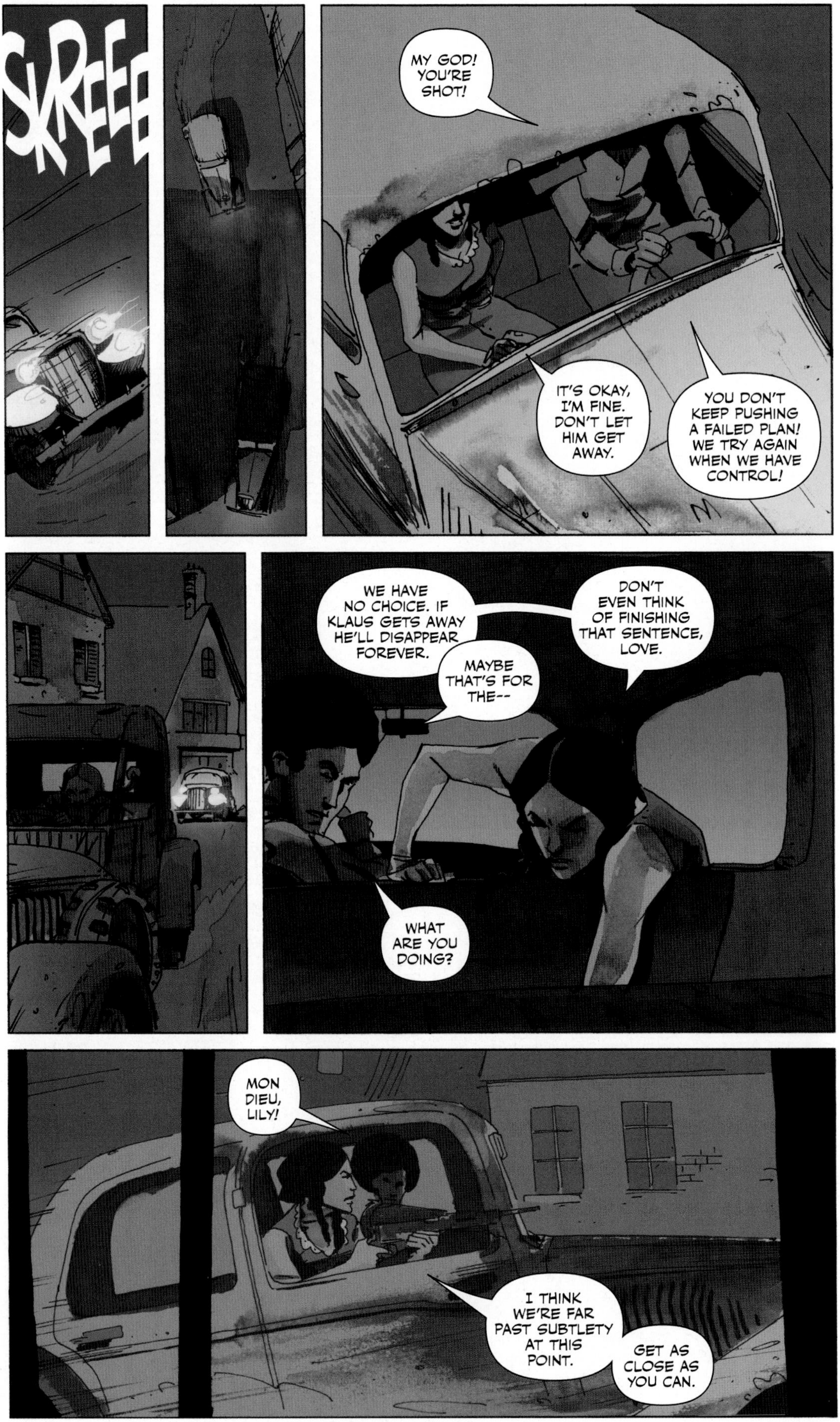
SKREEE
MY GOD! YOU'RE SHOT!
IT'S OKAY, I'M FINE. DON'T LET HIM GET AWAY.
YOU DON'T KEEP PUSHING A FAILED PLAN! WE TRY AGAIN WHEN WE HAVE CONTROL!
WE HAVE NO CHOICE. IF KLAUS GETS AWAY HE'LL DISAPPEAR FOREVER.
MAYBE THAT'S FOR THE--
DON'T EVEN THINK OF FINISHING THAT SENTENCE, LOVE.
WHAT ARE YOU DOING?
MON DIEU, LILY!
I THINK WE'RE FAR PAST SUBTLETY AT THIS POINT.
GET AS CLOSE AS YOU CAN.

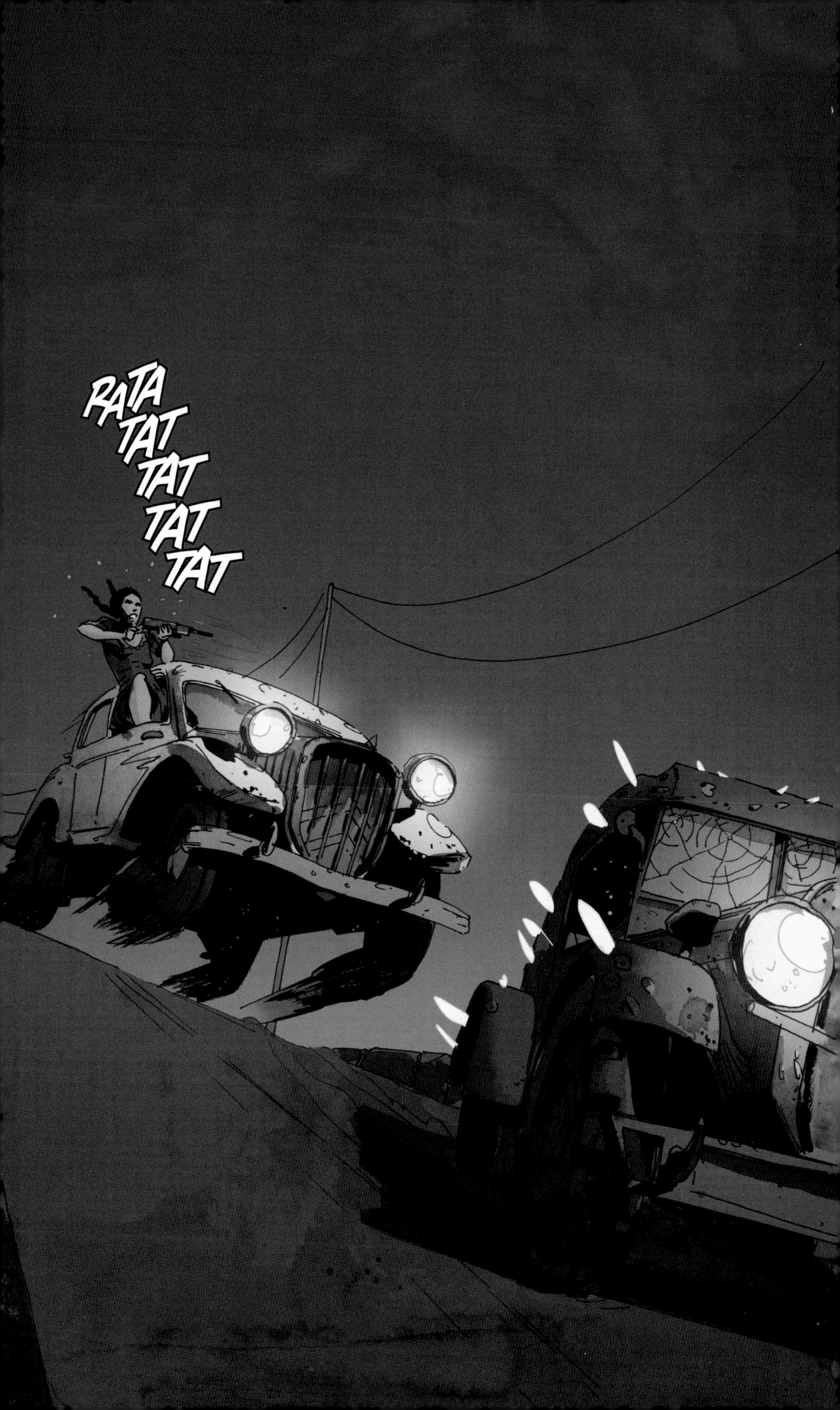
RATA TAT TAT TAT TAT

BANG
CRASH
SKREEEE

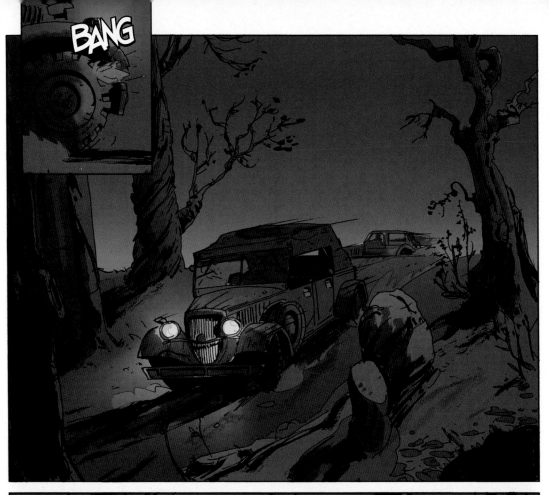

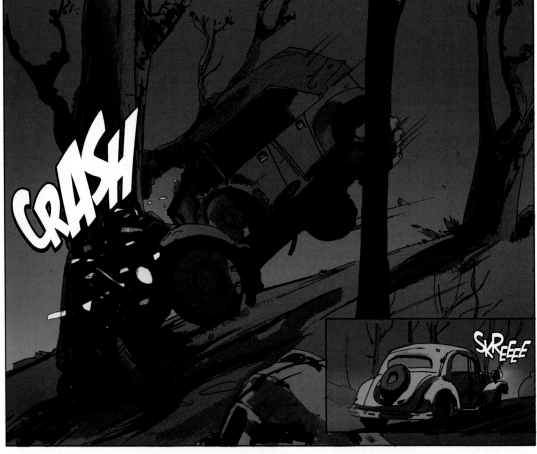

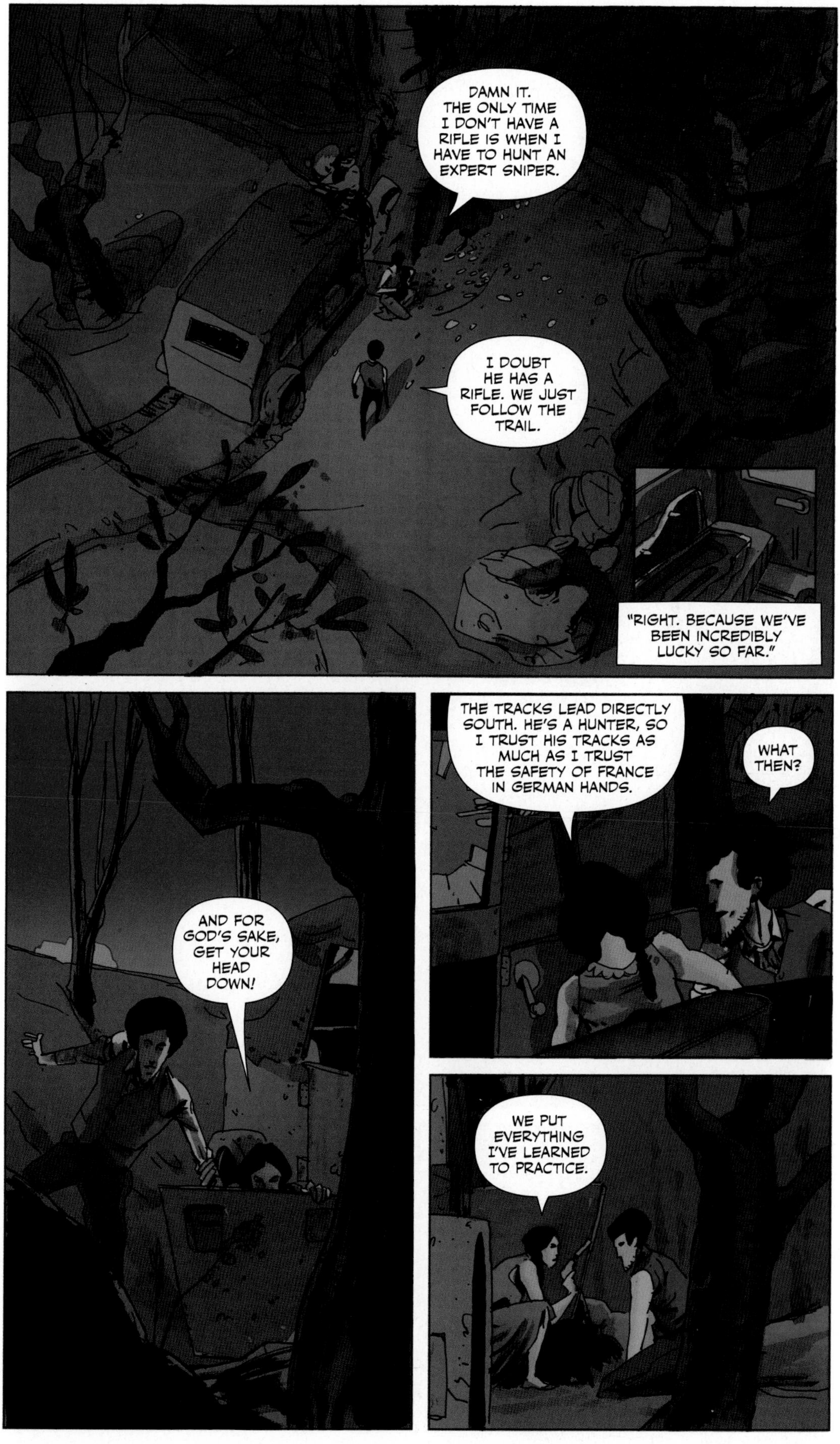
DAMN IT. THE ONLY TIME I DON'T HAVE A RIFLE IS WHEN I HAVE TO HUNT AN EXPERT SNIPER.
I DOUBT HE HAS A RIFLE. WE JUST FOLLOW THE TRAIL.
"RIGHT. BECAUSE WE'VE BEEN INCREDIBLY LUCKY SO FAR."
AND FOR GOD'S SAKE, GET YOUR HEAD DOWN!
THE TRACKS LEAD DIRECTLY SOUTH. HE'S A HUNTER, SO I TRUST HIS TRACKS AS MUCH AS I TRUST THE SAFETY OF FRANCE IN GERMAN HANDS.
WHAT THEN?
WE PUT EVERYTHING I'VE LEARNED TO PRACTICE.

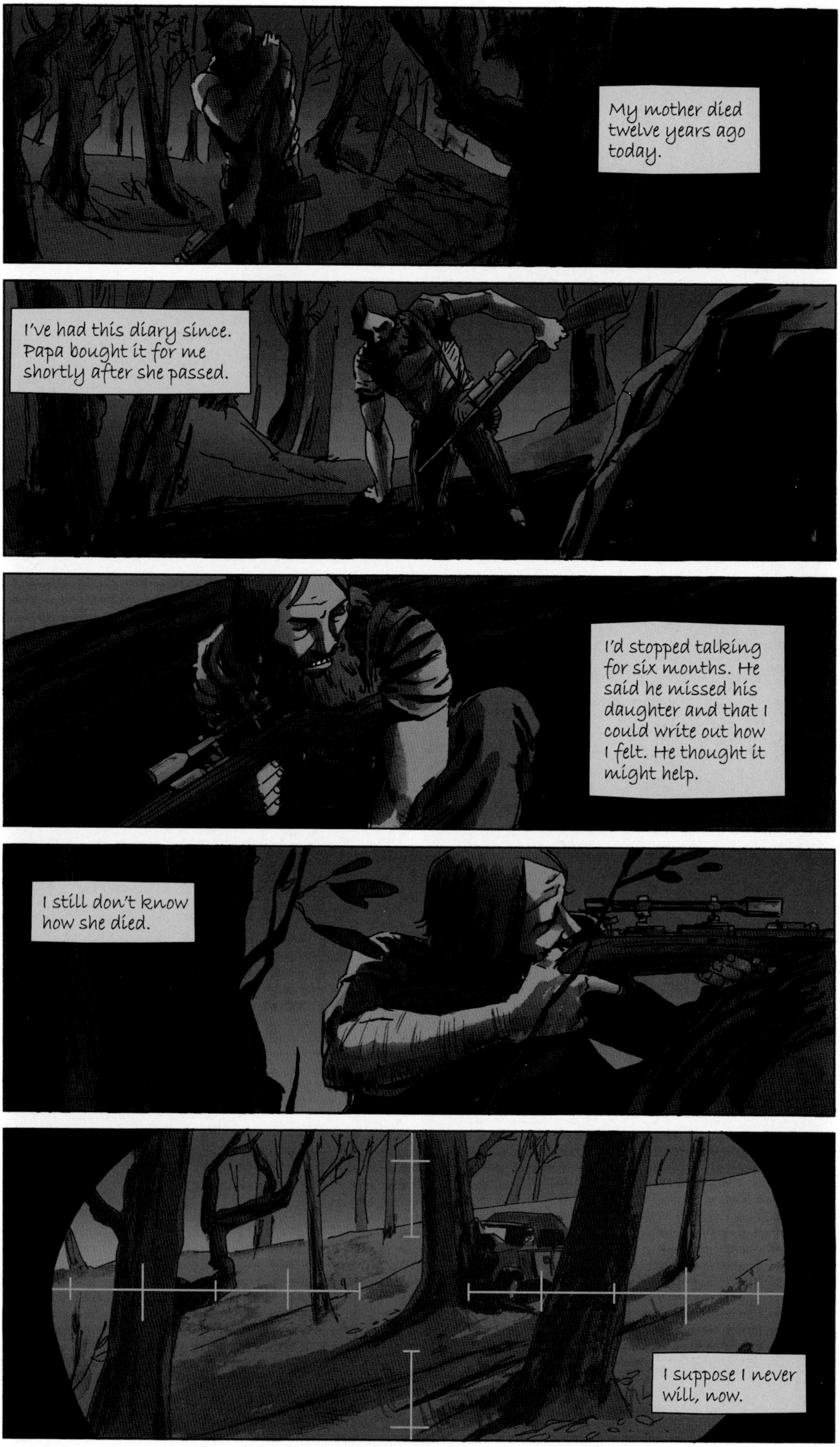
My mother died twelve years ago today.
I've had this diary since. Papa bought it for me shortly after she passed.
I'd stopped talking for six months. He said he missed his daughter and that I could write out how I felt. He thought it might help.
I still don't know how she died.
I suppose I never will, now.

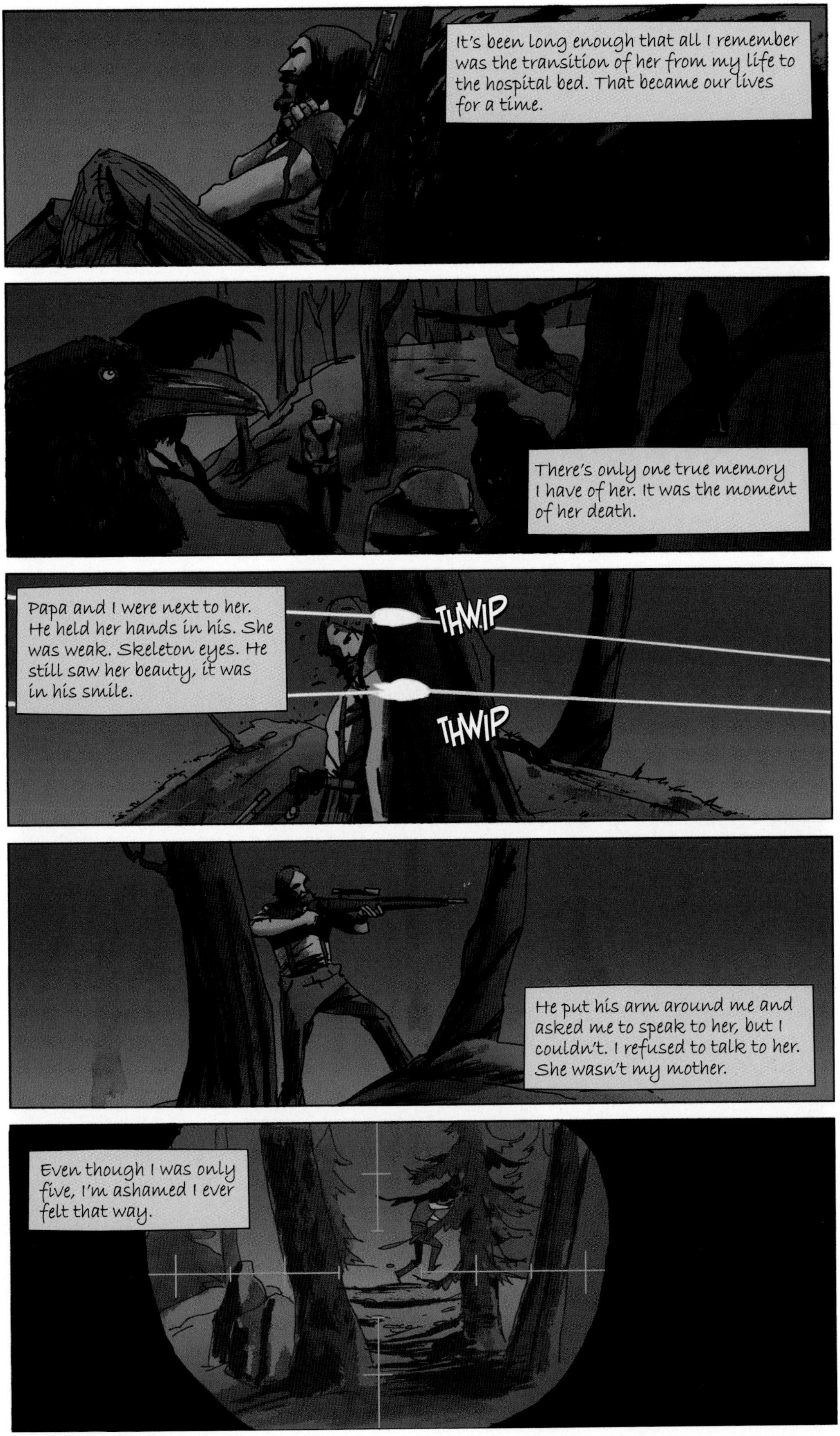
It's been long enough that all I remember was the transition of her from my life to the hospital bed. That became our lives for a time.
There's only one true memory I have of her. It was the moment of her death.
Papa and I were next to her. He held her hands in his. She was weak. Skeleton eyes. He still saw her beauty, it was in his smile.
THWIP
THWIP
He put his arm around me and asked me to speak to her, but I couldn't. I refused to talk to her. She wasn't my mother.
Even though I was only five, I'm ashamed I ever felt that way.

Father saved the moment.

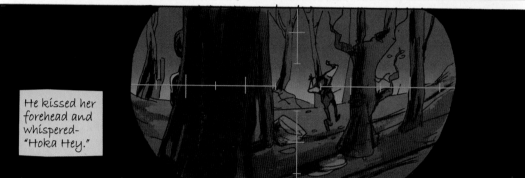

He kissed her forehead and whispered- "Hoka Hey."

Then she was gone. Sometimes I wish I missed her.

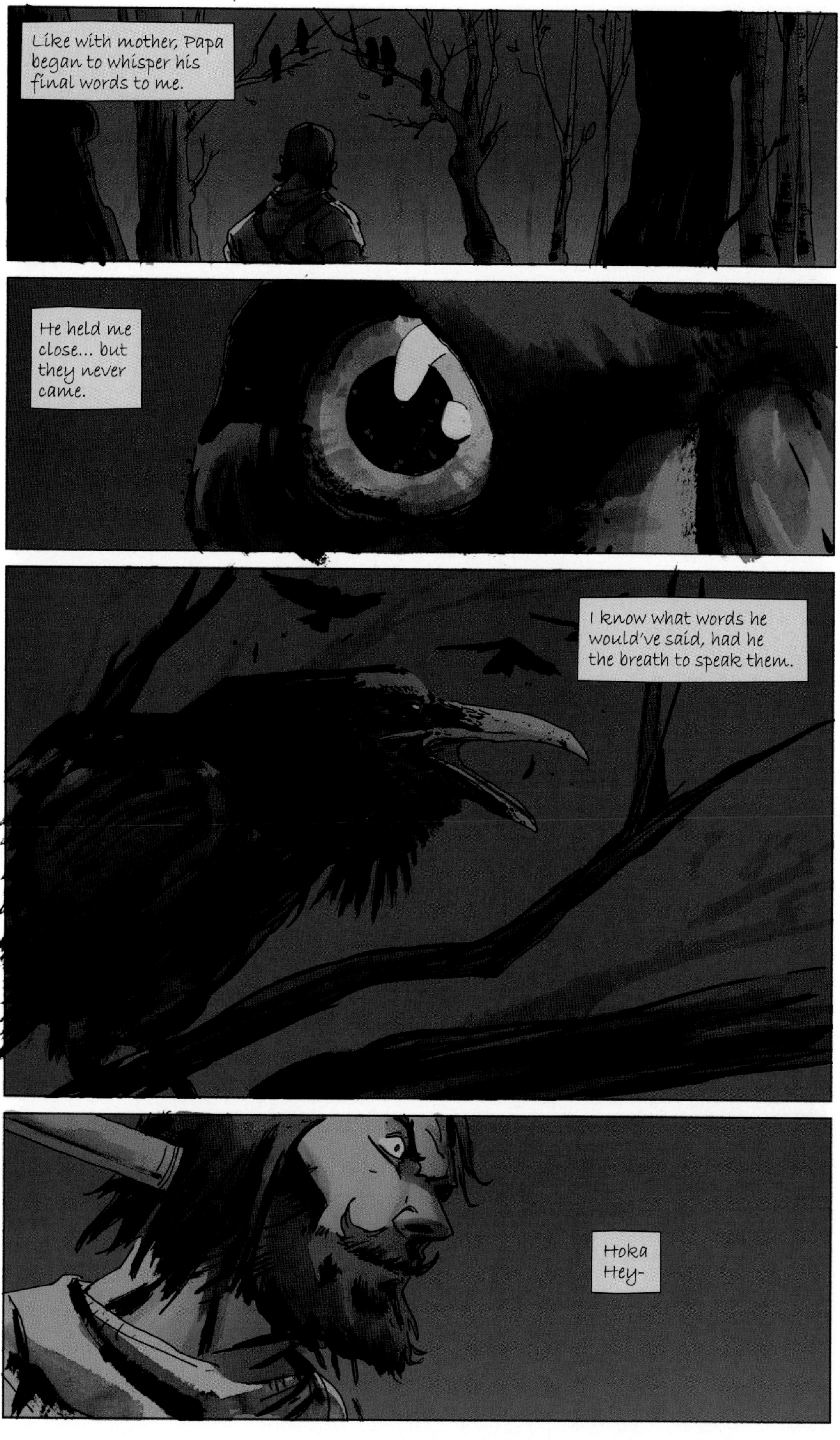
Like with mother, Papa began to whisper his final words to me.
He held me close... but they never came.
I know what words he would've said, had he the breath to speak them.
Hoka Hey-

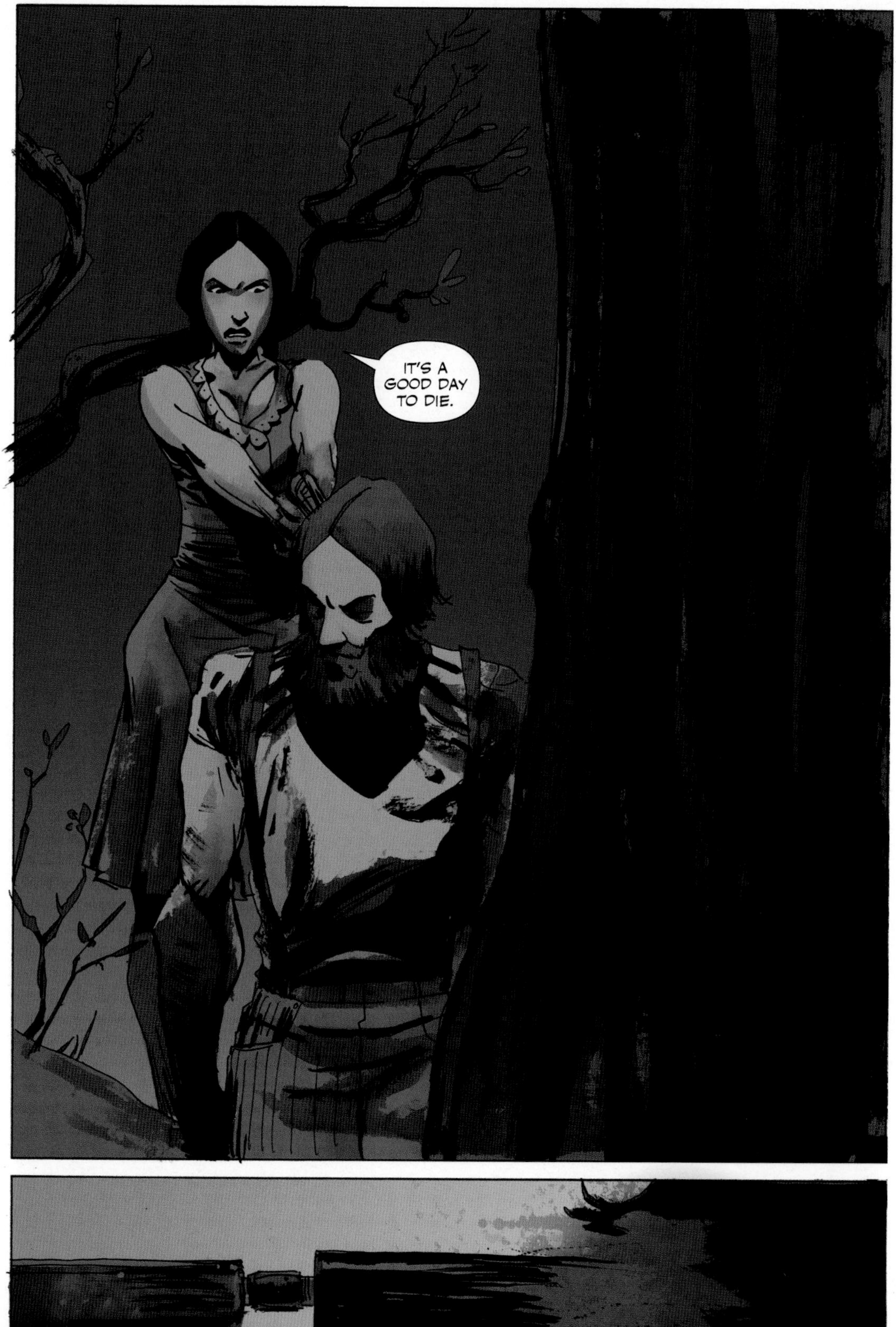
IT'S A GOOD DAY TO DIE.

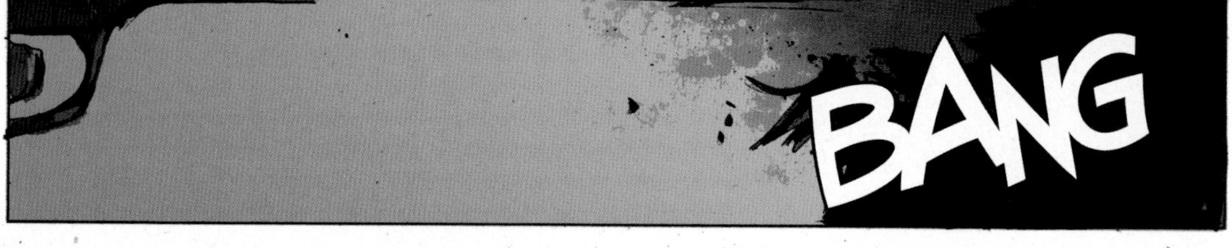
BANG

CHAPTER EIGHTEEN

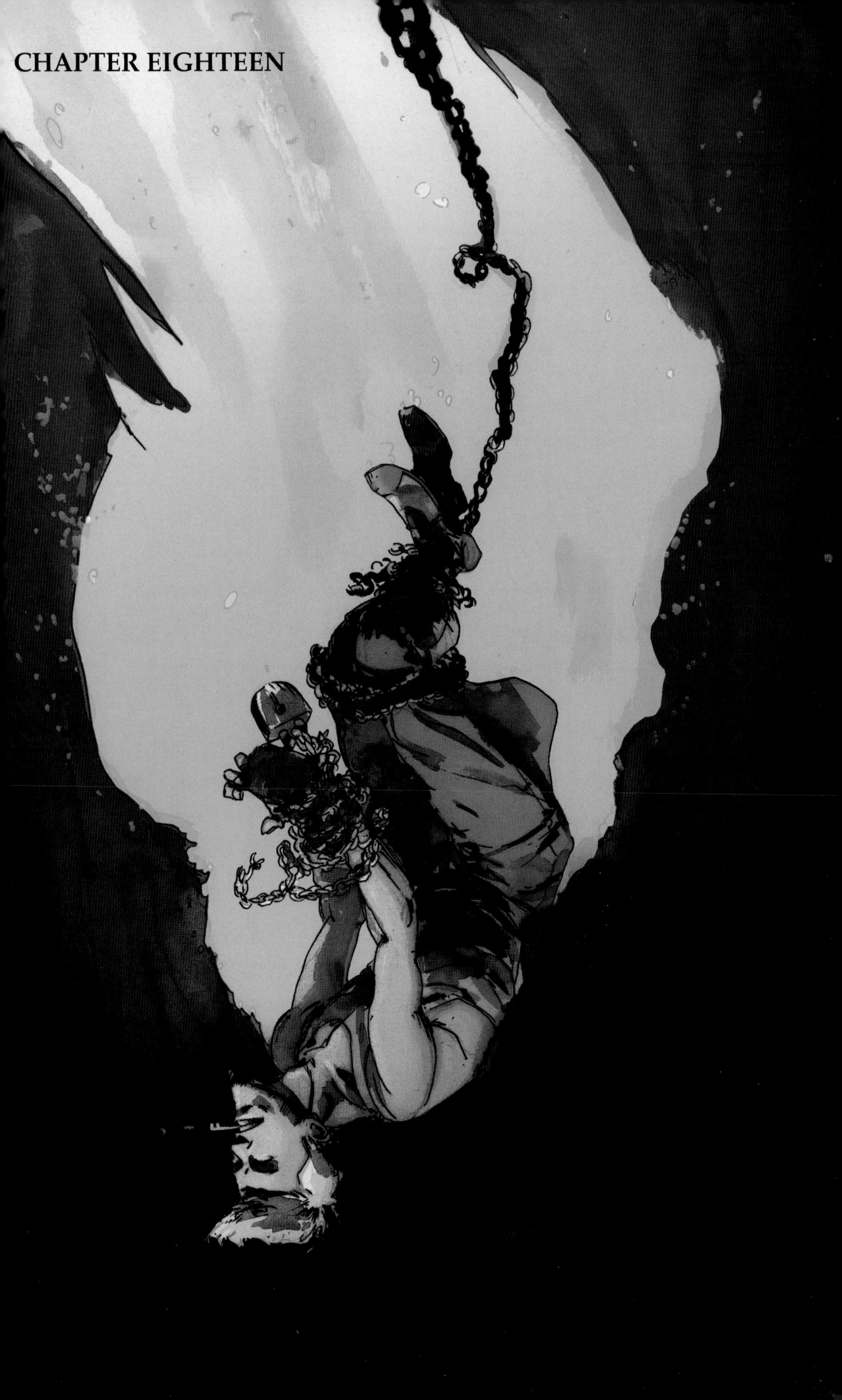

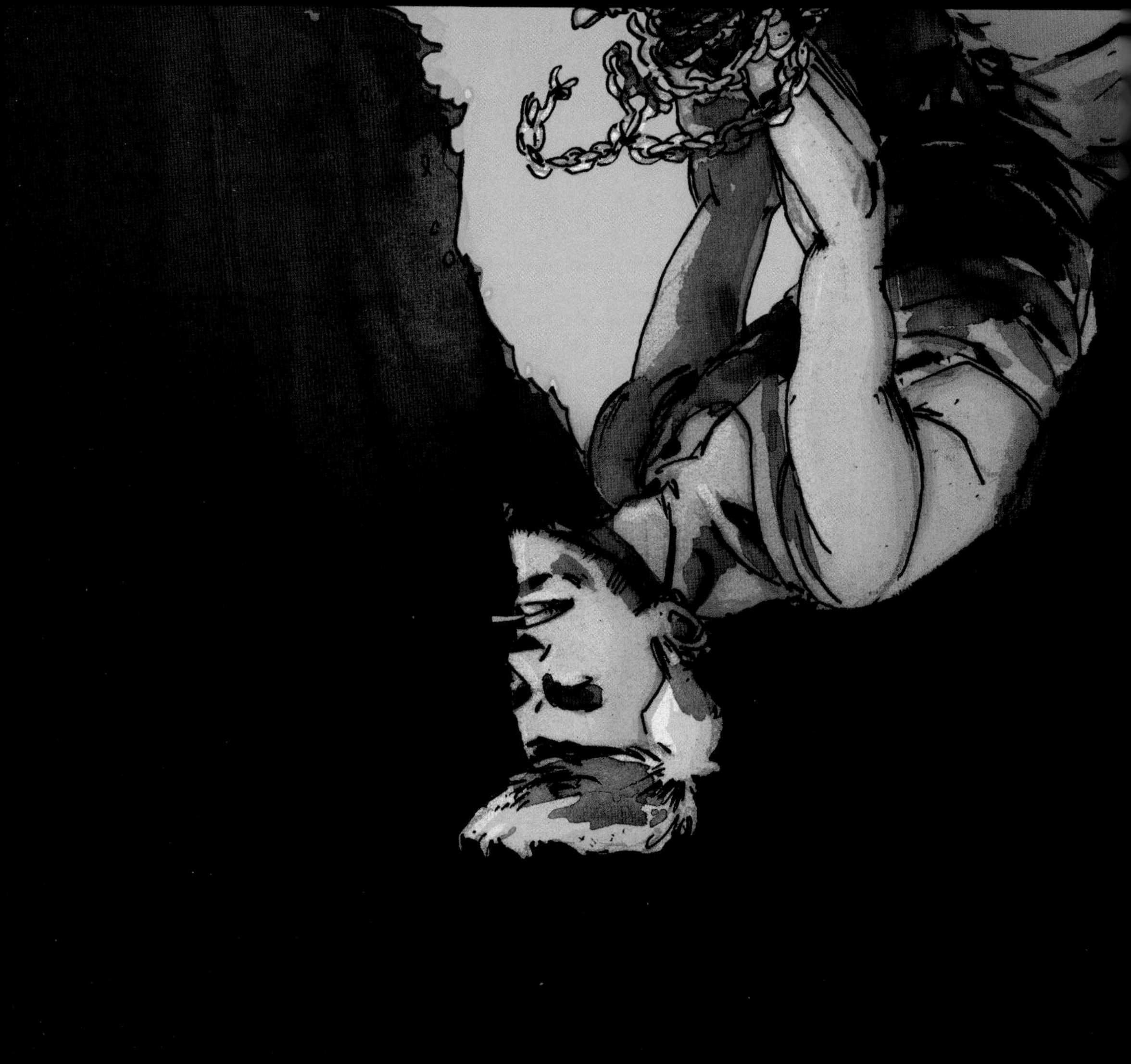

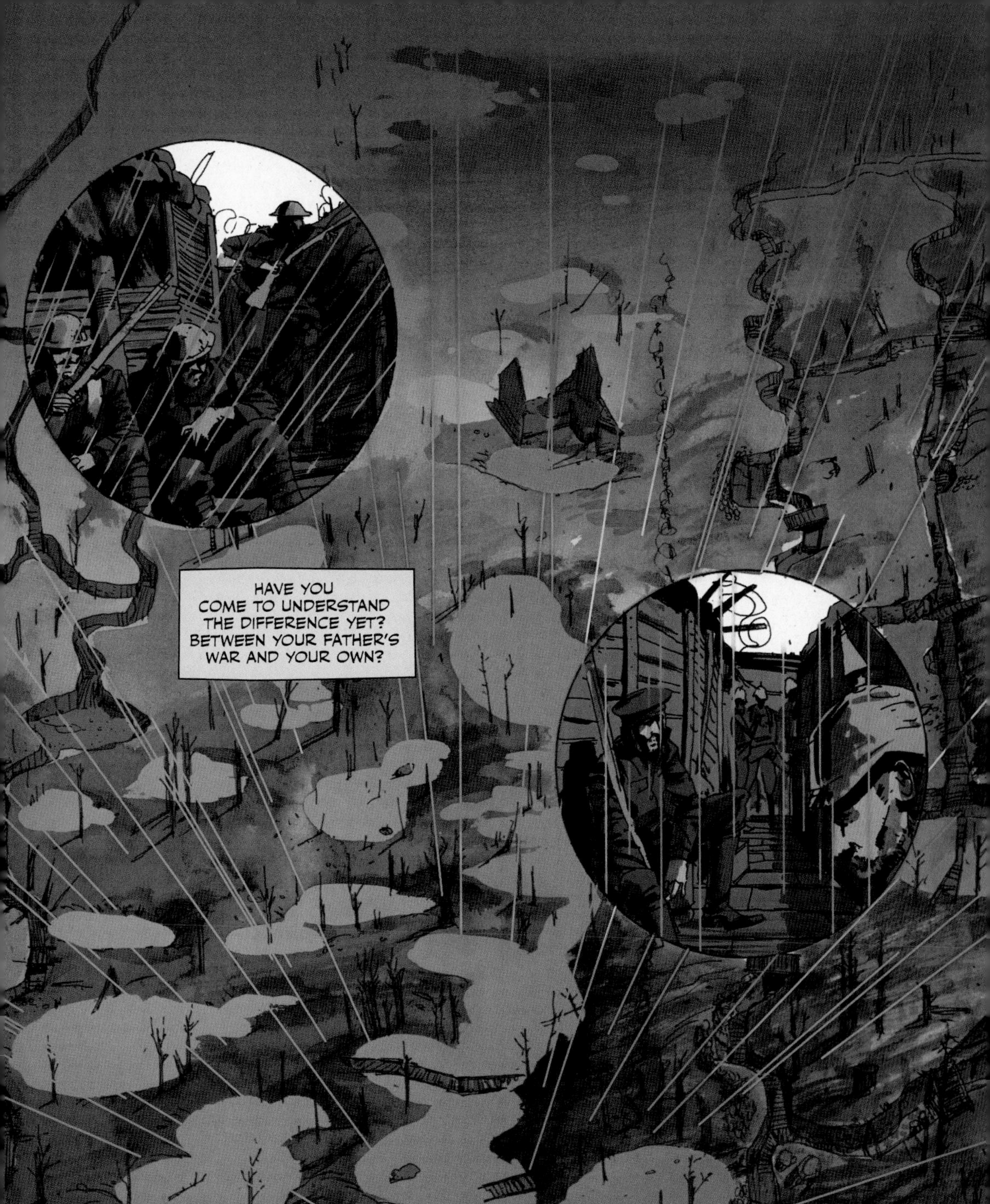
HAVE YOU COME TO UNDERSTAND THE DIFFERENCE YET? BETWEEN YOUR FATHER'S WAR AND YOUR OWN?

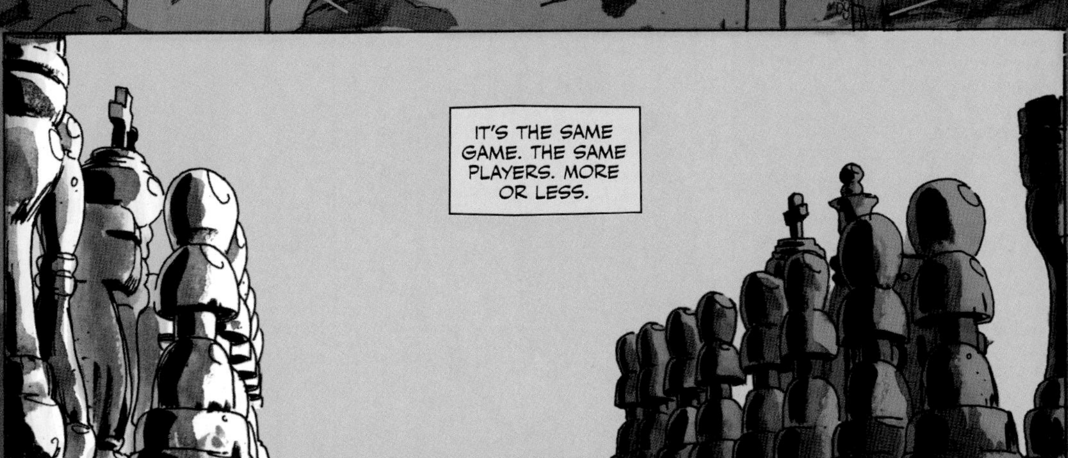
IT'S THE SAME GAME. THE SAME PLAYERS. MORE OR LESS.

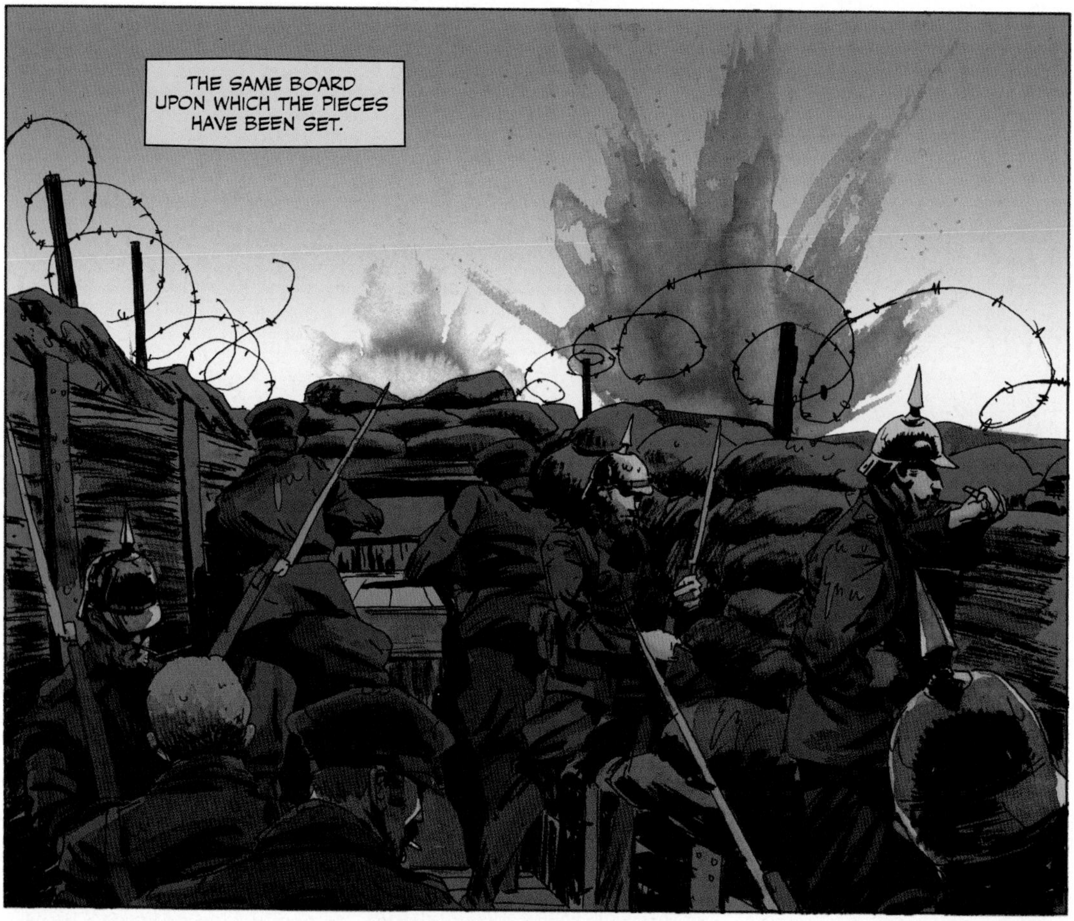
THE SAME BOARD UPON WHICH THE PIECES HAVE BEEN SET.

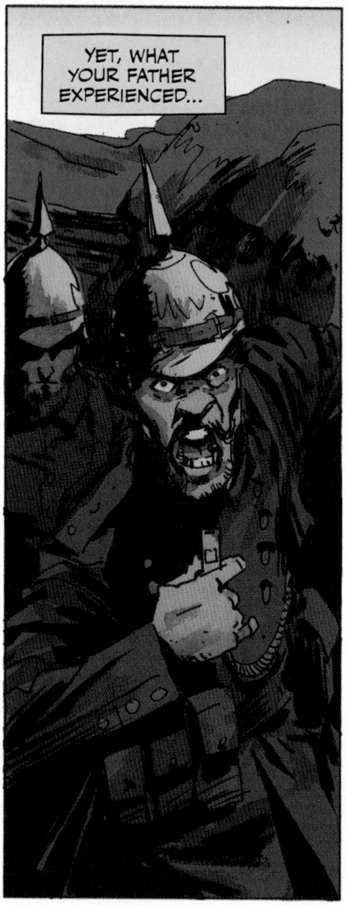
YET, WHAT YOUR FATHER EXPERIENCED...

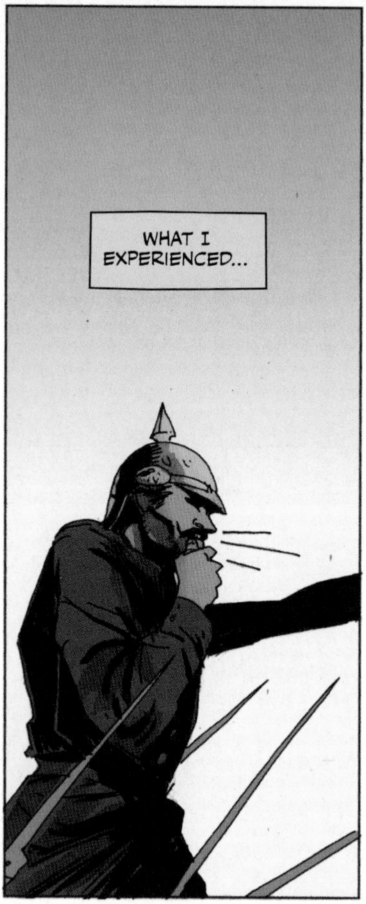
WHAT I EXPERIENCED...

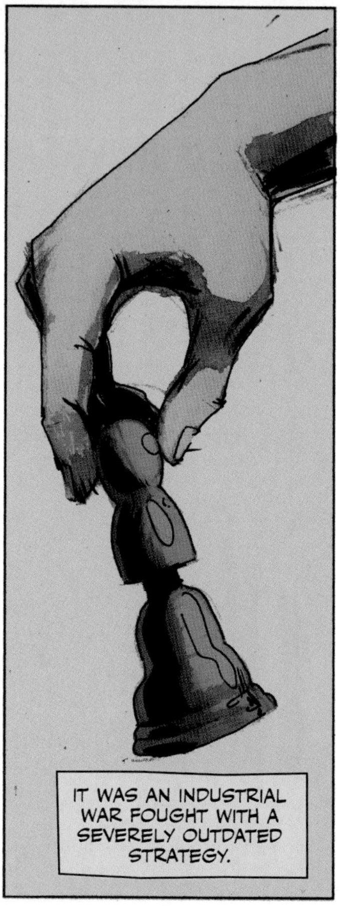
IT WAS AN INDUSTRIAL WAR FOUGHT WITH A SEVERELY OUTDATED STRATEGY.

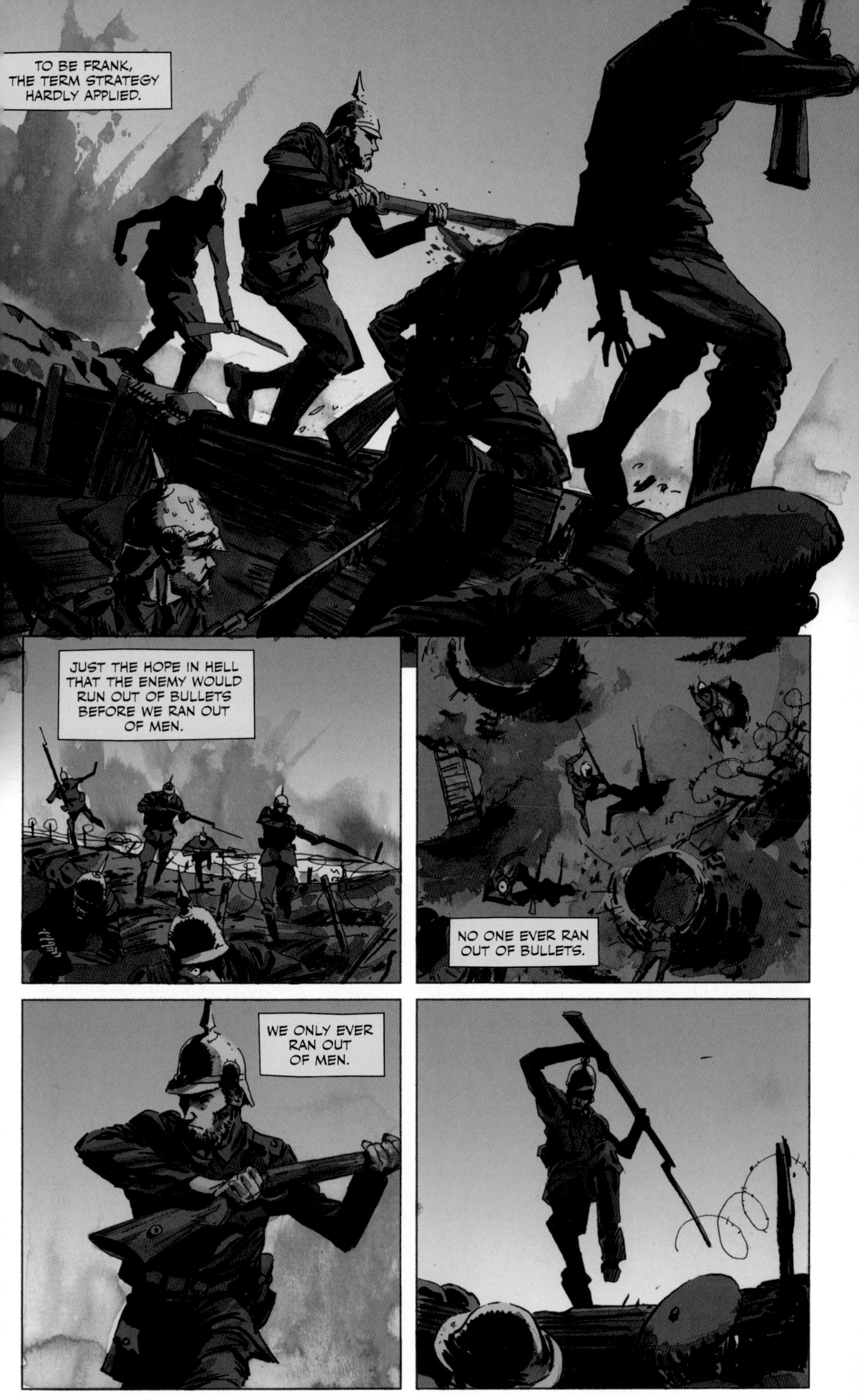
TO BE FRANK, THE TERM STRATEGY HARDLY APPLIED.
JUST THE HOPE IN HELL THAT THE ENEMY WOULD RUN OUT OF BULLETS BEFORE WE RAN OUT OF MEN.
NO ONE EVER RAN OUT OF BULLETS.
WE ONLY EVER RAN OUT OF MEN.

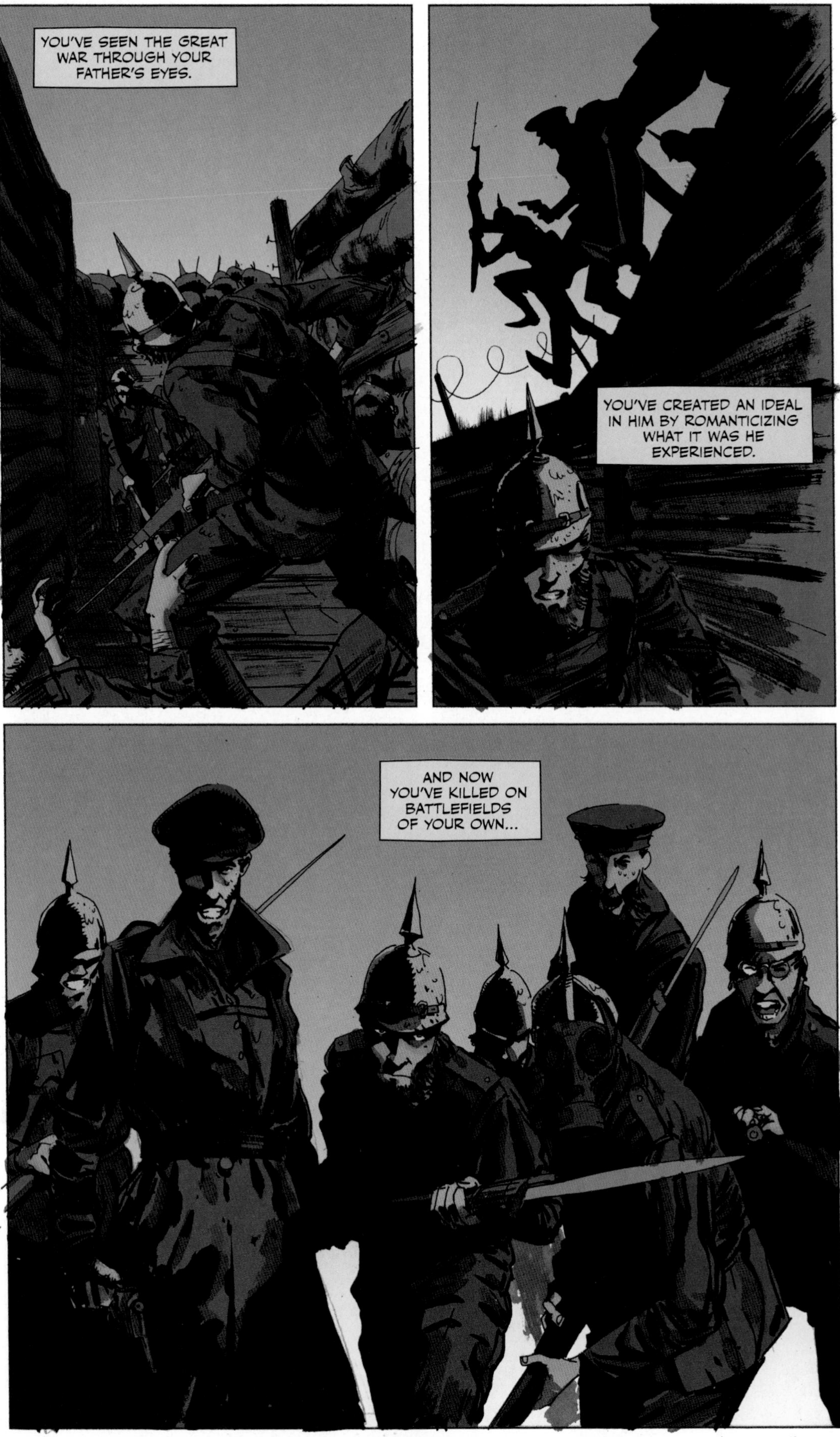
YOU'VE SEEN THE GREAT WAR THROUGH YOUR FATHER'S EYES.
YOU'VE CREATED AN IDEAL IN HIM BY ROMANTICIZING WHAT IT WAS HE EXPERIENCED.
AND NOW YOU'VE KILLED ON BATTLEFIELDS OF YOUR OWN...

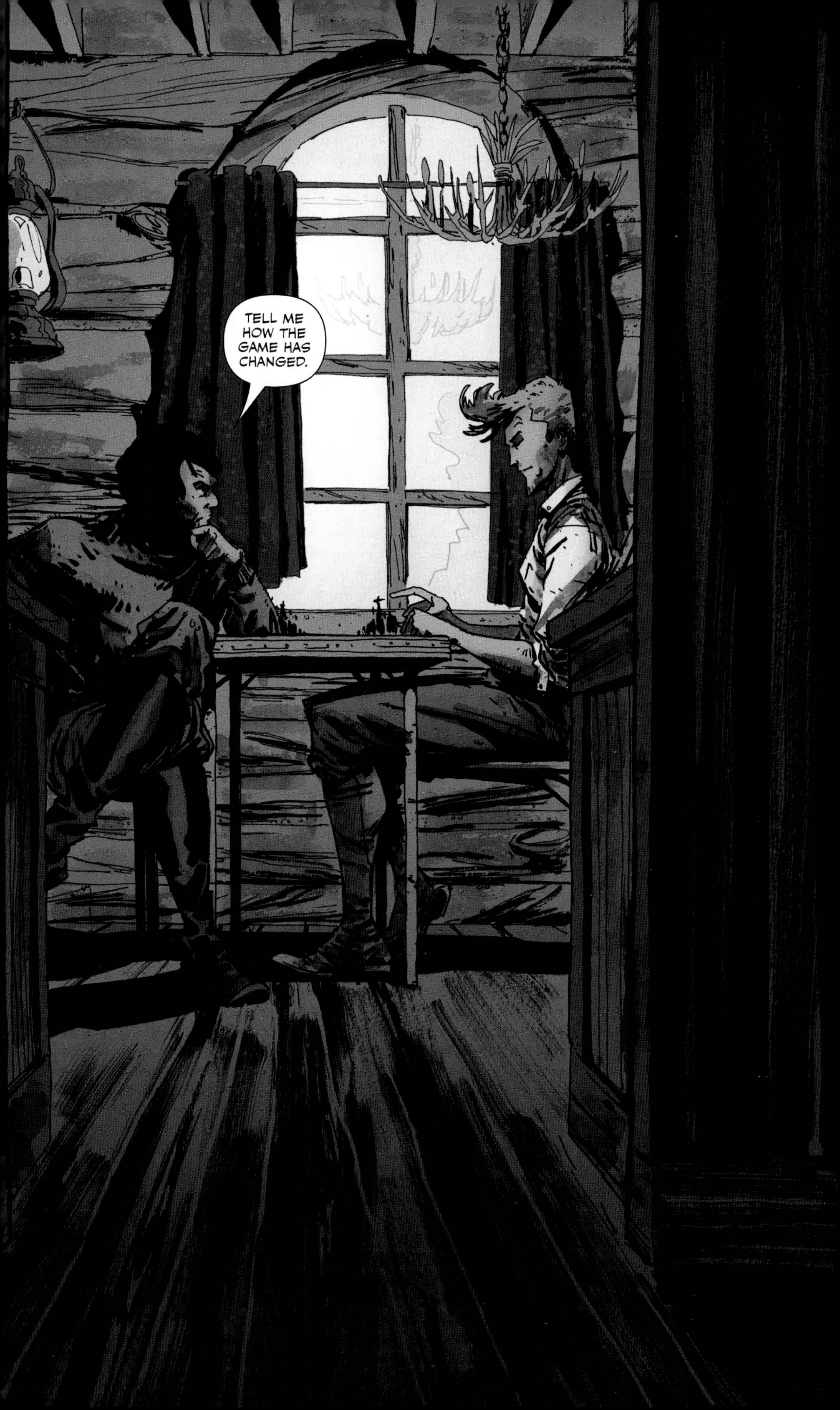
TELL ME HOW THE GAME HAS CHANGED.

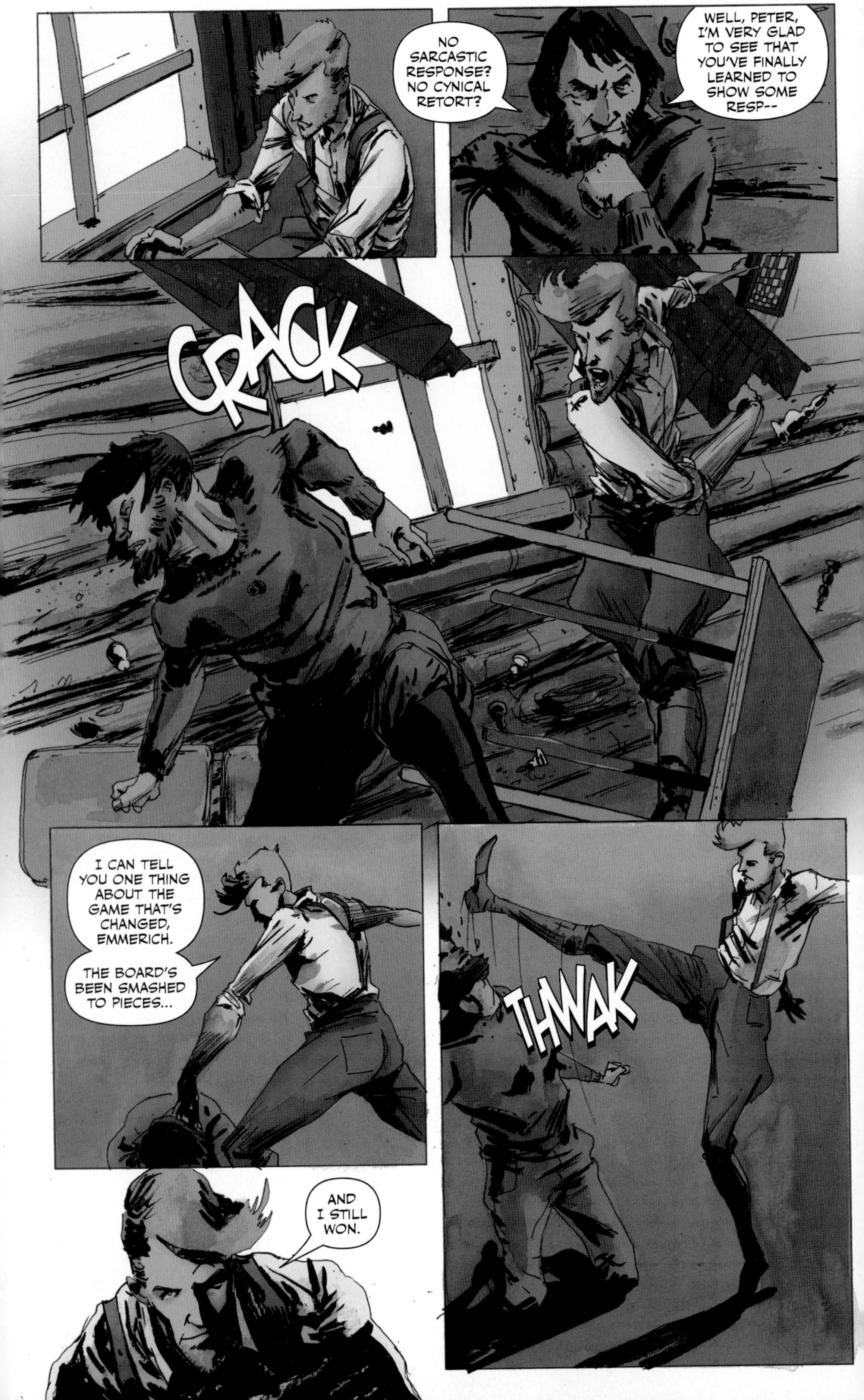
NO SARCASTIC RESPONSE? NO CYNICAL RETORT?
WELL, PETER, I'M VERY GLAD TO SEE THAT YOU'VE FINALLY LEARNED TO SHOW SOME RESP--
CRACK
I CAN TELL YOU ONE THING ABOUT THE GAME THAT'S CHANGED, EMMERICH.
THE BOARD'S BEEN SMASHED TO PIECES...
THWAK
AND I STILL WON.

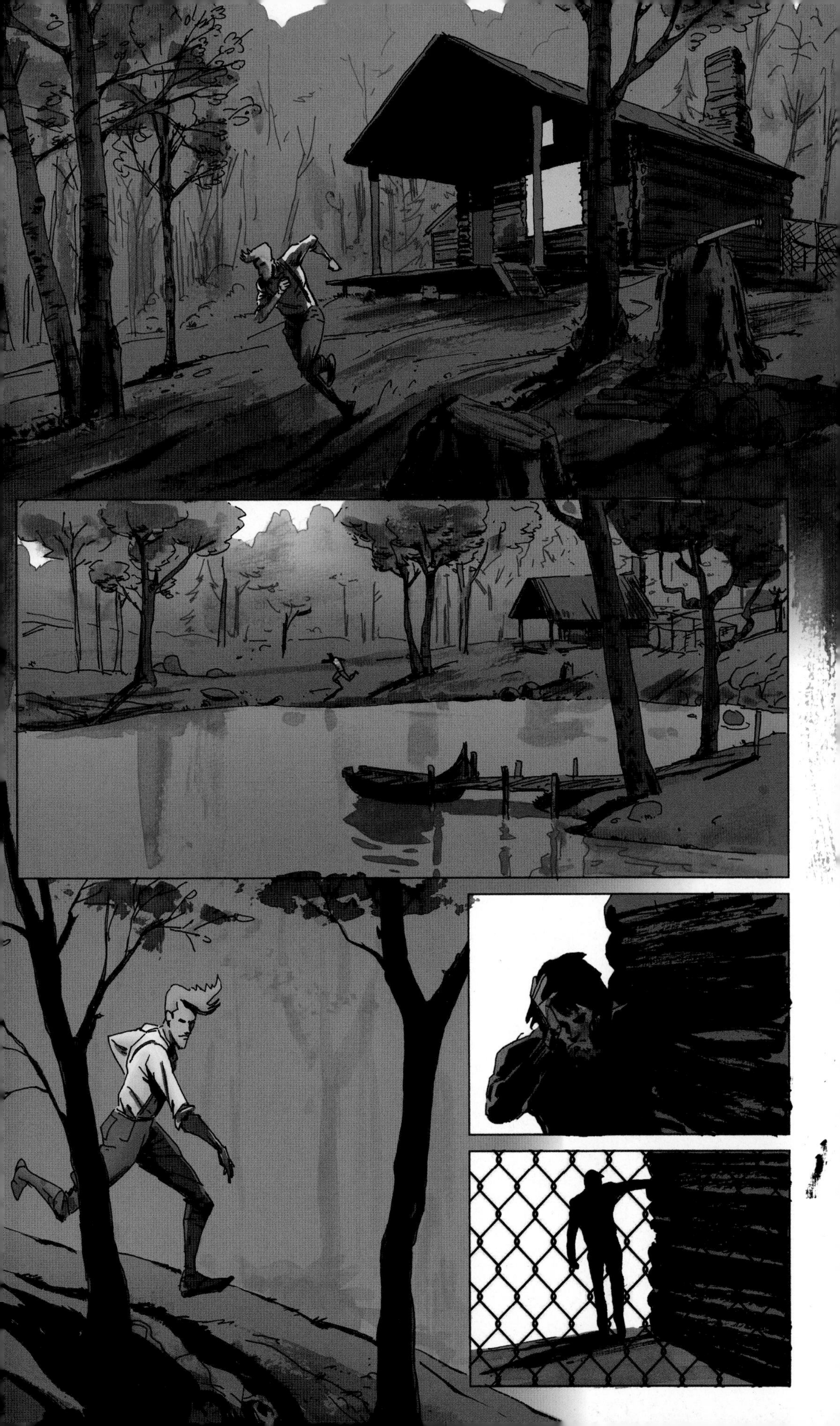

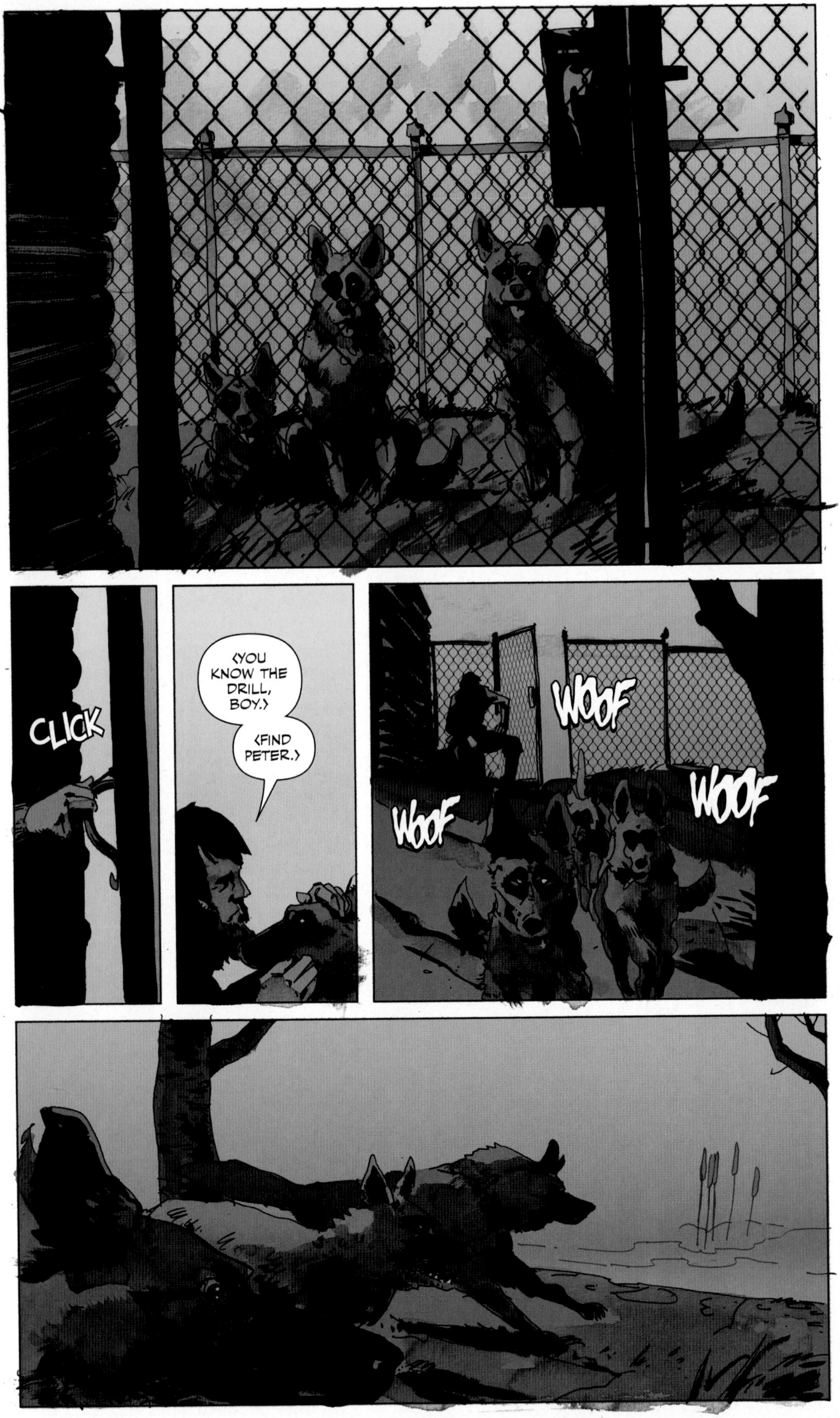
CLICK
<YOU KNOW THE DRILL, BOY.>
<FIND PETER.>
WOOF
WOOF
WOOF

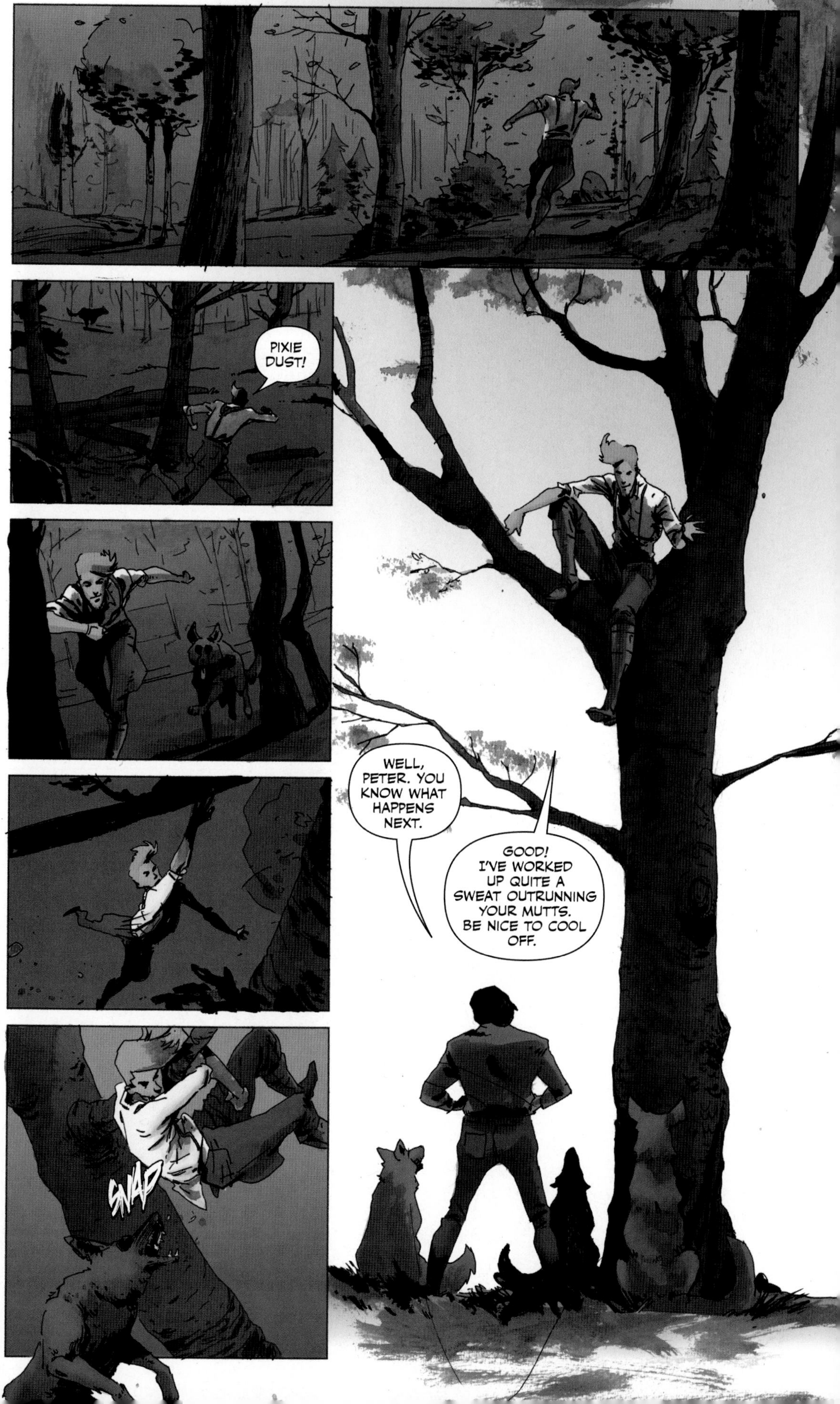
PIXIE DUST!
SNAP
WELL, PETER. YOU KNOW WHAT HAPPENS NEXT.
GOOD! I'VE WORKED UP QUITE A SWEAT OUTRUNNING YOUR MUTTS. BE NICE TO COOL OFF.

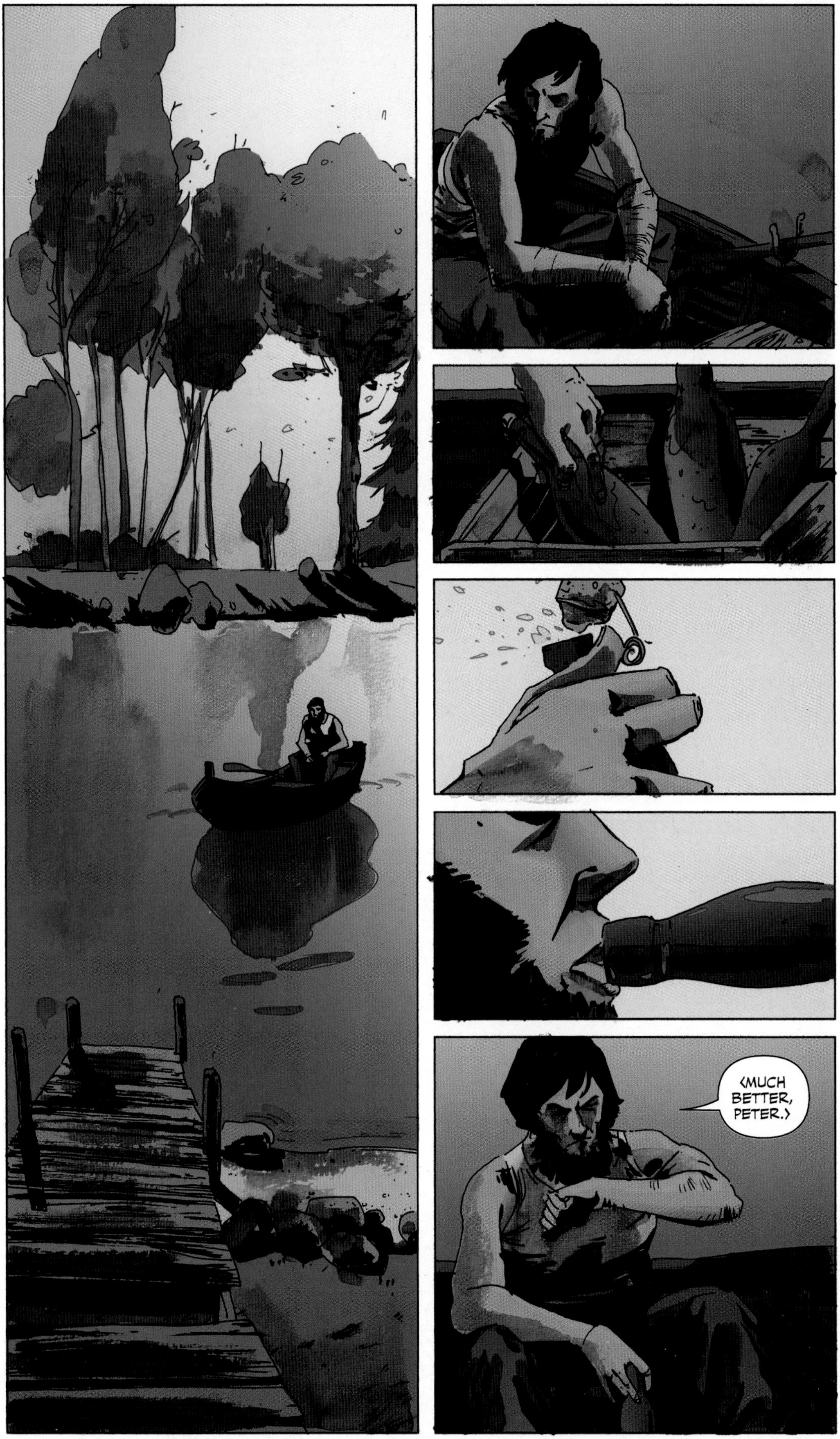
<MUCH BETTER, PETER.>

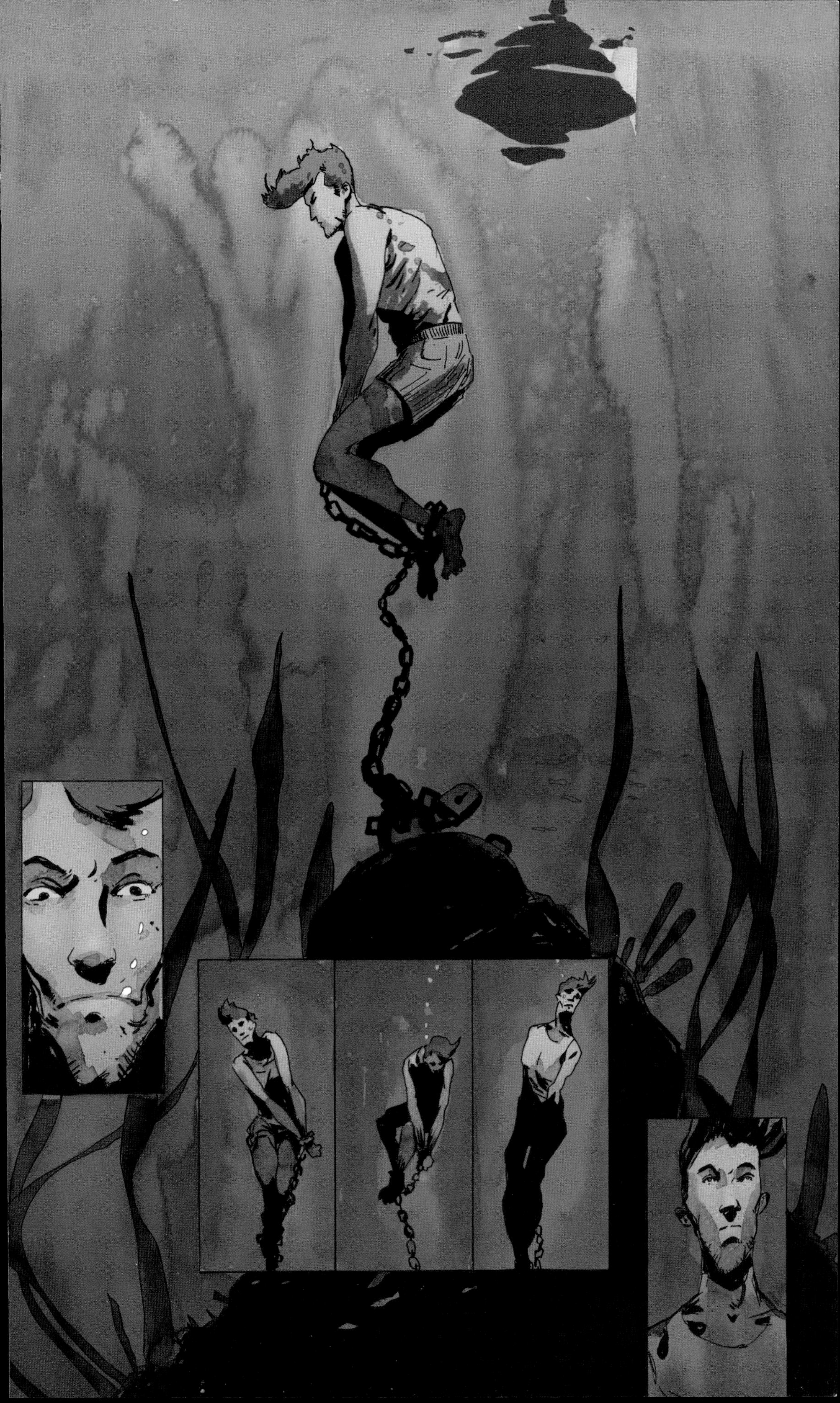

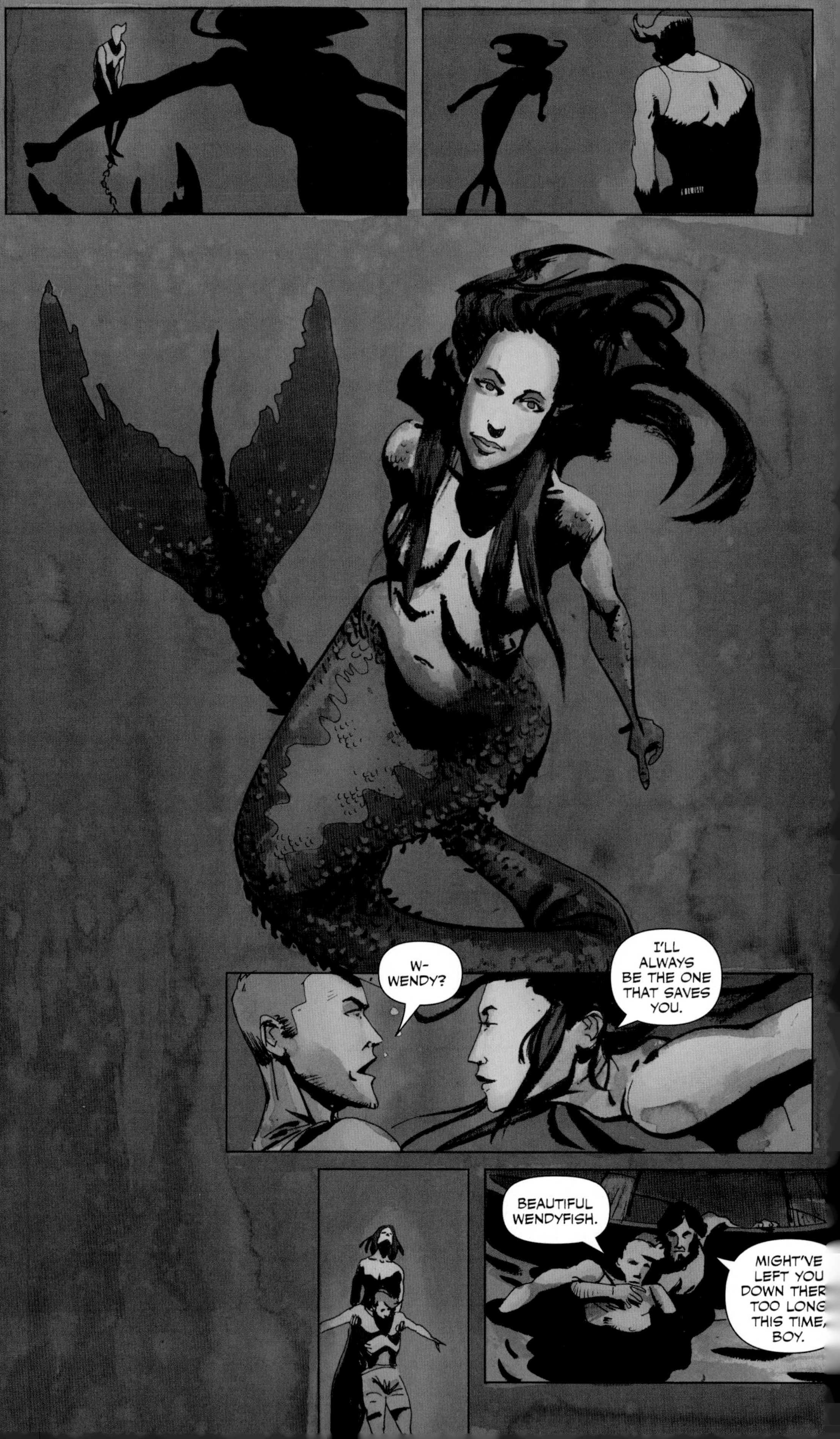
W-
WENDY?
I'LL ALWAYS BE THE ONE THAT SAVES YOU.
BEAUTIFUL WENDYFISH.
MIGHT'VE LEFT YOU DOWN THER TOO LONG THIS TIME, BOY.

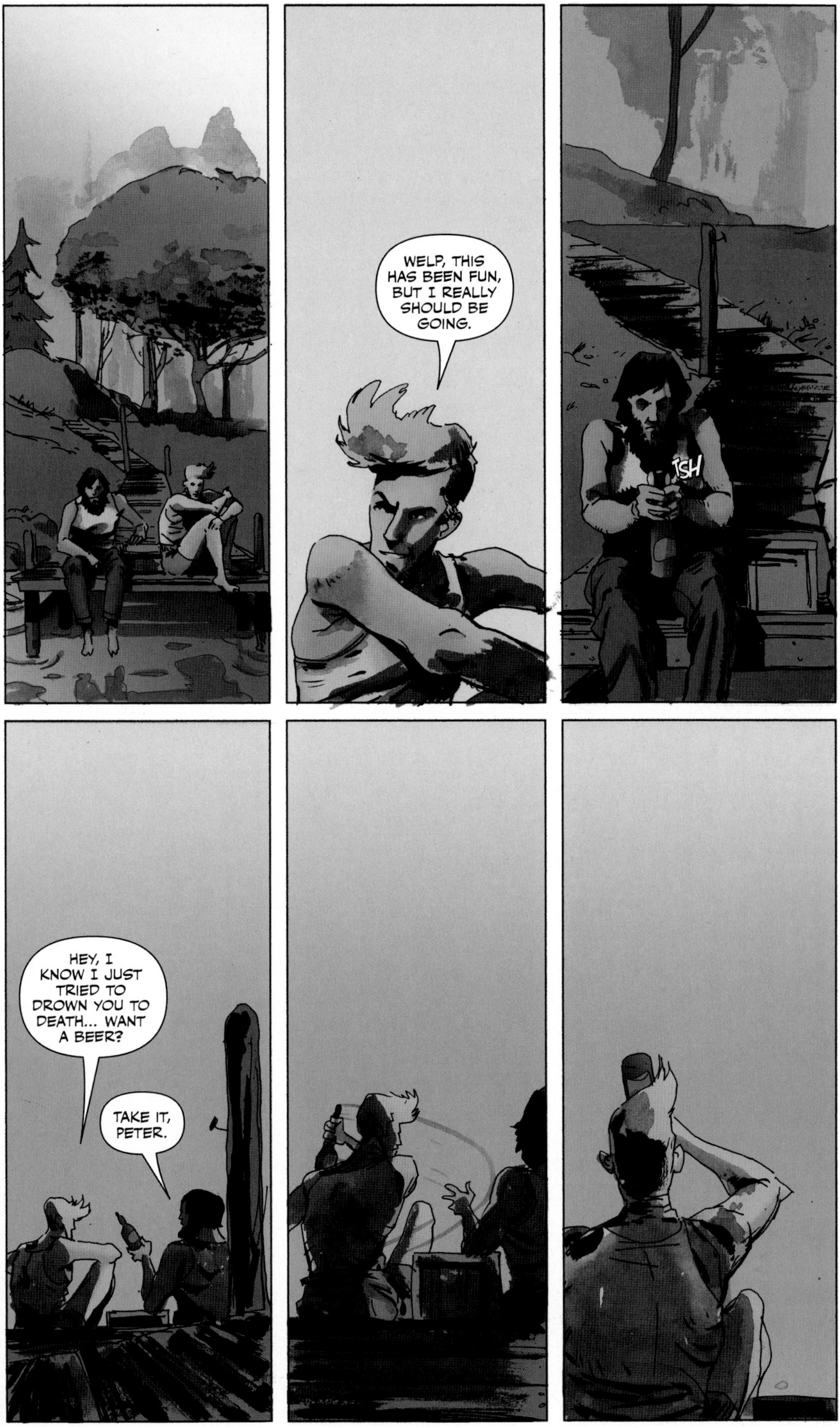
WELP, THIS HAS BEEN FUN, BUT I REALLY SHOULD BE GOING.
TSH
HEY, I KNOW I JUST TRIED TO DROWN YOU TO DEATH... WANT A BEER?
TAKE IT, PETER.

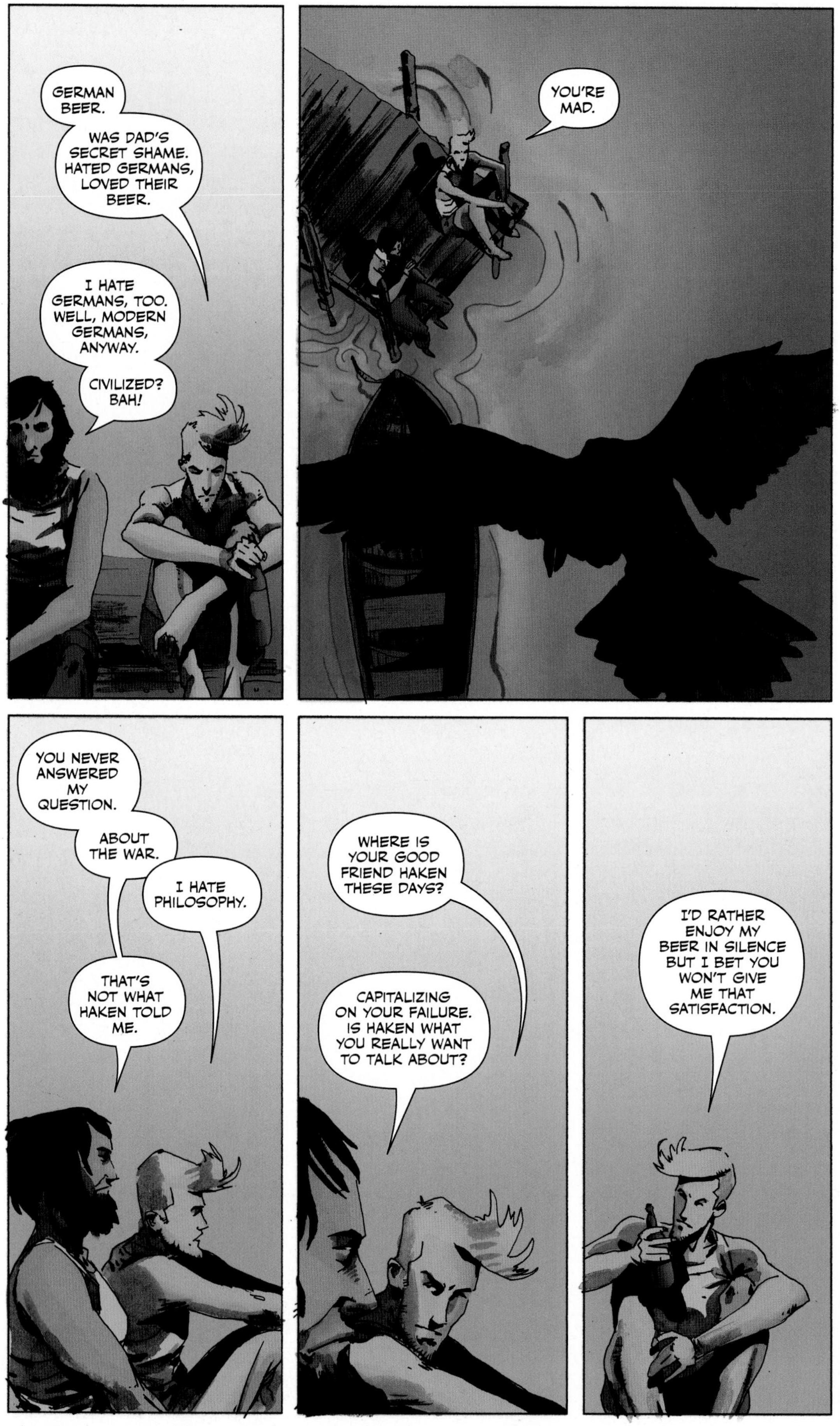
GERMAN BEER.
WAS DAD'S SECRET SHAME. HATED GERMANS, LOVED THEIR BEER.
I HATE GERMANS, TOO. WELL, MODERN GERMANS, ANYWAY.
CIVILIZED? BAH!
YOU'RE MAD.
YOU NEVER ANSWERED MY QUESTION.
ABOUT THE WAR.
I HATE PHILOSOPHY.
THAT'S NOT WHAT HAKEN TOLD ME.
WHERE IS YOUR GOOD FRIEND HAKEN THESE DAYS?
CAPITALIZING ON YOUR FAILURE. IS HAKEN WHAT YOU REALLY WANT TO TALK ABOUT?
I'D RATHER ENJOY MY BEER IN SILENCE BUT I BET YOU WON'T GIVE ME THAT SATISFACTION.

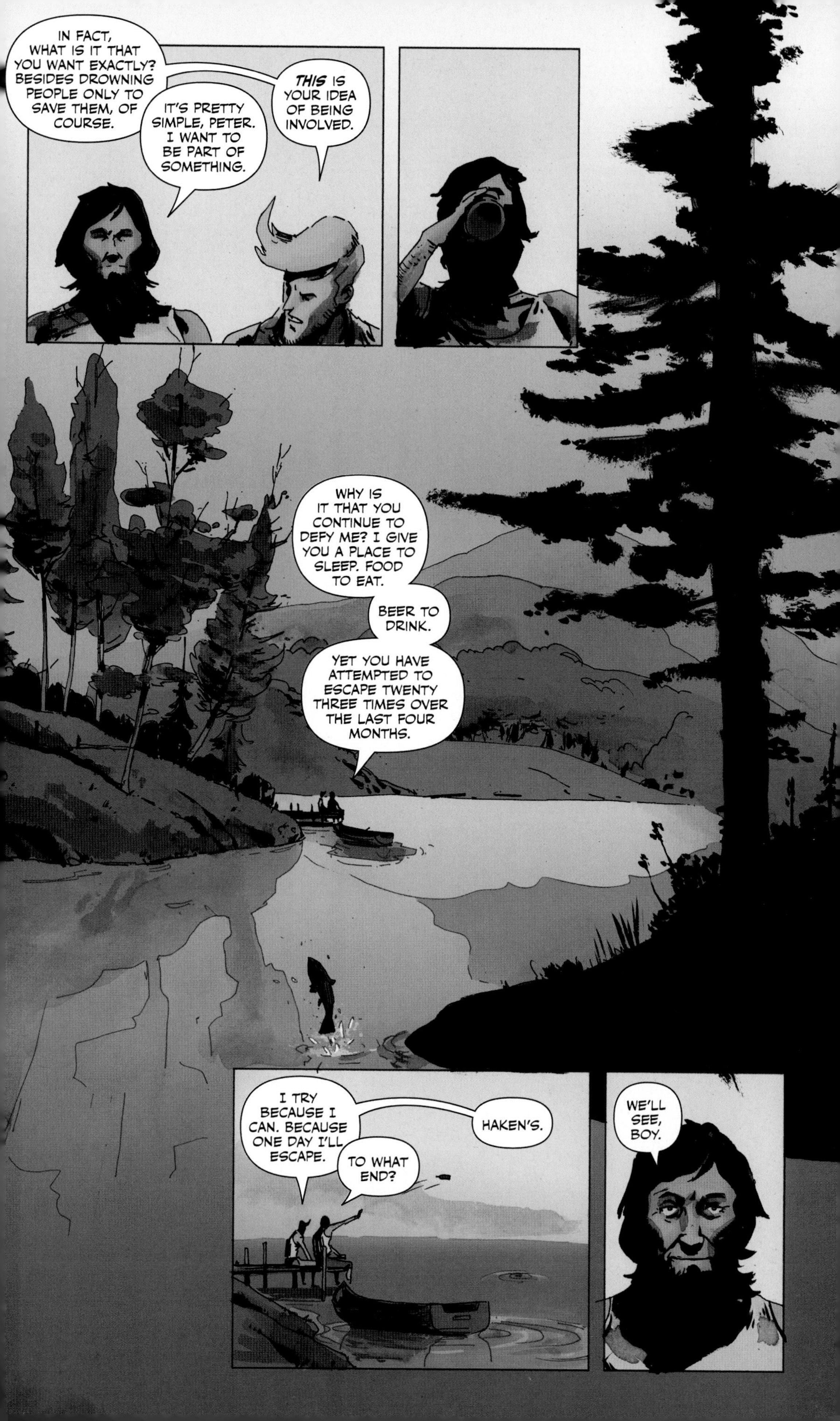
IN FACT, WHAT IS IT THAT YOU WANT EXACTLY? BESIDES DROWNING PEOPLE ONLY TO SAVE THEM, OF COURSE.
IT'S PRETTY SIMPLE, PETER. I WANT TO BE PART OF SOMETHING.
THIS IS YOUR IDEA OF BEING INVOLVED.
WHY IS IT THAT YOU CONTINUE TO DEFY ME? I GIVE YOU A PLACE TO SLEEP. FOOD TO EAT.
BEER TO DRINK.
YET YOU HAVE ATTEMPTED TO ESCAPE TWENTY THREE TIMES OVER THE LAST FOUR MONTHS.
I TRY BECAUSE I CAN. BECAUSE ONE DAY I'LL ESCAPE.
TO WHAT END?
HAKEN'S.
WE'LL SEE, BOY.

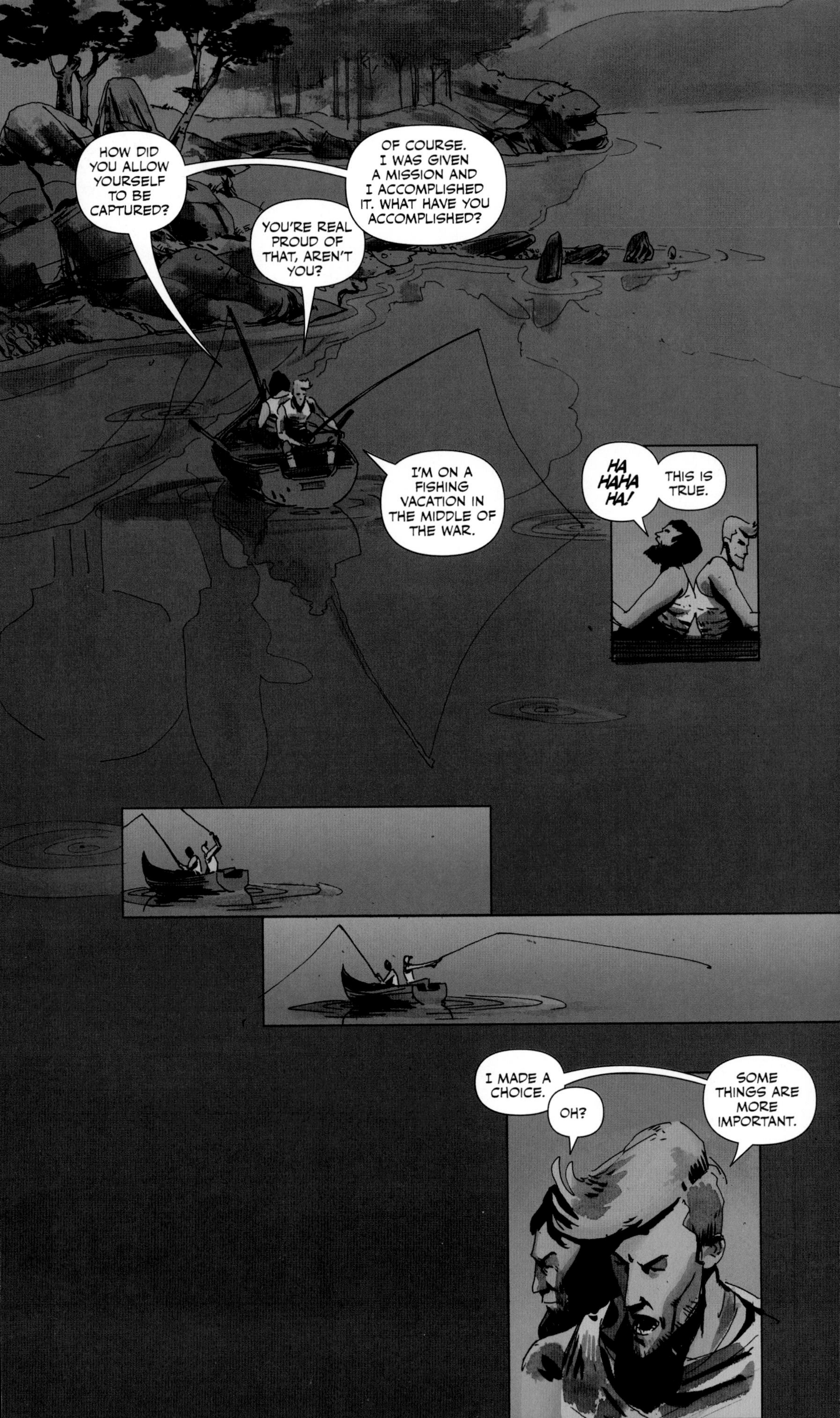
HOW DID YOU ALLOW YOURSELF TO BE CAPTURED?
OF COURSE. I WAS GIVEN A MISSION AND I ACCOMPLISHED IT. WHAT HAVE YOU ACCOMPLISHED?
YOU'RE REAL PROUD OF THAT, AREN'T YOU?
I'M ON A FISHING VACATION IN THE MIDDLE OF THE WAR.
HA HAHA HA!
THIS IS TRUE.
I MADE A CHOICE.
OH?
SOME THINGS ARE MORE IMPORTANT.

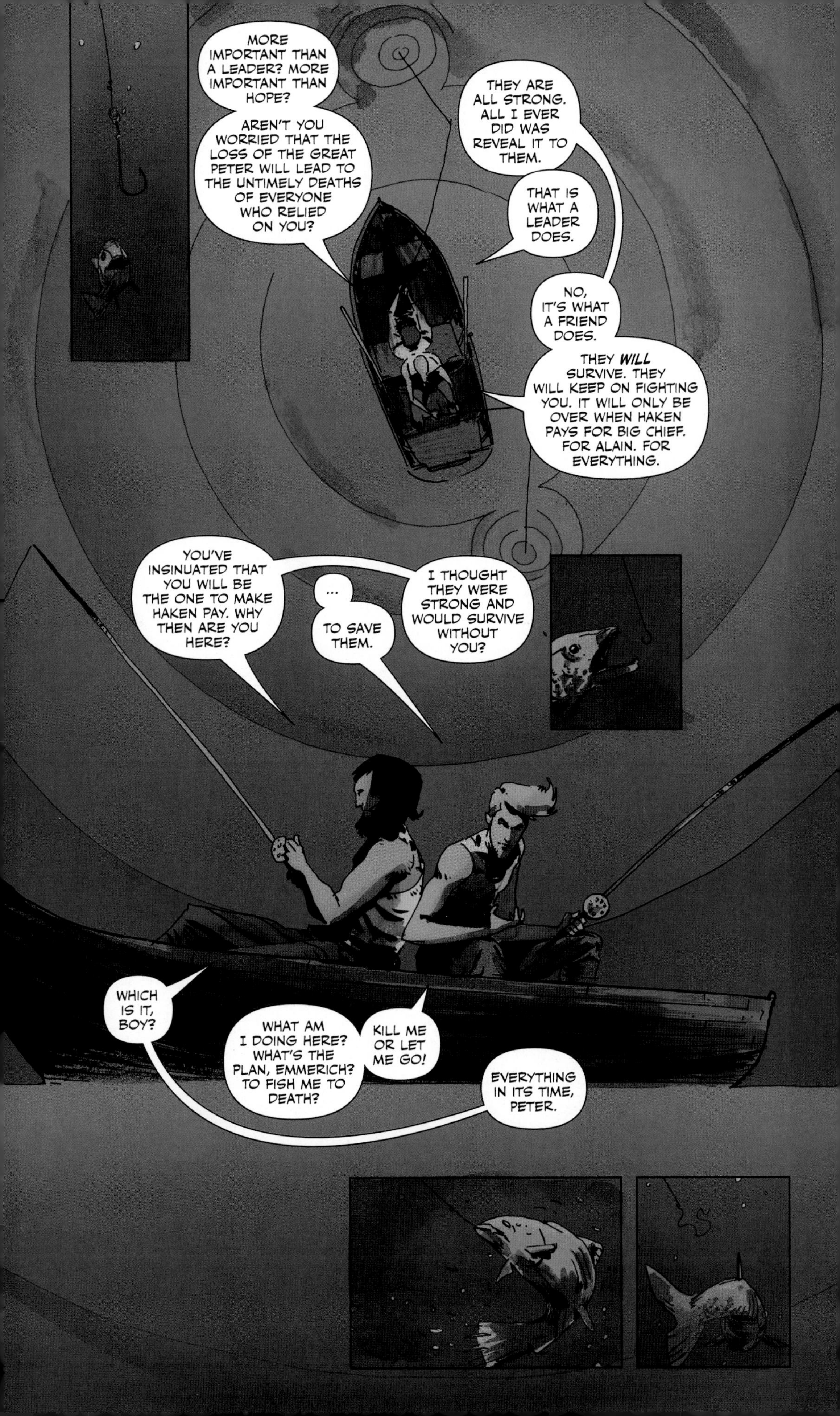

MORE IMPORTANT THAN A LEADER? MORE IMPORTANT THAN HOPE?
AREN'T YOU WORRIED THAT THE LOSS OF THE GREAT PETER WILL LEAD TO THE UNTIMELY DEATHS OF EVERYONE WHO RELIED ON YOU?
THEY ARE ALL STRONG. ALL I EVER DID WAS REVEAL IT TO THEM.
THAT IS WHAT A LEADER DOES.
NO, IT'S WHAT A FRIEND DOES.
THEY ***WILL*** SURVIVE. THEY WILL KEEP ON FIGHTING YOU. IT WILL ONLY BE OVER WHEN HAKEN PAYS FOR BIG CHIEF. FOR ALAIN. FOR EVERYTHING.
I THOUGHT THEY WERE STRONG AND WOULD SURVIVE WITHOUT YOU?
...
TO SAVE THEM.
YOU'VE INSINUATED THAT YOU WILL BE THE ONE TO MAKE HAKEN PAY. WHY THEN ARE YOU HERE?
KILL ME OR LET ME GO!
WHAT AM I DOING HERE? WHAT'S THE PLAN, EMMERICH? TO FISH ME TO DEATH?
WHICH IS IT, BOY?
EVERYTHING IN ITS TIME, PETER.

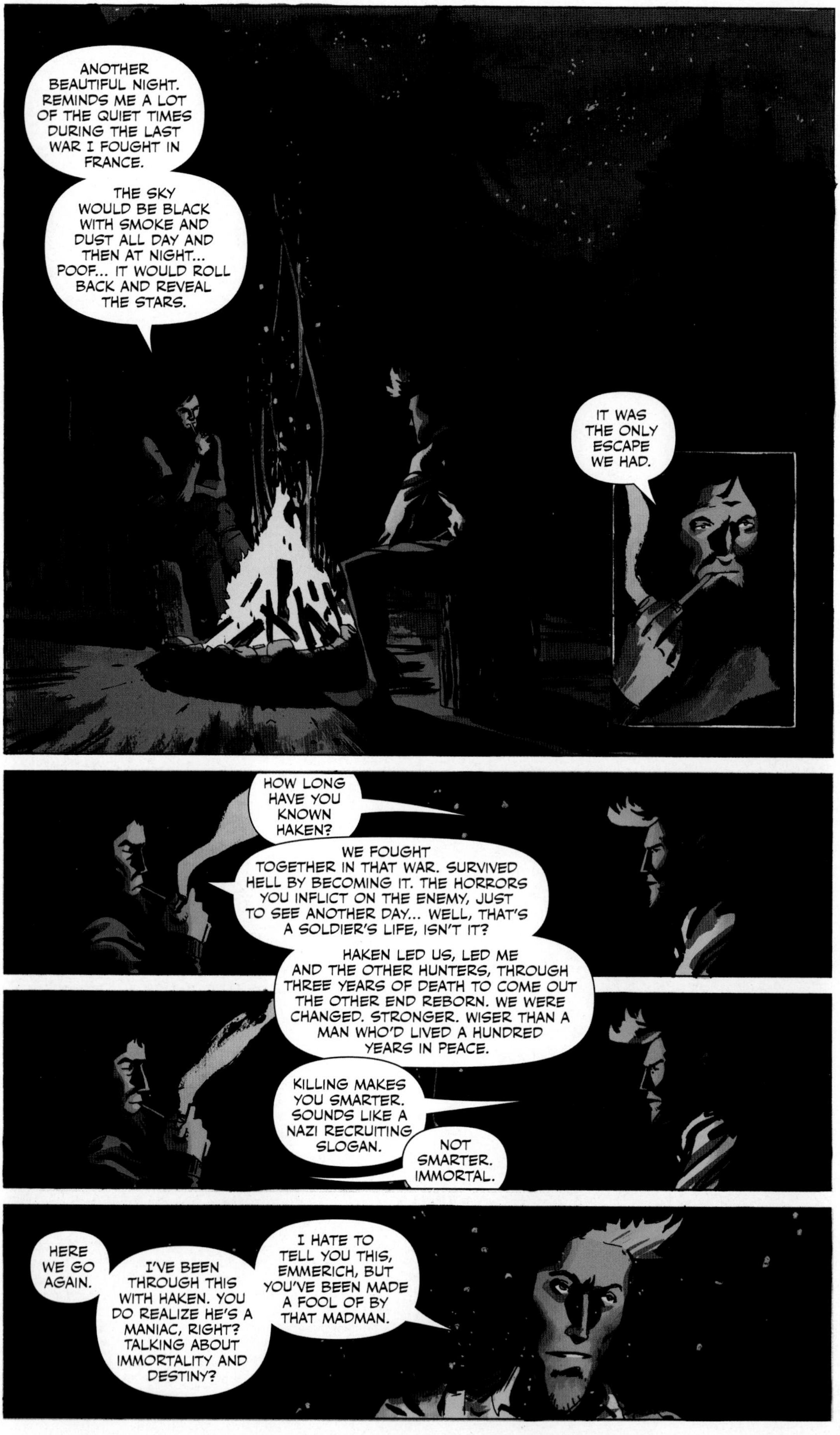
ANOTHER BEAUTIFUL NIGHT. REMINDS ME A LOT OF THE QUIET TIMES DURING THE LAST WAR I FOUGHT IN FRANCE.
THE SKY WOULD BE BLACK WITH SMOKE AND DUST ALL DAY AND THEN AT NIGHT... POOF... IT WOULD ROLL BACK AND REVEAL THE STARS.
IT WAS THE ONLY ESCAPE WE HAD.
HOW LONG HAVE YOU KNOWN HAKEN?
WE FOUGHT TOGETHER IN THAT WAR. SURVIVED HELL BY BECOMING IT. THE HORRORS YOU INFLICT ON THE ENEMY, JUST TO SEE ANOTHER DAY... WELL, THAT'S A SOLDIER'S LIFE, ISN'T IT?
HAKEN LED US, LED ME AND THE OTHER HUNTERS, THROUGH THREE YEARS OF DEATH TO COME OUT THE OTHER END REBORN. WE WERE CHANGED. STRONGER. WISER THAN A MAN WHO'D LIVED A HUNDRED YEARS IN PEACE.
KILLING MAKES YOU SMARTER. SOUNDS LIKE A NAZI RECRUITING SLOGAN.
NOT SMARTER. IMMORTAL.
HERE WE GO AGAIN.
I'VE BEEN THROUGH THIS WITH HAKEN. YOU DO REALIZE HE'S A MANIAC, RIGHT? TALKING ABOUT IMMORTALITY AND DESTINY?
I HATE TO TELL YOU THIS, EMMERICH, BUT YOU'VE BEEN MADE A FOOL OF BY THAT MADMAN.

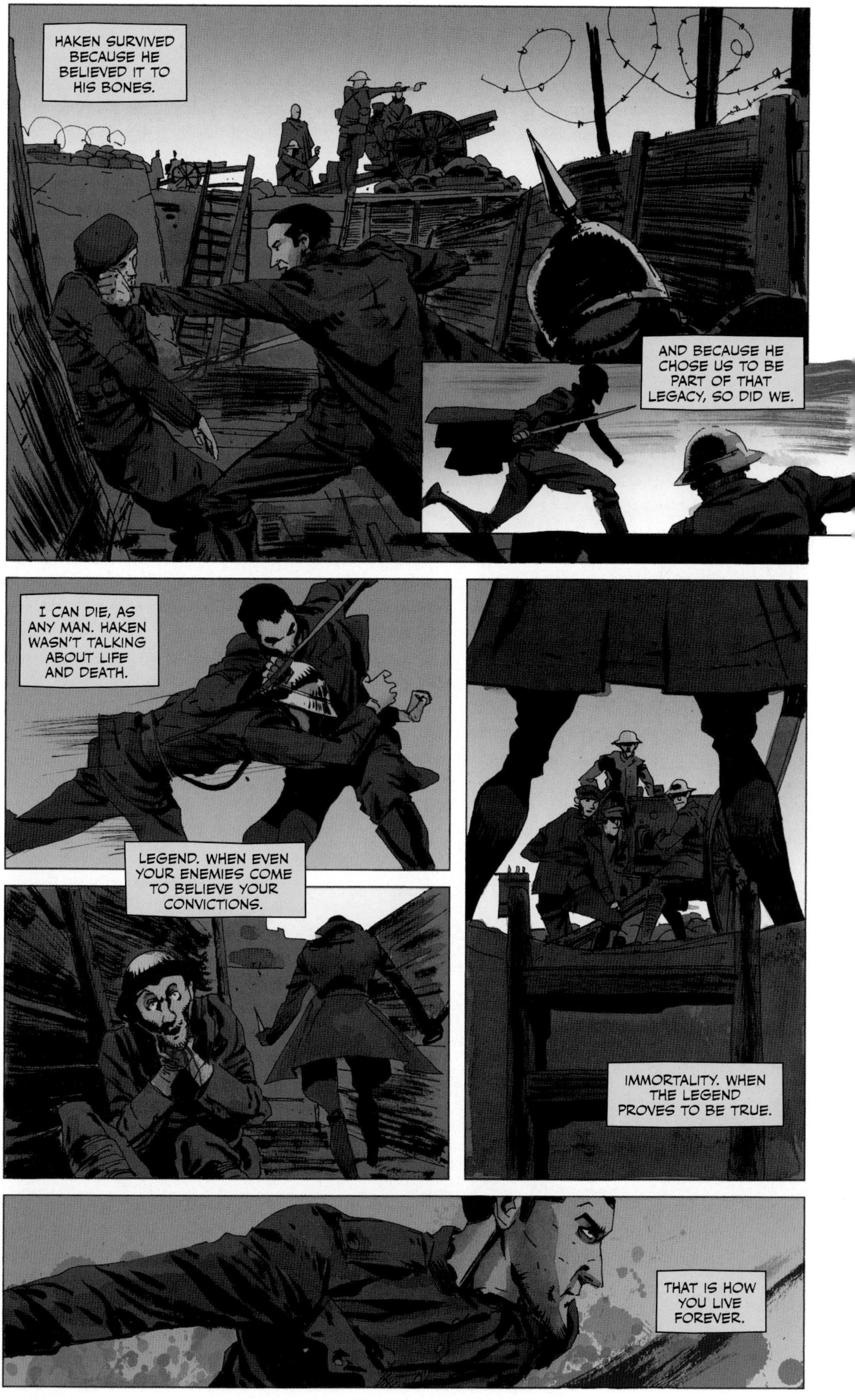
HAKEN SURVIVED BECAUSE HE BELIEVED IT TO HIS BONES.
AND BECAUSE HE CHOSE US TO BE PART OF THAT LEGACY, SO DID WE.
I CAN DIE, AS ANY MAN. HAKEN WASN'T TALKING ABOUT LIFE AND DEATH.
LEGEND. WHEN EVEN YOUR ENEMIES COME TO BELIEVE YOUR CONVICTIONS.
IMMORTALITY. WHEN THE LEGEND PROVES TO BE TRUE.
THAT IS HOW YOU LIVE FOREVER.

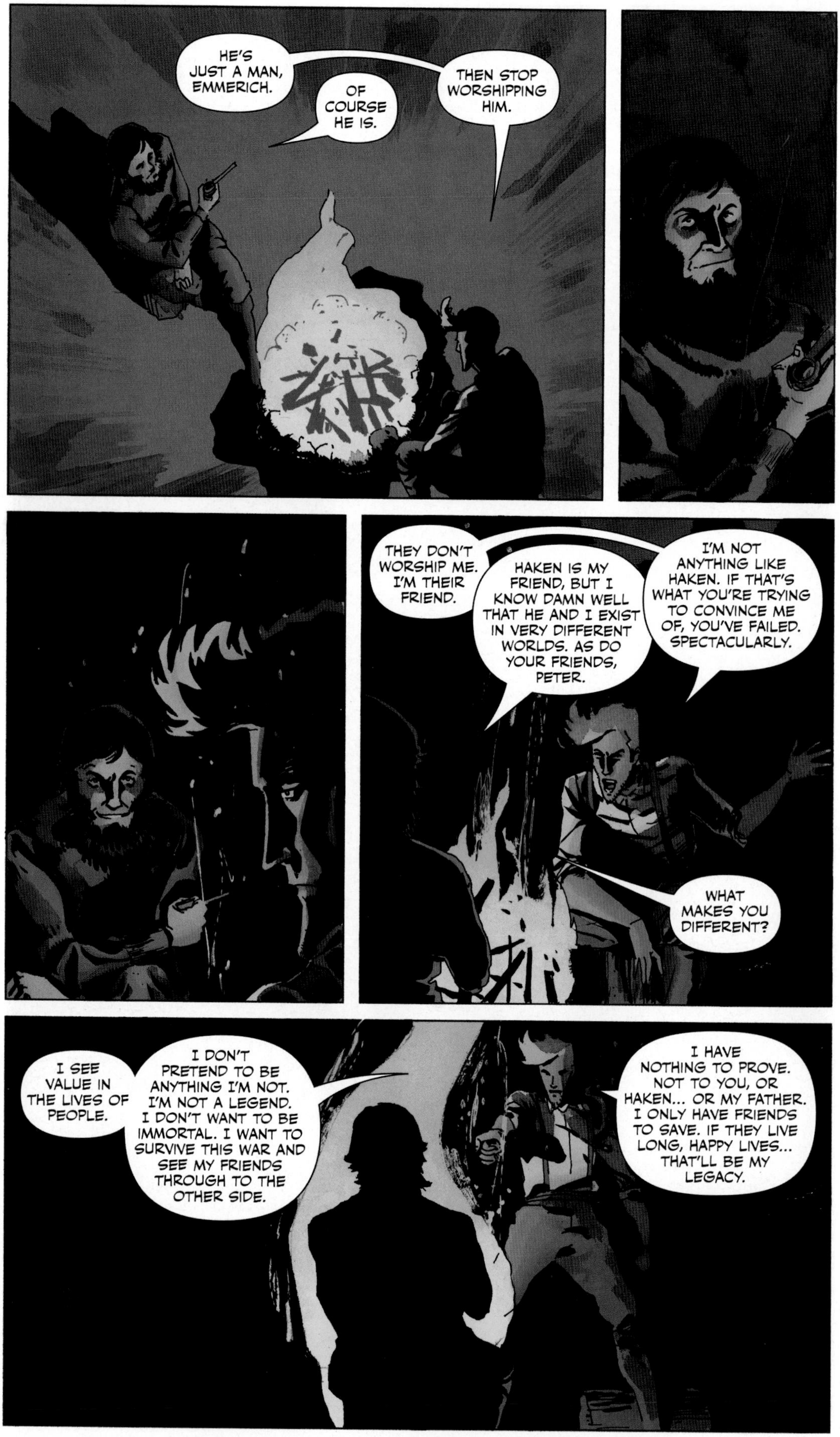
HE'S JUST A MAN, EMMERICH.
OF COURSE HE IS.
THEN STOP WORSHIPPING HIM.
THEY DON'T WORSHIP ME. I'M THEIR FRIEND.
HAKEN IS MY FRIEND, BUT I KNOW DAMN WELL THAT HE AND I EXIST IN VERY DIFFERENT WORLDS. AS DO YOUR FRIENDS, PETER.
I'M NOT ANYTHING LIKE HAKEN. IF THAT'S WHAT YOU'RE TRYING TO CONVINCE ME OF, YOU'VE FAILED. SPECTACULARLY.
WHAT MAKES YOU DIFFERENT?
I SEE VALUE IN THE LIVES OF PEOPLE.
I DON'T PRETEND TO BE ANYTHING I'M NOT. I'M NOT A LEGEND. I DON'T WANT TO BE IMMORTAL. I WANT TO SURVIVE THIS WAR AND SEE MY FRIENDS THROUGH TO THE OTHER SIDE.
I HAVE NOTHING TO PROVE. NOT TO YOU, OR HAKEN... OR MY FATHER. I ONLY HAVE FRIENDS TO SAVE. IF THEY LIVE LONG, HAPPY LIVES... THAT'LL BE MY LEGACY.

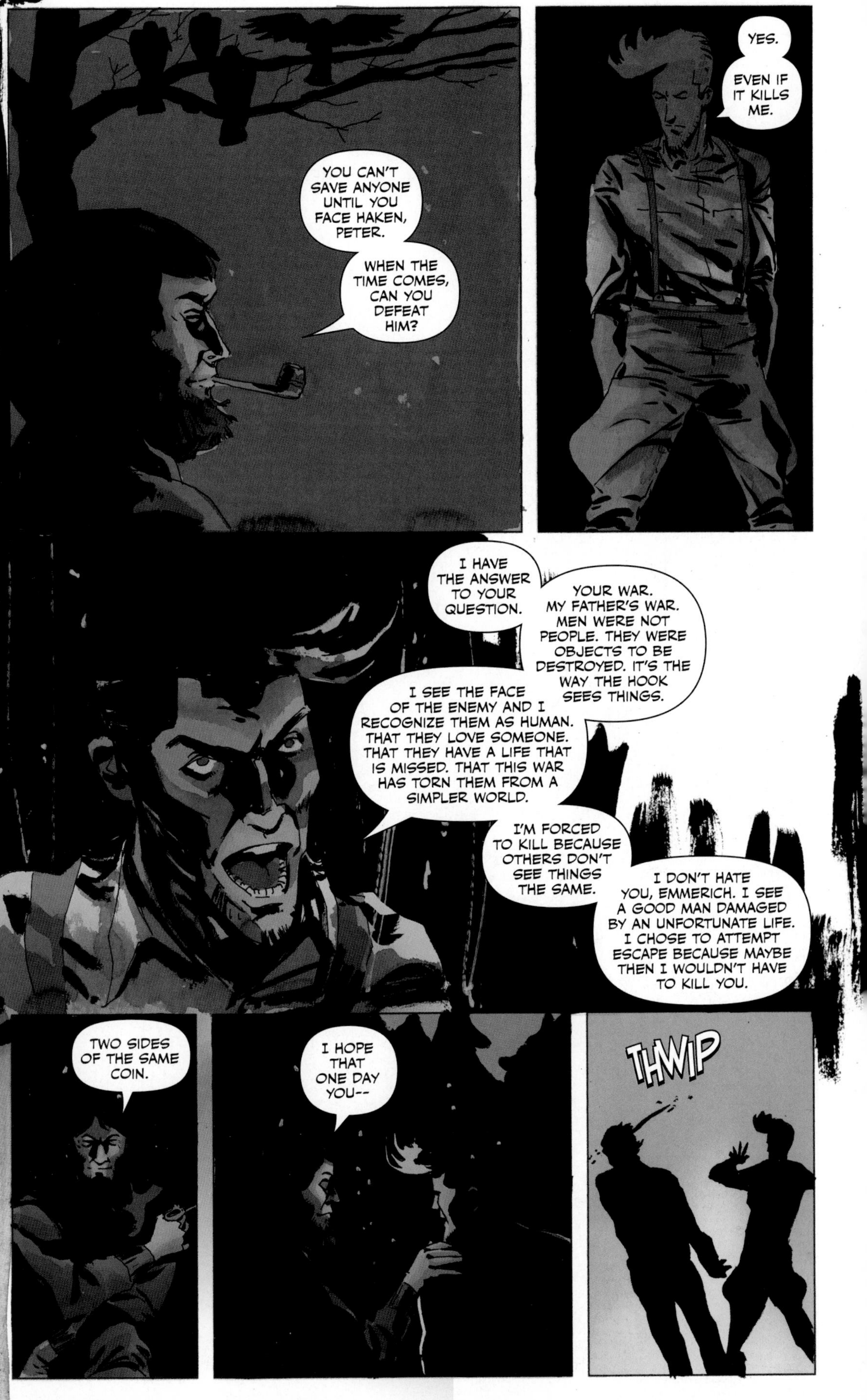
YOU CAN'T SAVE ANYONE UNTIL YOU FACE HAKEN, PETER.
WHEN THE TIME COMES, CAN YOU DEFEAT HIM?
YES.
EVEN IF IT KILLS ME.
I HAVE THE ANSWER TO YOUR QUESTION.
YOUR WAR. MY FATHER'S WAR. MEN WERE NOT PEOPLE. THEY WERE OBJECTS TO BE DESTROYED. IT'S THE WAY THE HOOK SEES THINGS.
I SEE THE FACE OF THE ENEMY AND I RECOGNIZE THEM AS HUMAN. THAT THEY LOVE SOMEONE. THAT THEY HAVE A LIFE THAT IS MISSED. THAT THIS WAR HAS TORN THEM FROM A SIMPLER WORLD.
I'M FORCED TO KILL BECAUSE OTHERS DON'T SEE THINGS THE SAME.
I DON'T HATE YOU, EMMERICH. I SEE A GOOD MAN DAMAGED BY AN UNFORTUNATE LIFE. I CHOSE TO ATTEMPT ESCAPE BECAUSE MAYBE THEN I WOULDN'T HAVE TO KILL YOU.
TWO SIDES OF THE SAME COIN.
I HOPE THAT ONE DAY YOU--
THWIP

THAT'S TWO YOU OWE ME.

TIME TO GO, PETER.

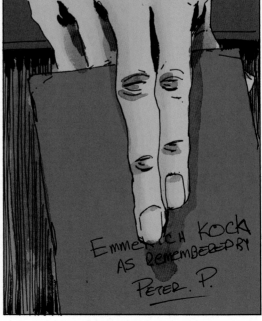

EMMERICH KOCK AS REMEMBERED BY PETER. P.

HAPTER NINETEEN

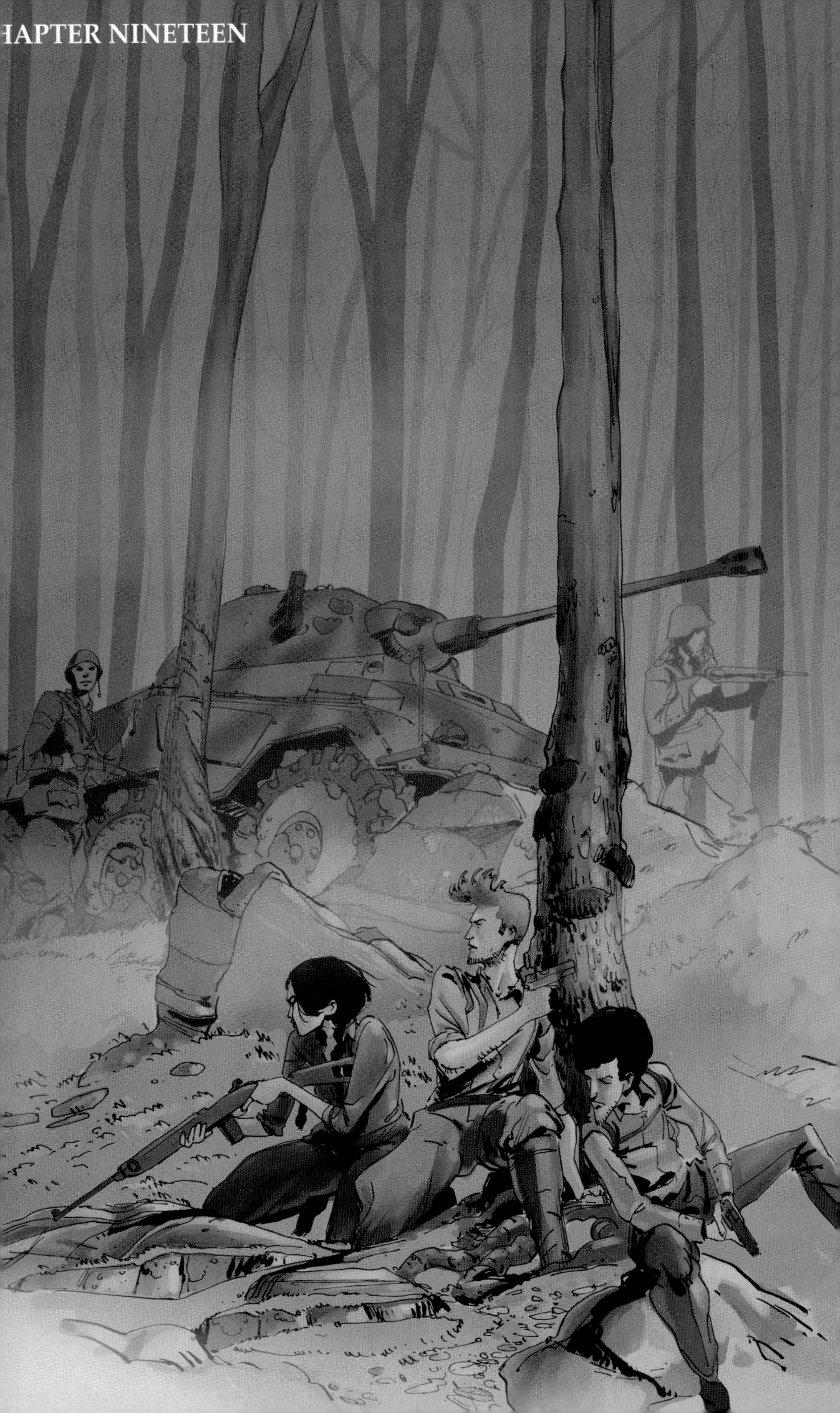

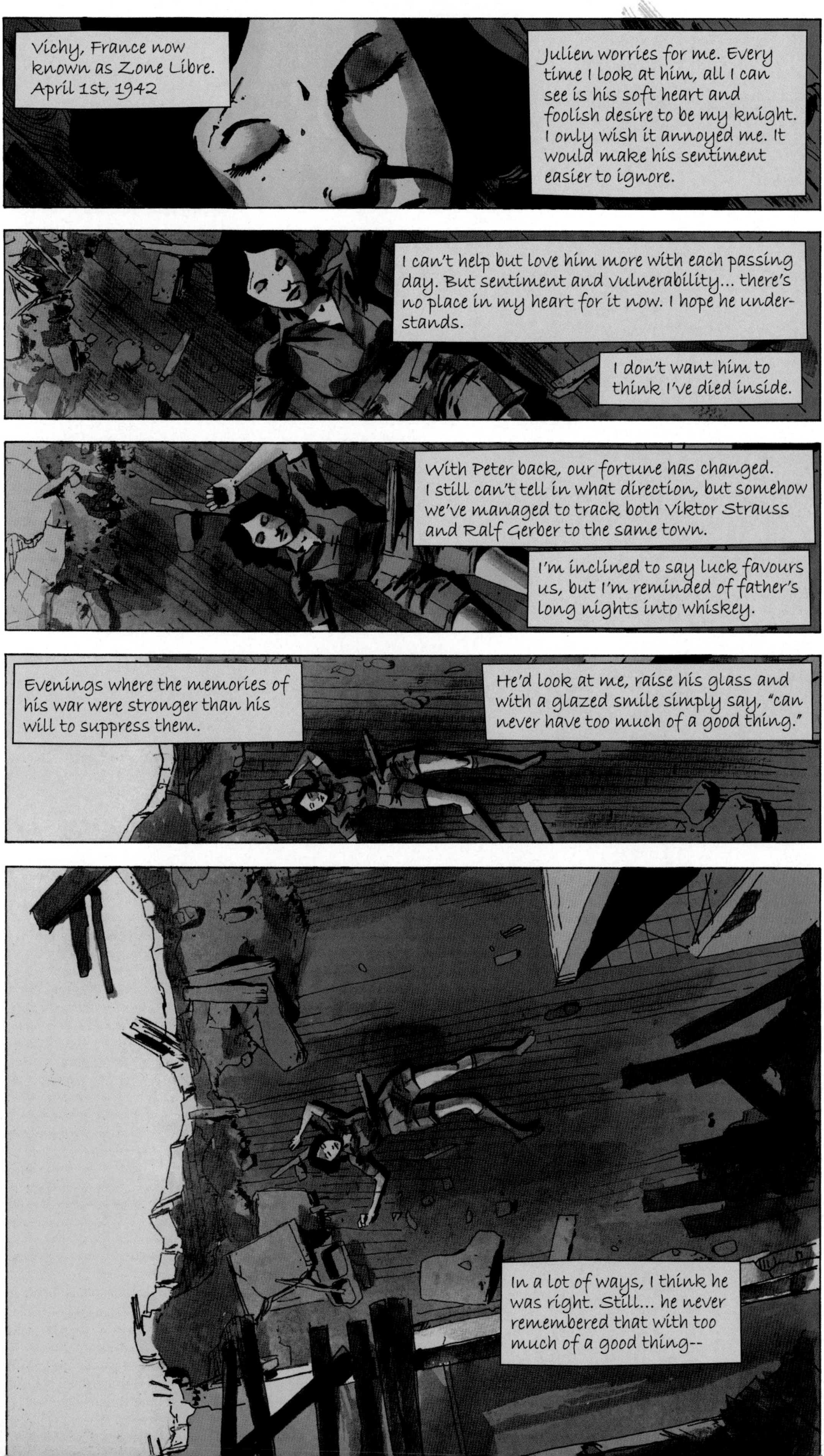
Vichy, France now known as Zone Libre. April 1st, 1942
Julien worries for me. Every time I look at him, all I can see is his soft heart and foolish desire to be my knight. I only wish it annoyed me. It would make his sentiment easier to ignore.
I can't help but love him more with each passing day. But sentiment and vulnerability... there's no place in my heart for it now. I hope he understands.
I don't want him to think I've died inside.
With Peter back, our fortune has changed. I still can't tell in what direction, but somehow we've managed to track both Viktor Strauss and Ralf Gerber to the same town.
I'm inclined to say luck favours us, but I'm reminded of father's long nights into whiskey.
Evenings where the memories of his war were stronger than his will to suppress them.
He'd look at me, raise his glass and with a glazed smile simply say, "can never have too much of a good thing."
In a lot of ways, I think he was right. Still... he never remembered that with too much of a good thing--

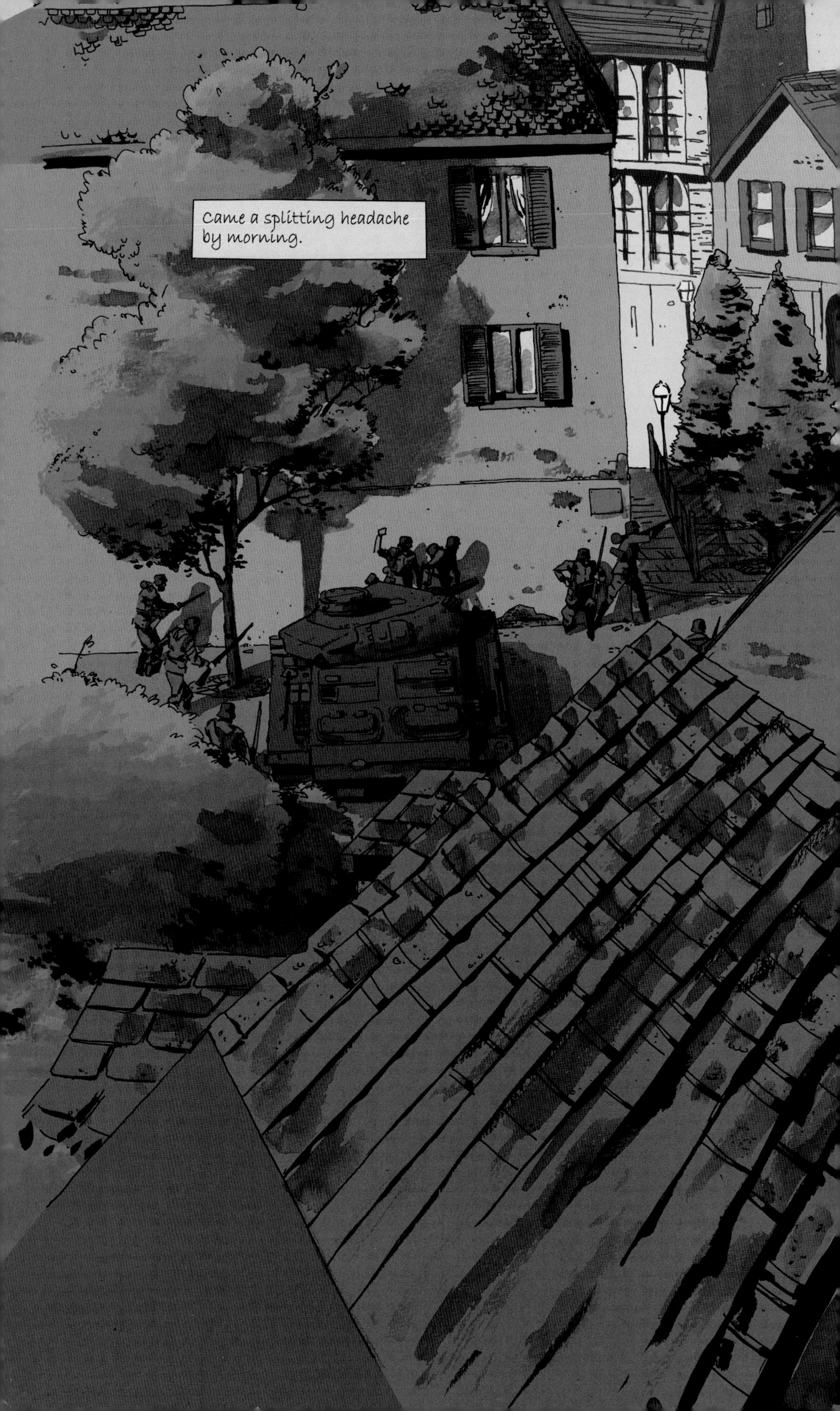
Came a splitting headache by morning.

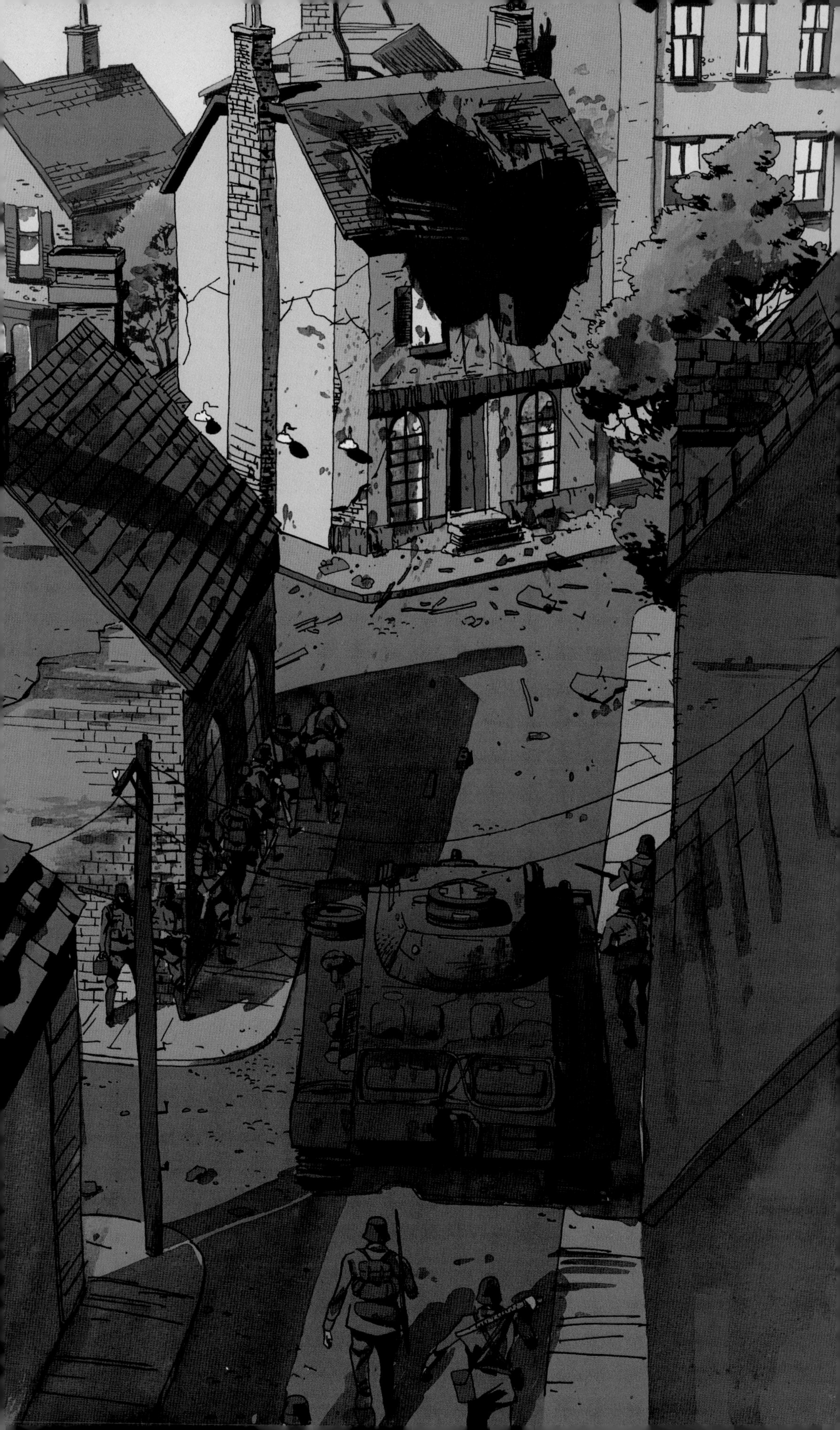

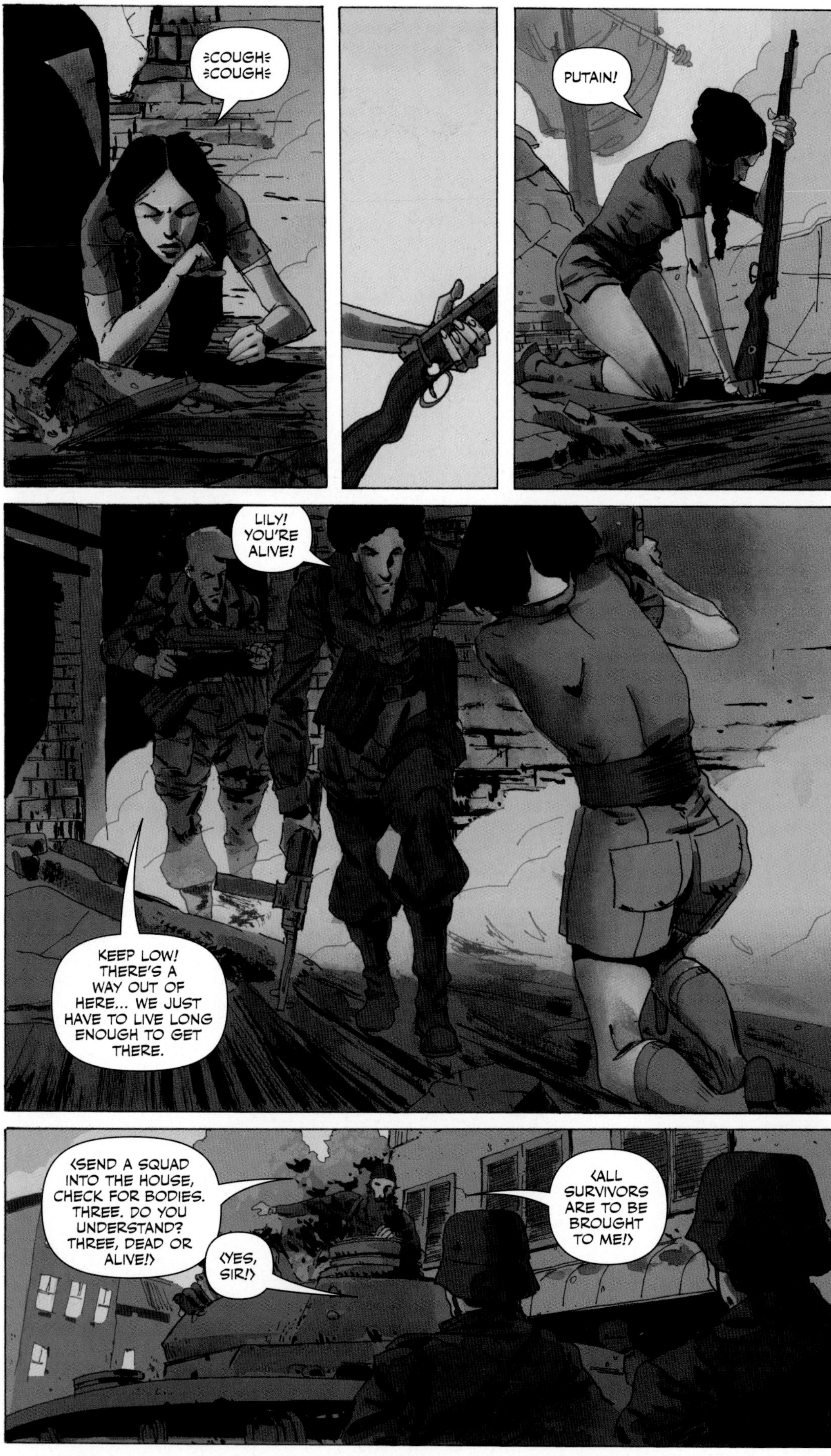
=COUGH=
=COUGH=
PUTAIN!
LILY! YOU'RE ALIVE!
KEEP LOW! THERE'S A WAY OUT OF HERE... WE JUST HAVE TO LIVE LONG ENOUGH TO GET THERE.
‹SEND A SQUAD INTO THE HOUSE, CHECK FOR BODIES. THREE. DO YOU UNDERSTAND? THREE, DEAD OR ALIVE!›
‹YES, SIR!›
‹ALL SURVIVORS ARE TO BE BROUGHT TO ME!›

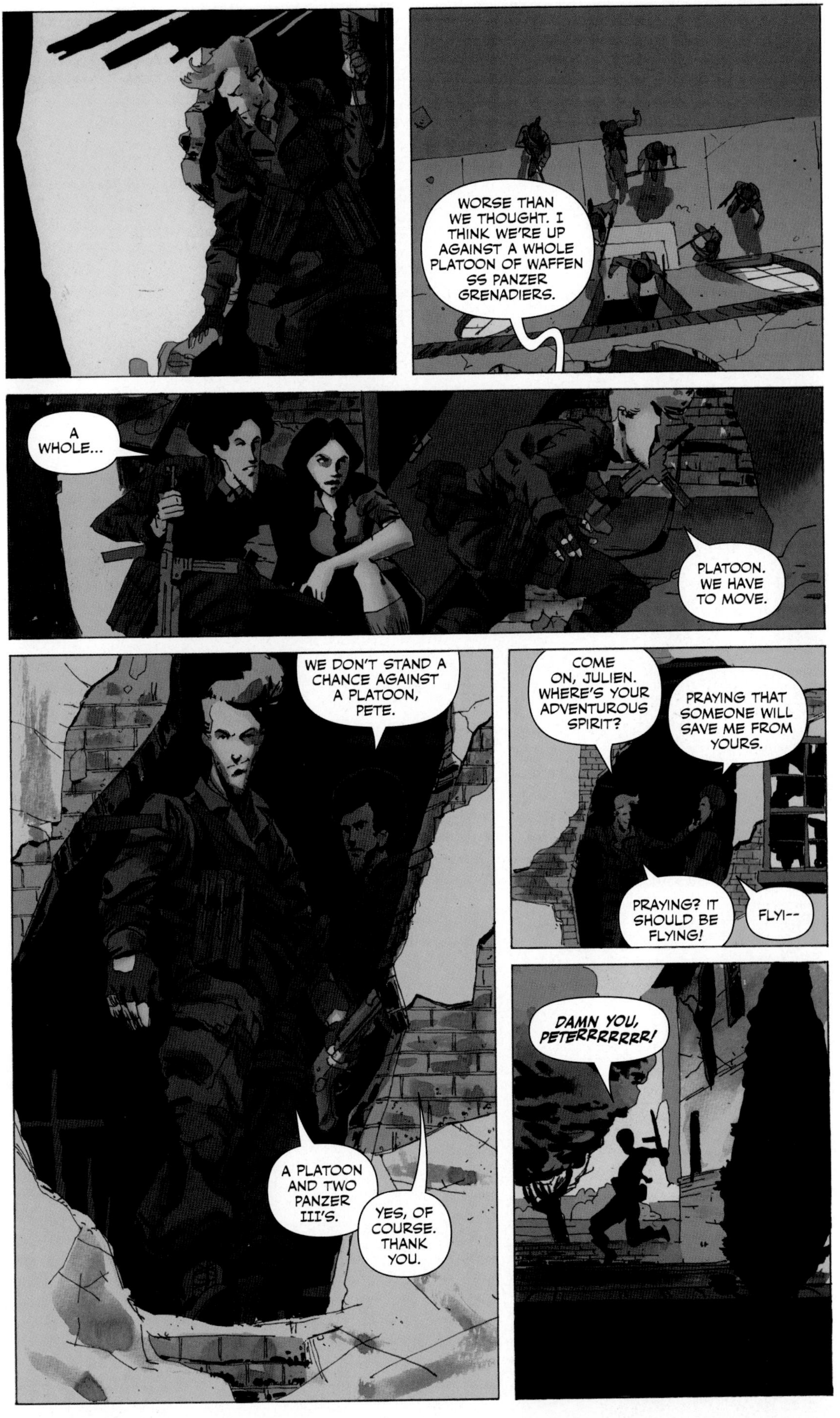
WORSE THAN WE THOUGHT. I THINK WE'RE UP AGAINST A WHOLE PLATOON OF WAFFEN SS PANZER GRENADIERS.
A WHOLE...
PLATOON. WE HAVE TO MOVE.
WE DON'T STAND A CHANCE AGAINST A PLATOON, PETE.
A PLATOON AND TWO PANZER III'S.
YES, OF COURSE. THANK YOU.
COME ON, JULIEN. WHERE'S YOUR ADVENTUROUS SPIRIT?
PRAYING THAT SOMEONE WILL SAVE ME FROM YOURS.
PRAYING? IT SHOULD BE FLYING!
FLYI--
DAMN YOU, PETERRRRRRR!

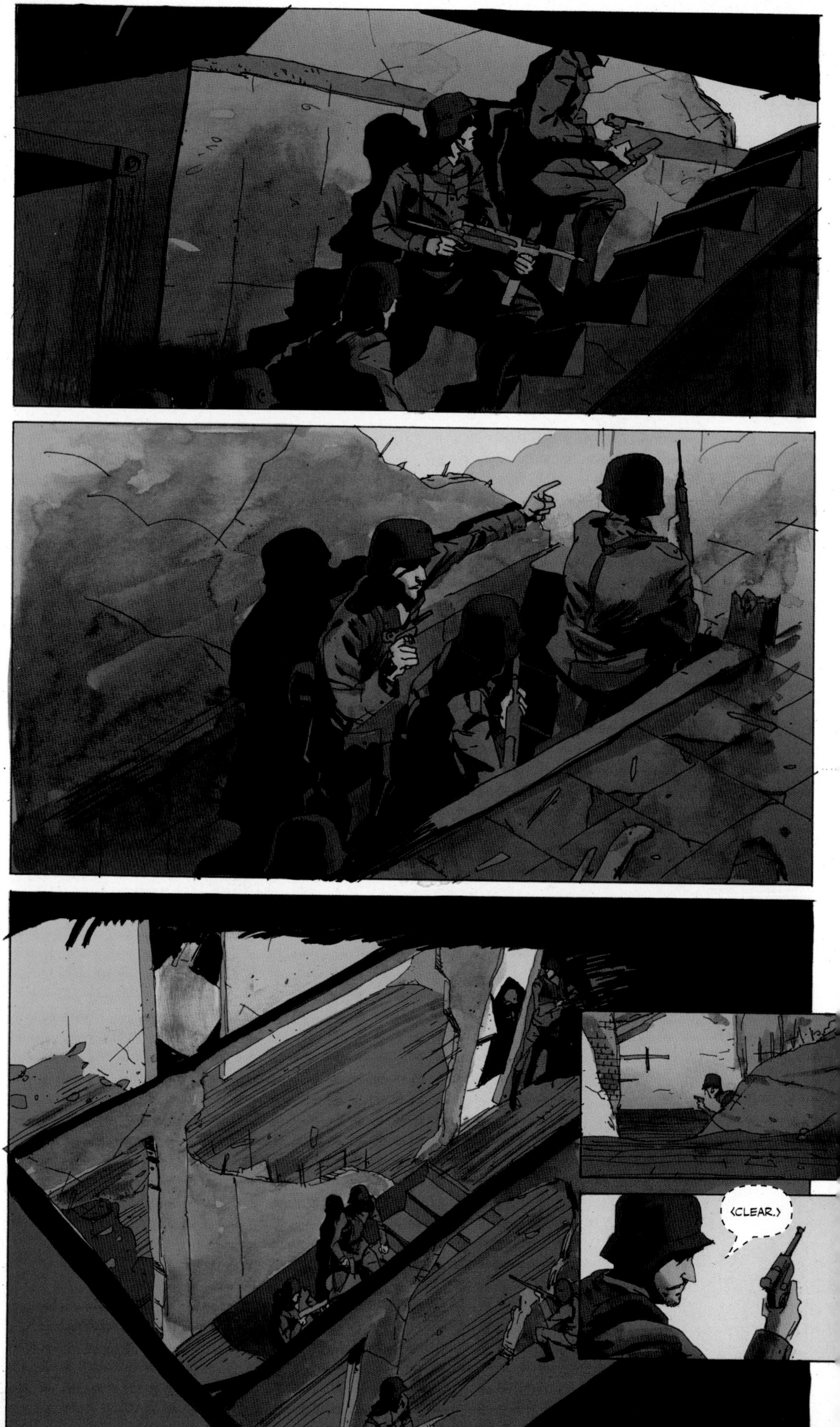
‹CLEAR.›

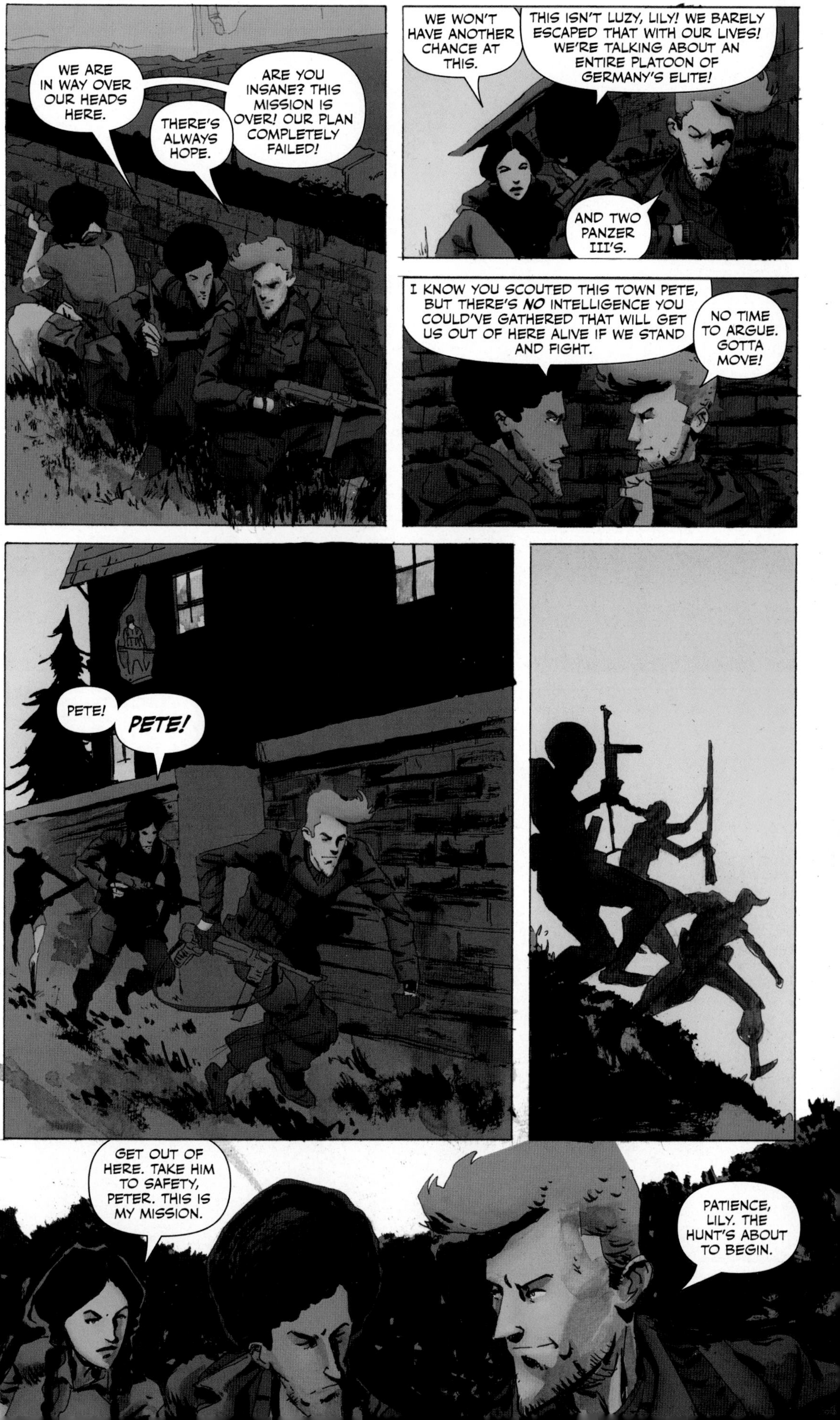
WE ARE IN WAY OVER OUR HEADS HERE.
ARE YOU INSANE? THIS MISSION IS OVER! OUR PLAN COMPLETELY FAILED!
THERE'S ALWAYS HOPE.
WE WON'T HAVE ANOTHER CHANCE AT THIS.
THIS ISN'T LUZY, LILY! WE BARELY ESCAPED THAT WITH OUR LIVES! WE'RE TALKING ABOUT AN ENTIRE PLATOON OF GERMANY'S ELITE!
AND TWO PANZER III'S.
I KNOW YOU SCOUTED THIS TOWN PETE, BUT THERE'S NO INTELLIGENCE YOU COULD'VE GATHERED THAT WILL GET US OUT OF HERE ALIVE IF WE STAND AND FIGHT.
NO TIME TO ARGUE. GOTTA MOVE!
PETE!
PETE!
GET OUT OF HERE. TAKE HIM TO SAFETY, PETER. THIS IS MY MISSION.
PATIENCE, LILY. THE HUNT'S ABOUT TO BEGIN.

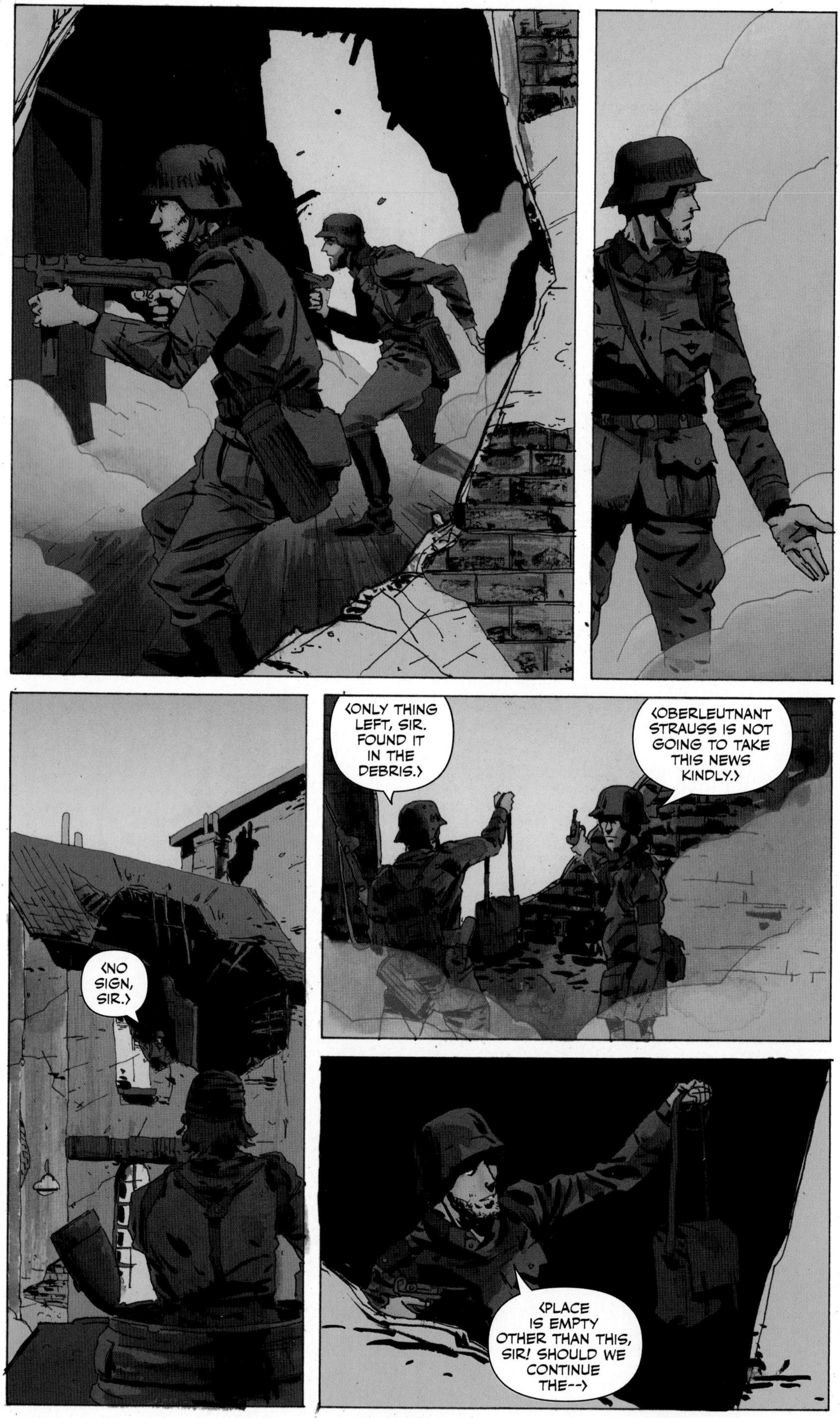
<NO SIGN, SIR.>
<ONLY THING LEFT, SIR. FOUND IT IN THE DEBRIS.>
<OBERLEUTNANT STRAUSS IS NOT GOING TO TAKE THIS NEWS KINDLY.>
<PLACE IS EMPTY OTHER THAN THIS, SIR! SHOULD WE CONTINUE THE-->

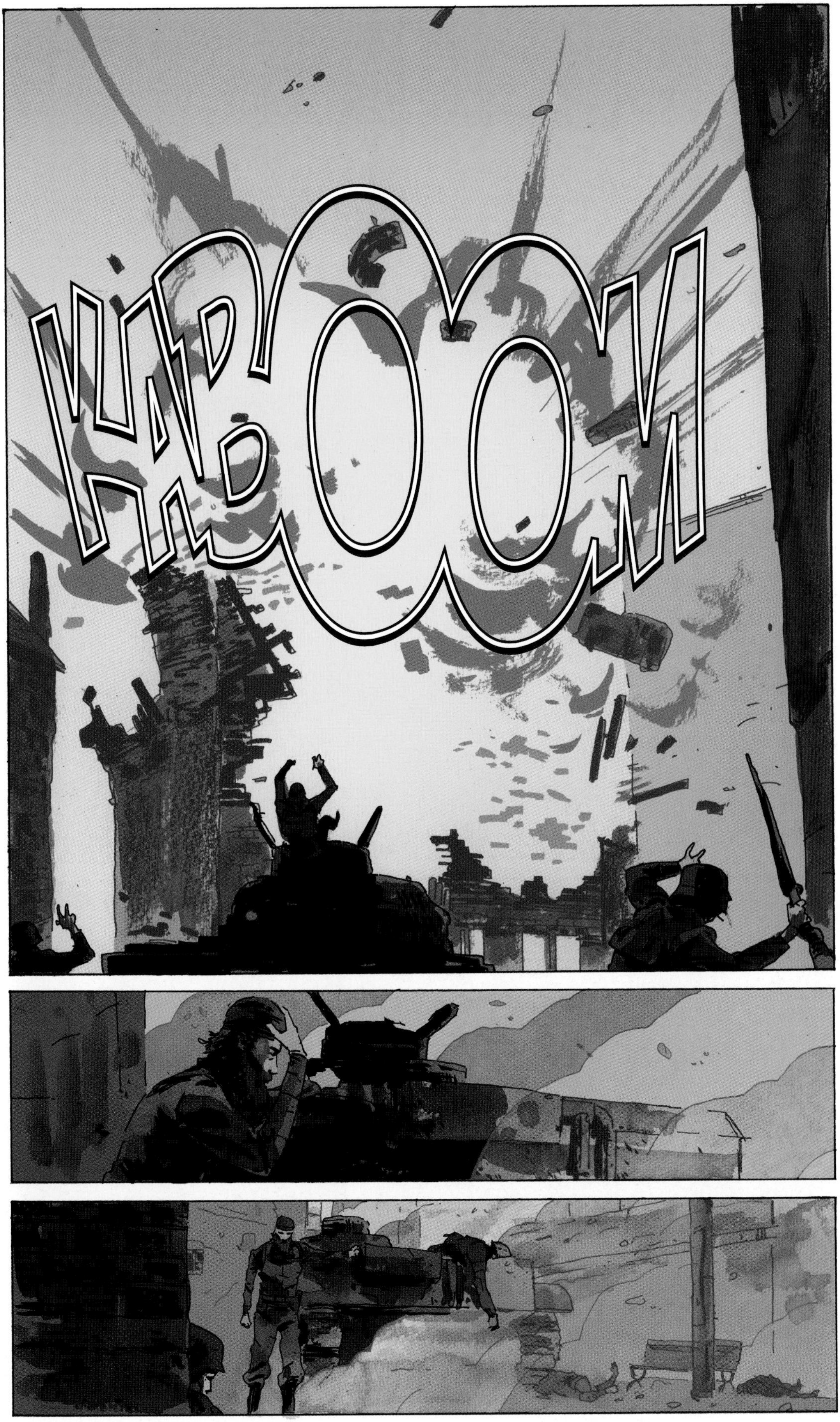
KABOOM

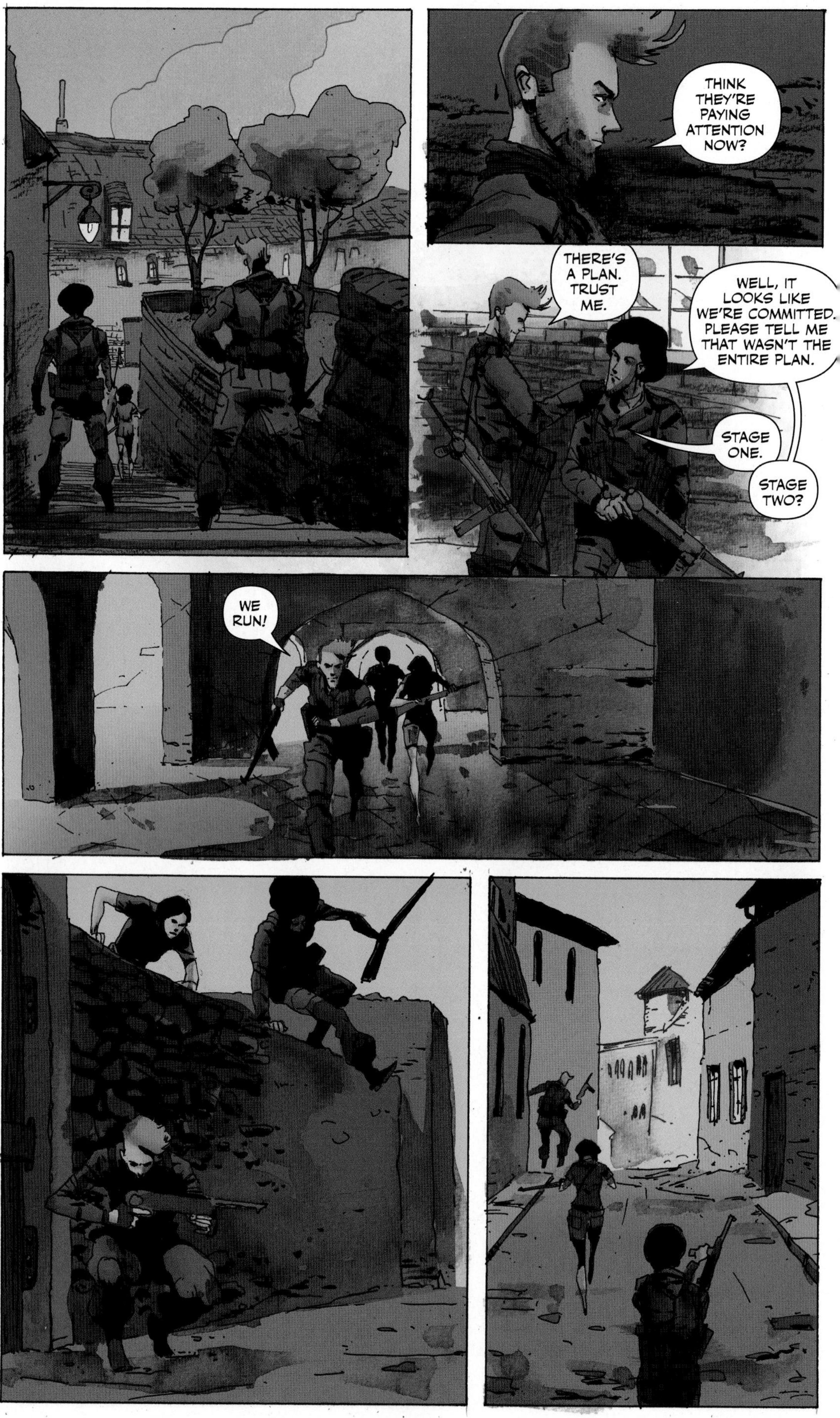
THINK THEY'RE PAYING ATTENTION NOW?
THERE'S A PLAN. TRUST ME.
WELL, IT LOOKS LIKE WE'RE COMMITTED. PLEASE TELL ME THAT WASN'T THE ENTIRE PLAN.
STAGE ONE.
STAGE TWO?
WE RUN!

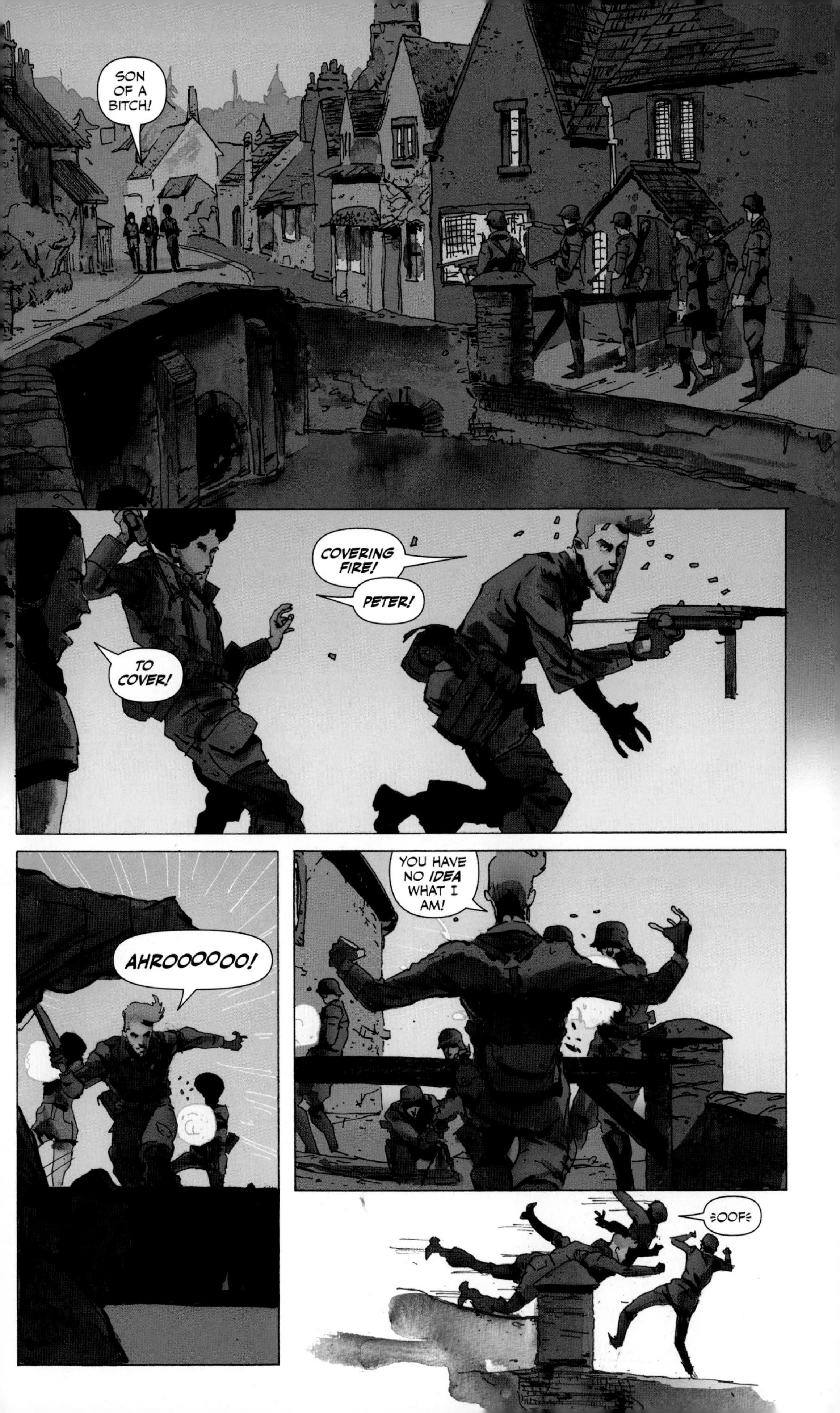
SON OF A BITCH!
COVERING FIRE!
PETER!
TO COVER!
AHROOOOOO!
YOU HAVE NO IDEA WHAT I AM!
OOF

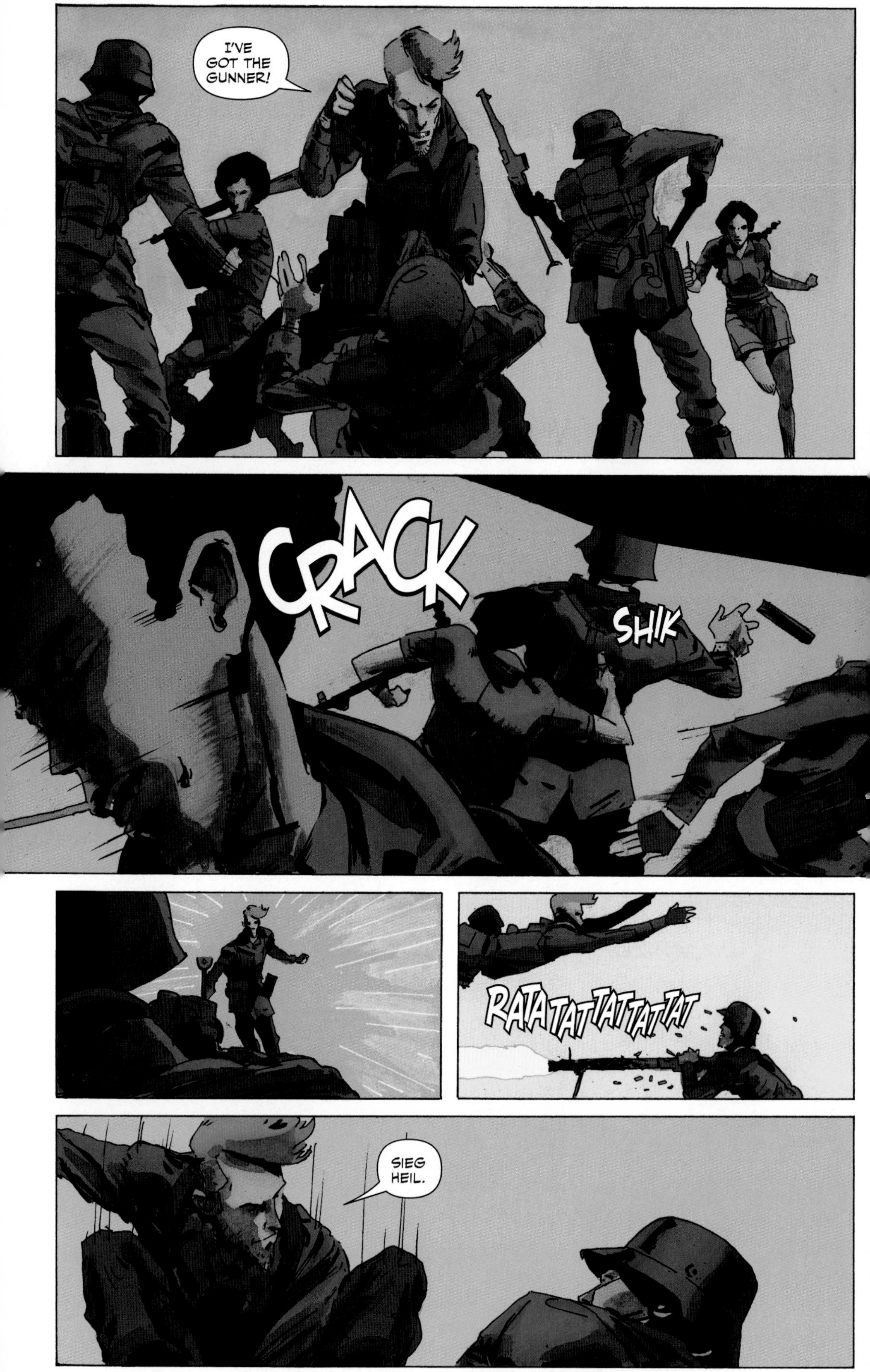
I'VE GOT THE GUNNER!
CRACK
SHIK
RATATATTATTATTAT
SIEG HEIL.

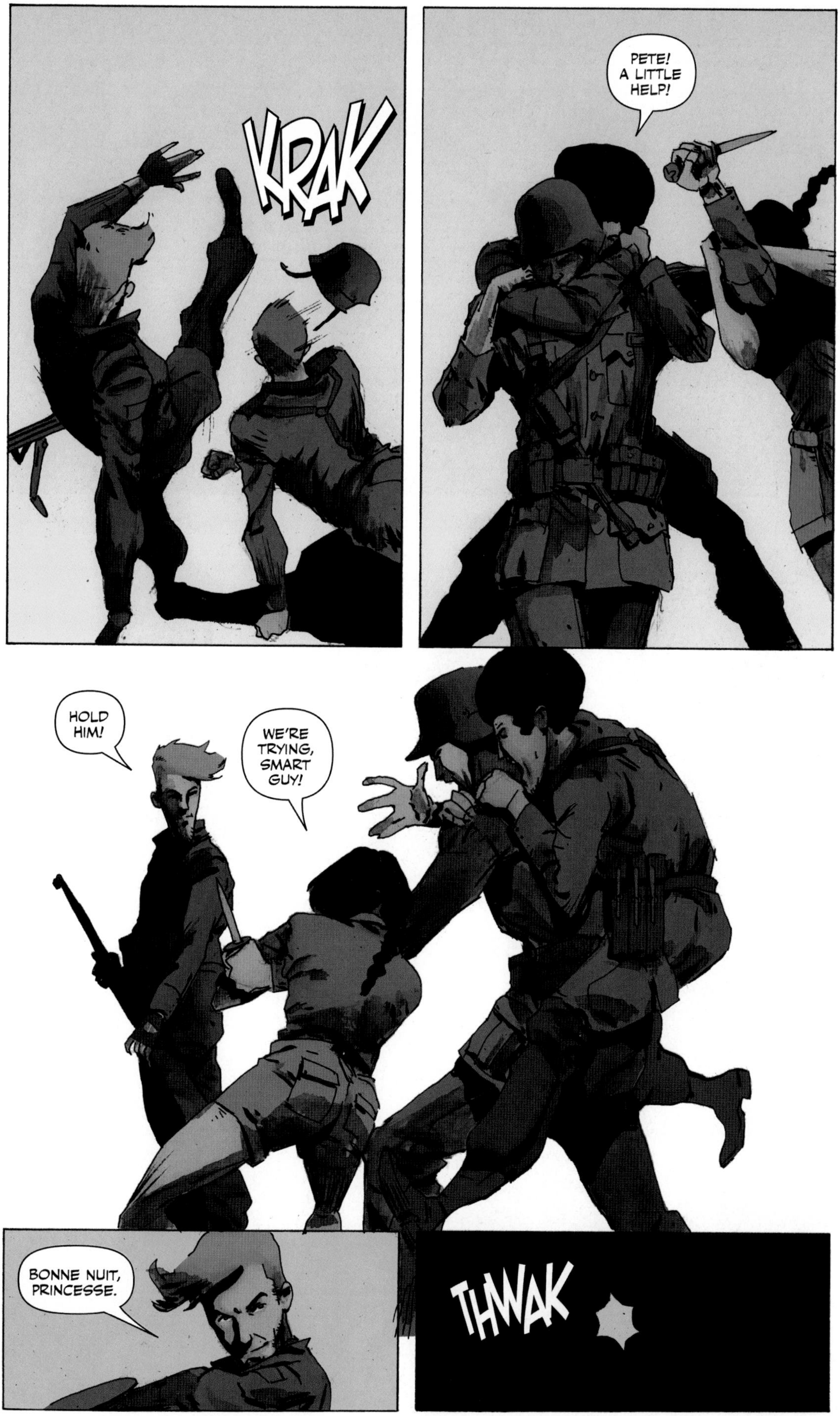
KRAK
PETE! A LITTLE HELP!
HOLD HIM!
WE'RE TRYING, SMART GUY!
BONNE NUIT, PRINCESSE.
THWAK

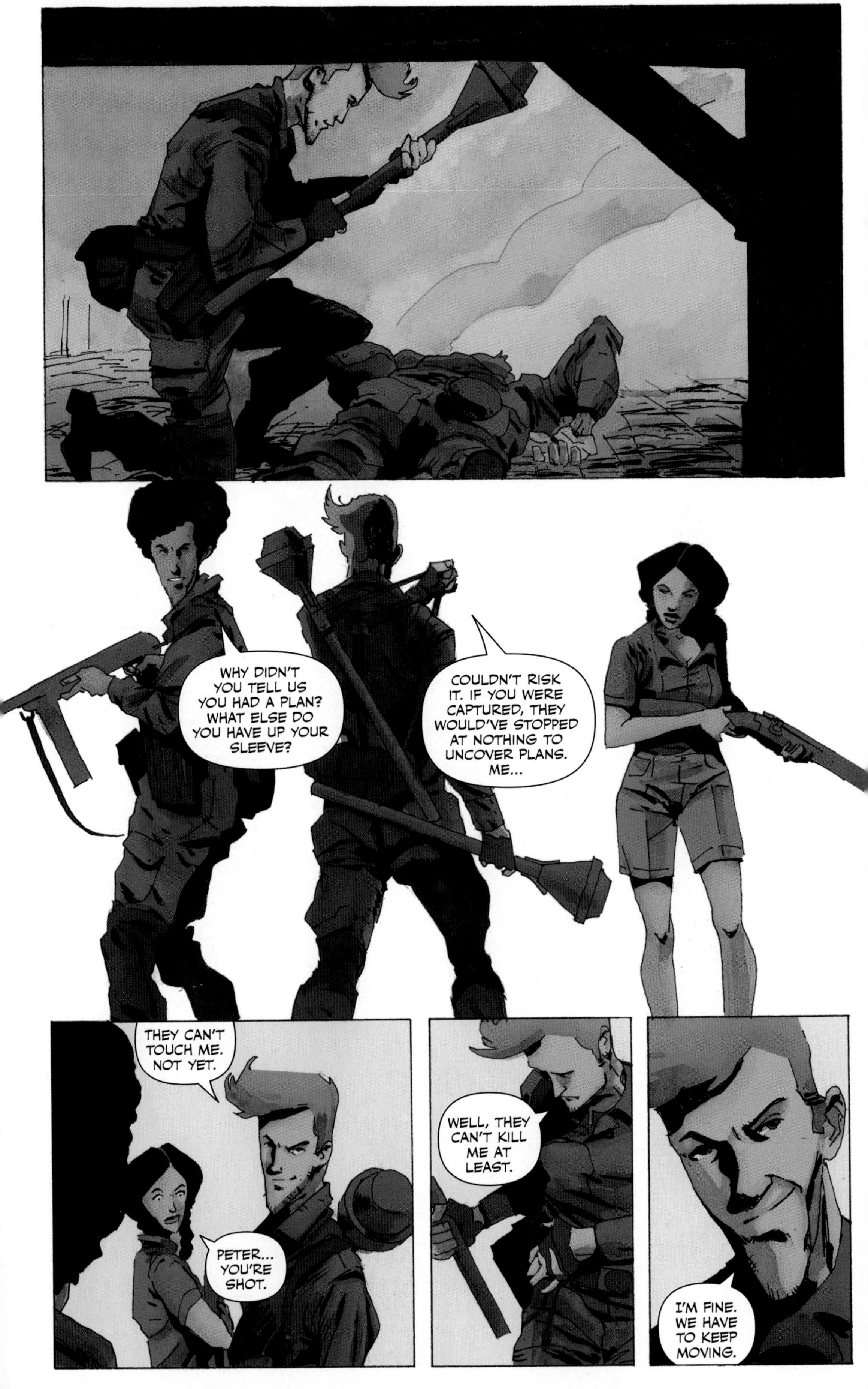
WHY DIDN'T YOU TELL US YOU HAD A PLAN? WHAT ELSE DO YOU HAVE UP YOUR SLEEVE?
COULDN'T RISK IT. IF YOU WERE CAPTURED, THEY WOULD'VE STOPPED AT NOTHING TO UNCOVER PLANS. ME...
THEY CAN'T TOUCH ME. NOT YET.
PETER... YOU'RE SHOT.
WELL, THEY CAN'T KILL ME AT LEAST.
I'M FINE. WE HAVE TO KEEP MOVING.

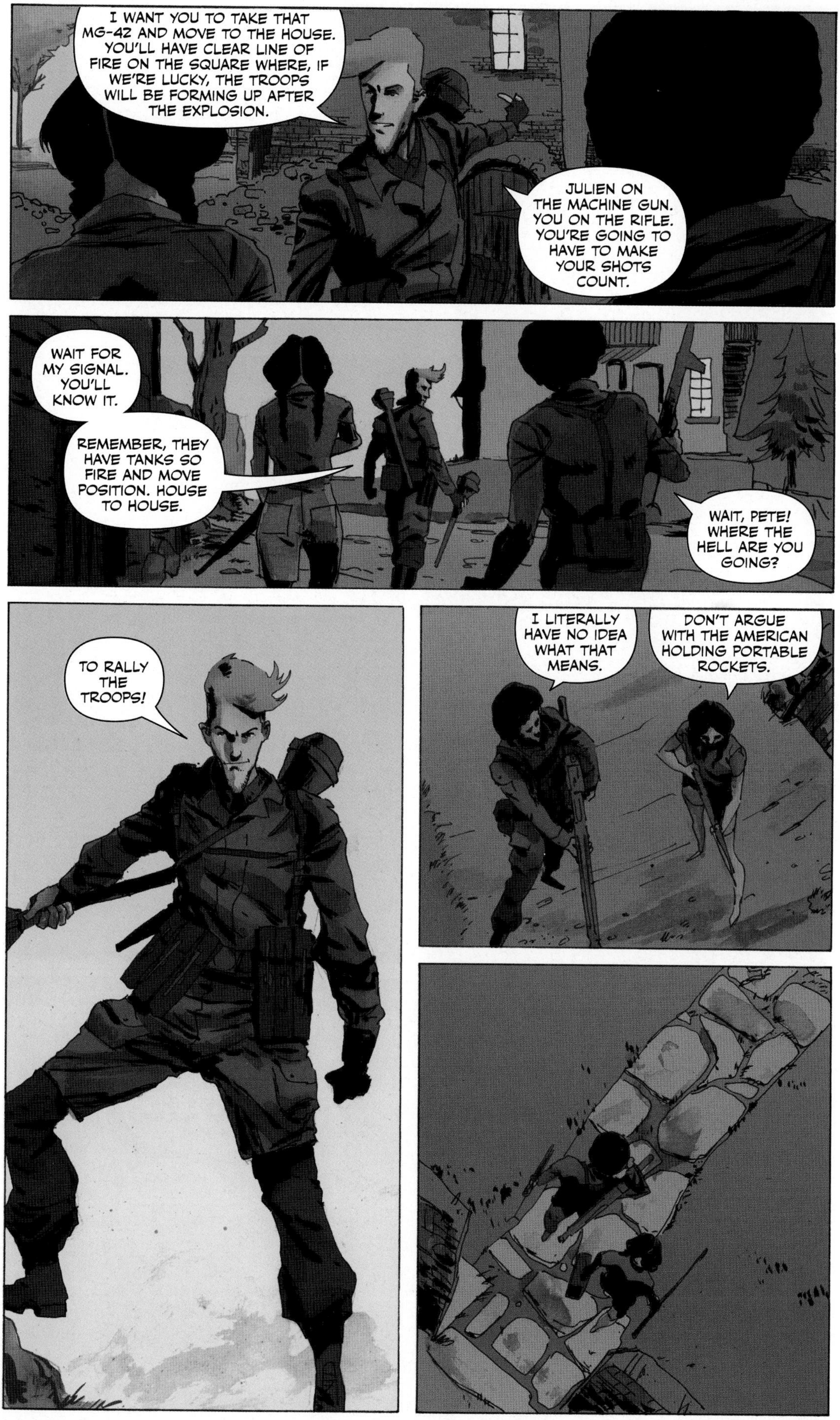
I WANT YOU TO TAKE THAT MG-42 AND MOVE TO THE HOUSE. YOU'LL HAVE CLEAR LINE OF FIRE ON THE SQUARE WHERE, IF WE'RE LUCKY, THE TROOPS WILL BE FORMING UP AFTER THE EXPLOSION.
JULIEN ON THE MACHINE GUN. YOU ON THE RIFLE. YOU'RE GOING TO HAVE TO MAKE YOUR SHOTS COUNT.
WAIT FOR MY SIGNAL. YOU'LL KNOW IT.
REMEMBER, THEY HAVE TANKS SO FIRE AND MOVE POSITION. HOUSE TO HOUSE.
WAIT, PETE! WHERE THE HELL ARE YOU GOING?
TO RALLY THE TROOPS!
I LITERALLY HAVE NO IDEA WHAT THAT MEANS.
DON'T ARGUE WITH THE AMERICAN HOLDING PORTABLE ROCKETS.

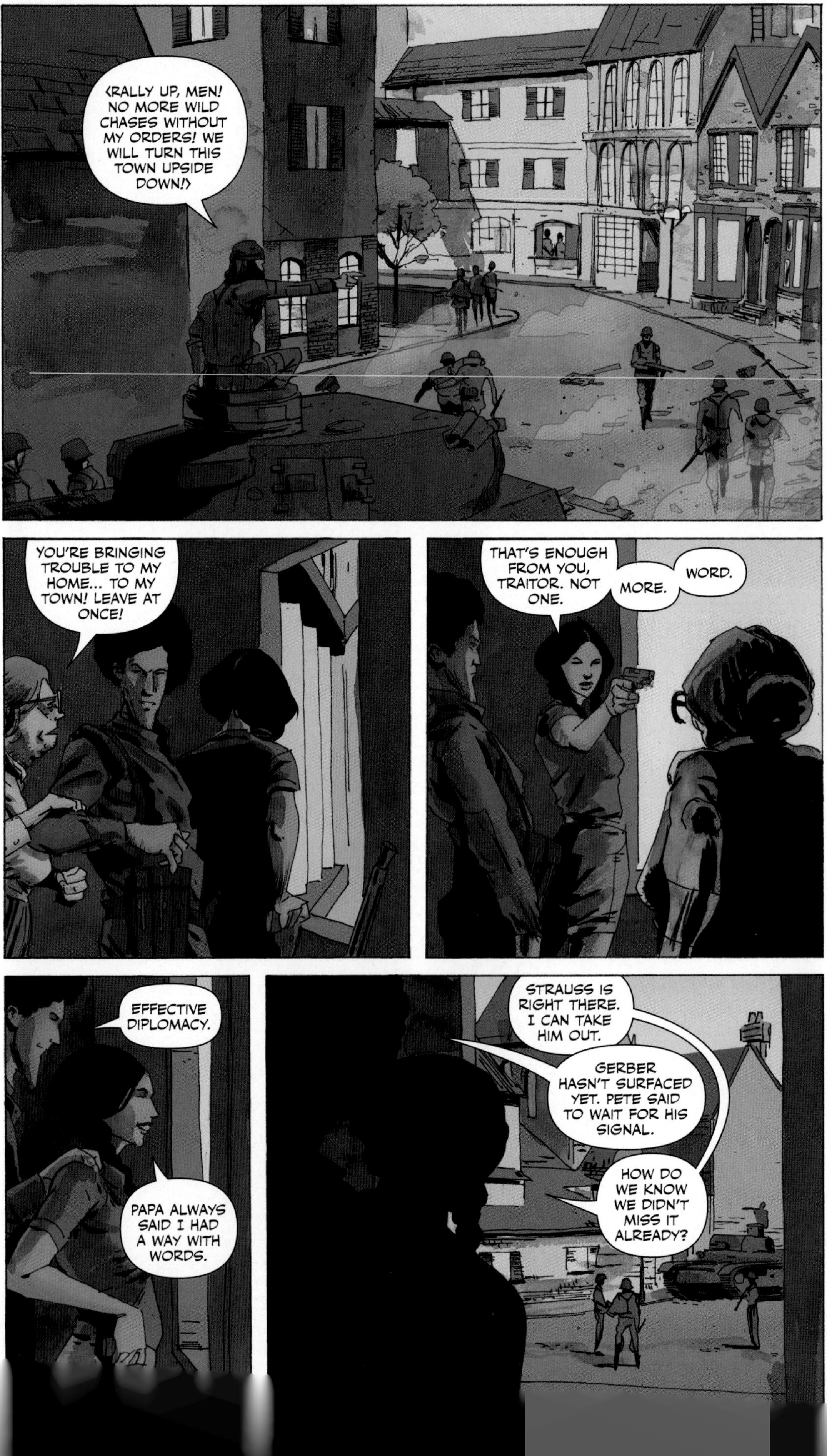
‹RALLY UP, MEN! NO MORE WILD CHASES WITHOUT MY ORDERS! WE WILL TURN THIS TOWN UPSIDE DOWN!›
YOU'RE BRINGING TROUBLE TO MY HOME... TO MY TOWN! LEAVE AT ONCE!
THAT'S ENOUGH FROM YOU, TRAITOR. NOT ONE.
MORE.
WORD.
EFFECTIVE DIPLOMACY.
PAPA ALWAYS SAID I HAD A WAY WITH WORDS.
STRAUSS IS RIGHT THERE. I CAN TAKE HIM OUT.
GERBER HASN'T SURFACED YET. PETE SAID TO WAIT FOR HIS SIGNAL.
HOW DO WE KNOW WE DIDN'T MISS IT ALREADY?

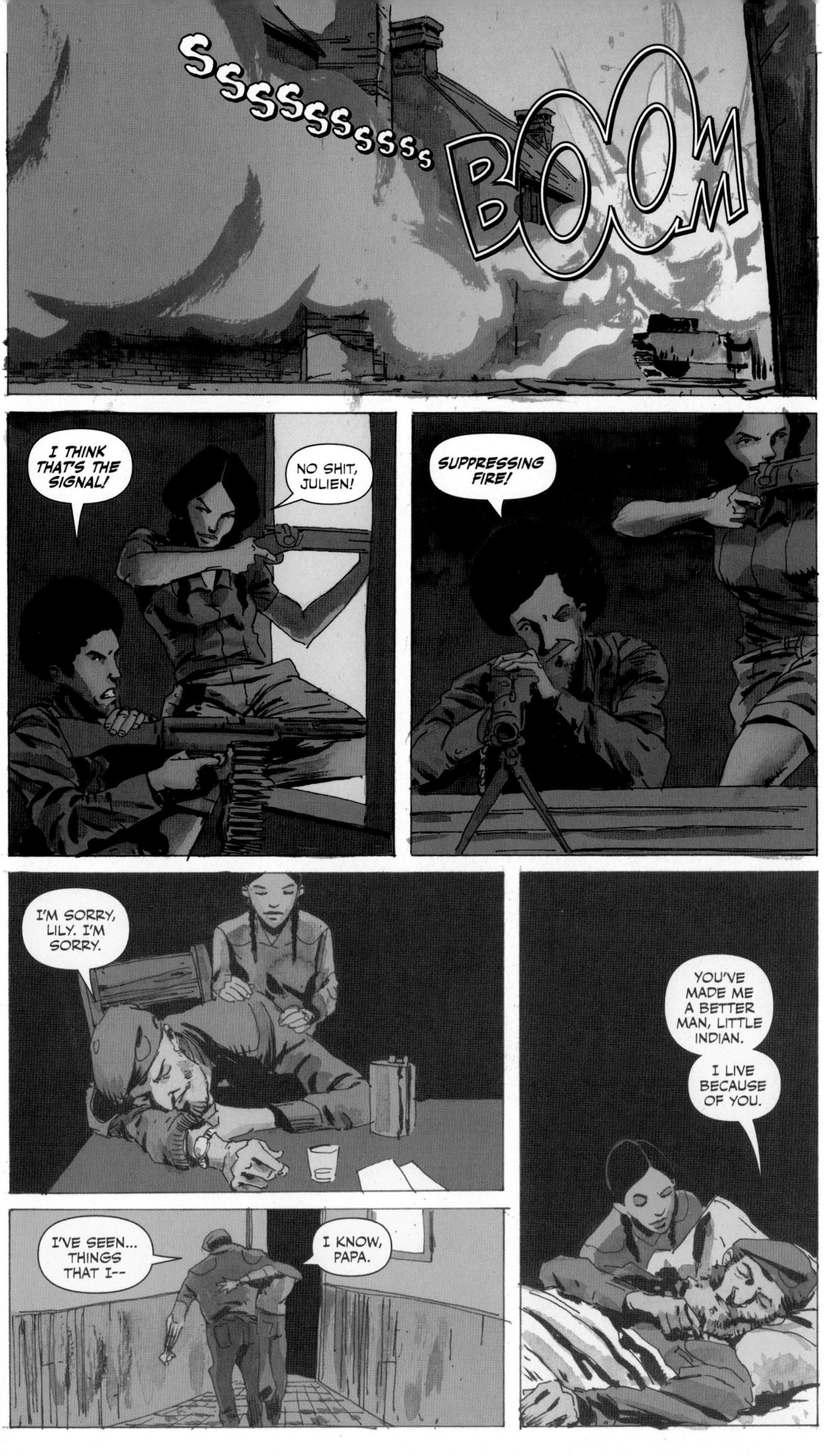
SSSSSSSSSSSS
BOOOM
I THINK THAT'S THE SIGNAL!
NO SHIT, JULIEN!
SUPPRESSING FIRE!
I'M SORRY, LILY. I'M SORRY.
I'VE SEEN... THINGS THAT I--
I KNOW, PAPA.
YOU'VE MADE ME A BETTER MAN, LITTLE INDIAN.
I LIVE BECAUSE OF YOU.

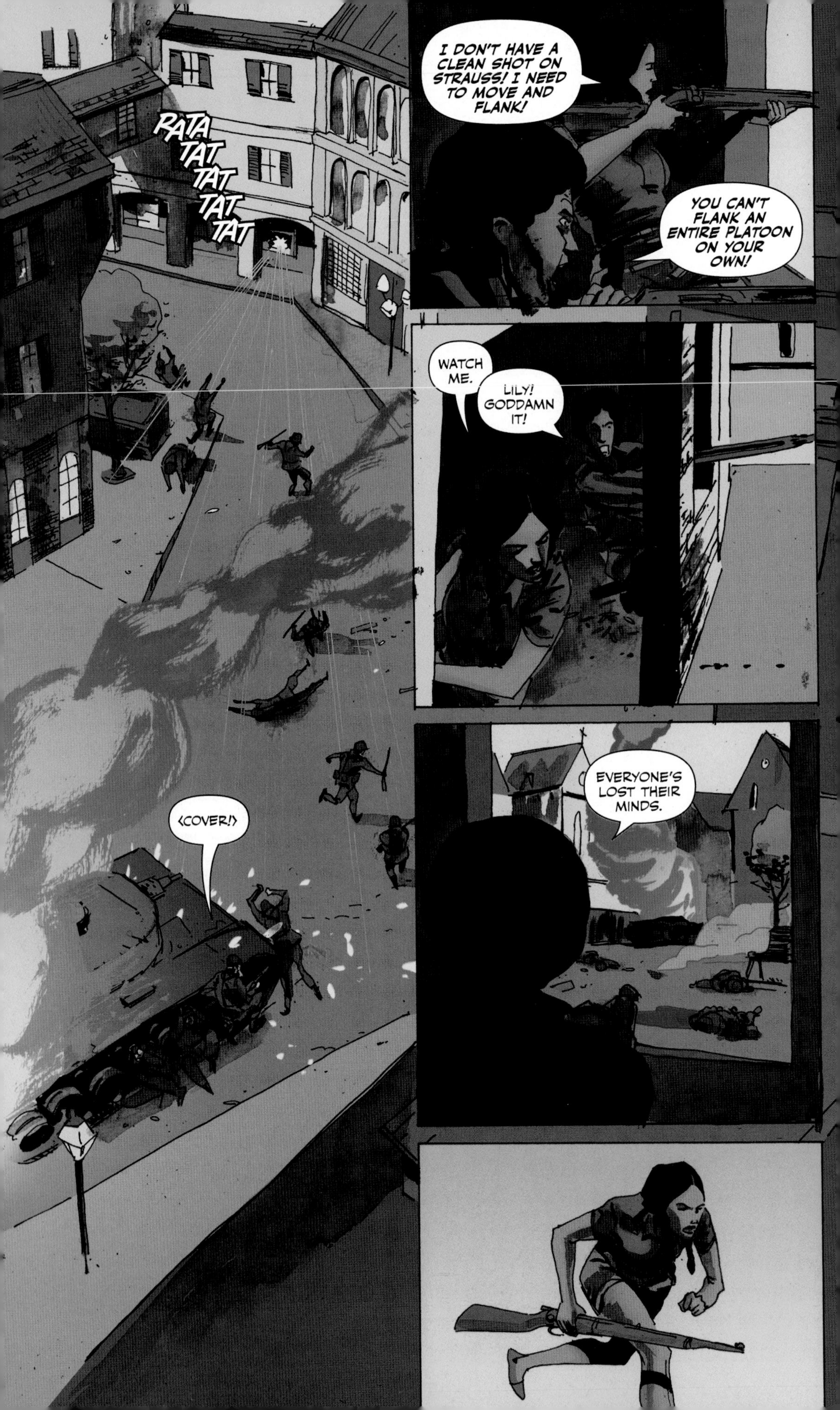
RATA TAT TAT TAT TAT
<COVER!>
I DON'T HAVE A CLEAN SHOT ON STRAUSS! I NEED TO MOVE AND FLANK!
YOU CAN'T FLANK AN ENTIRE PLATOON ON YOUR OWN!
WATCH ME.
LILY! GODDAMN IT!
EVERYONE'S LOST THEIR MINDS.

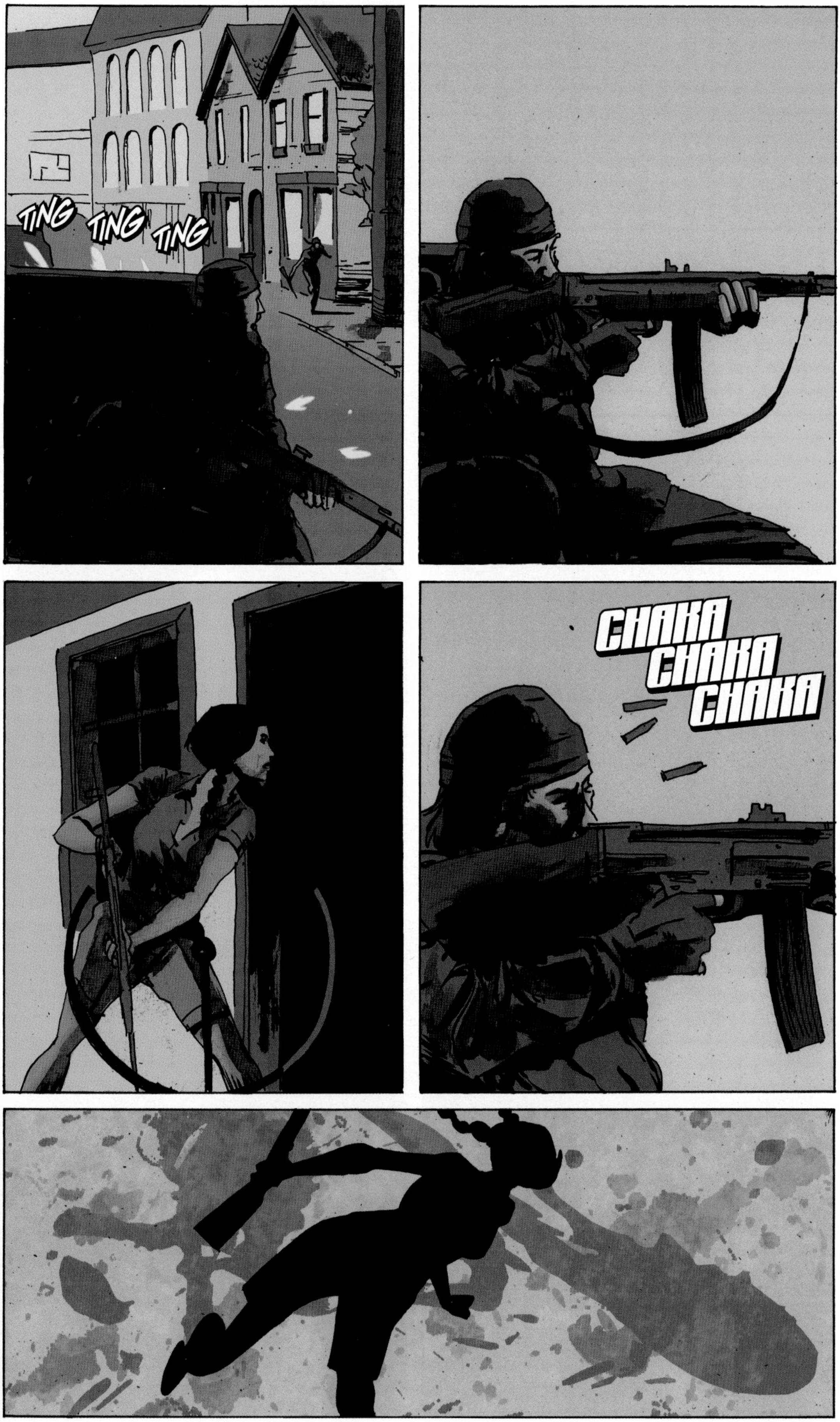
TING TING TING
CHAKA CHAKA CHAKA

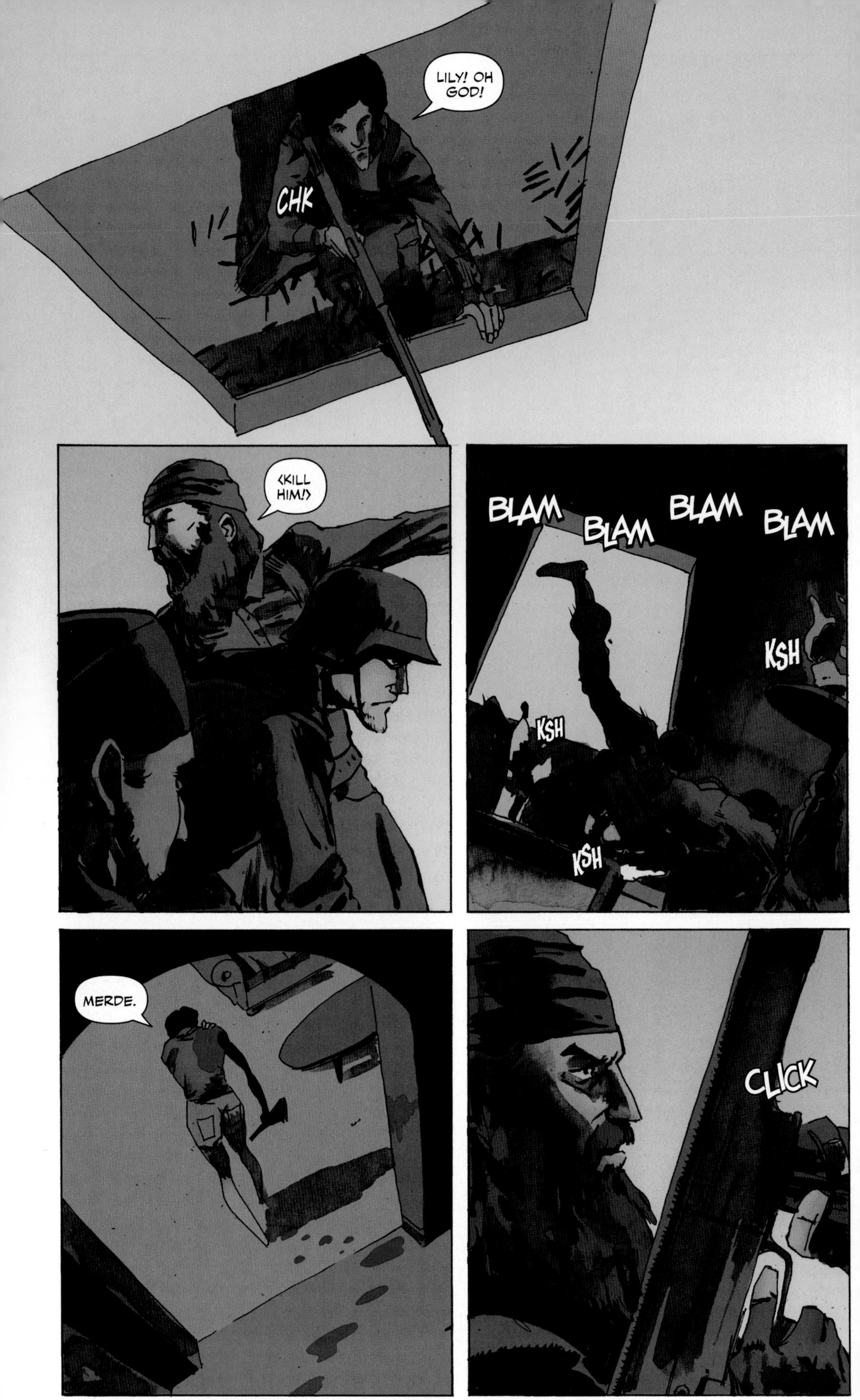
LILY! OH GOD!
CHK
<KILL HIM!>
BLAM BLAM BLAM BLAM
KSH
KSH
KSH
MERDE.
CLICK

April 1st, 1946
Julien and I spent a wonderful evening at Bois de Boulogne tonight.

We shared a bottle of Côté Tariquet that led to much public affection and an embarrassed husband.

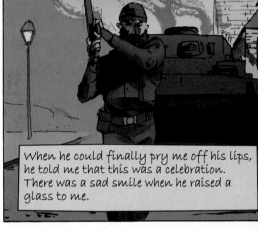

When he could finally pry me off his lips, he told me that this was a celebration. There was a sad smile when he raised a glass to me.

"It's been four years to the day. Four years since you were nearly taken from me," was all he could muster through a cracking voice.

I never remember such things. But Julien, my one love... he is a romantic to his very bones. There was a time when my heart had no place for such sentiment.

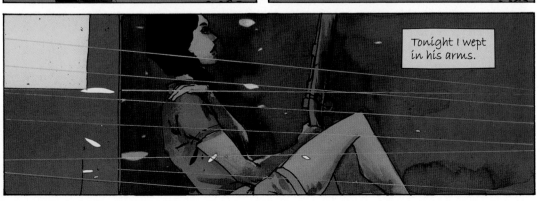

Tonight I wept in his arms.

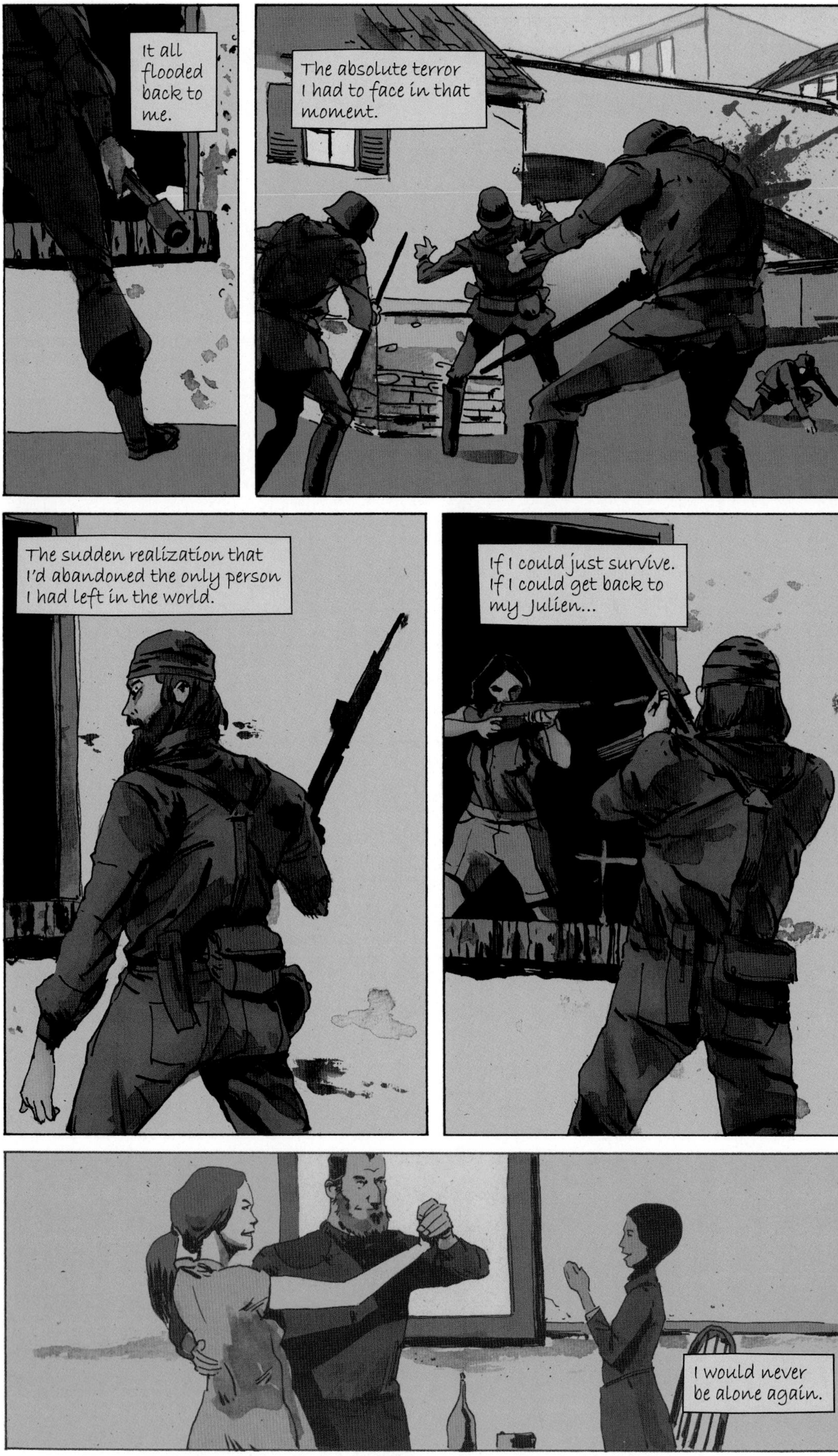
It all flooded back to me.
The absolute terror I had to face in that moment.
The sudden realization that I'd abandoned the only person I had left in the world.
If I could just survive. If I could get back to my Julien...
I would never be alone again.

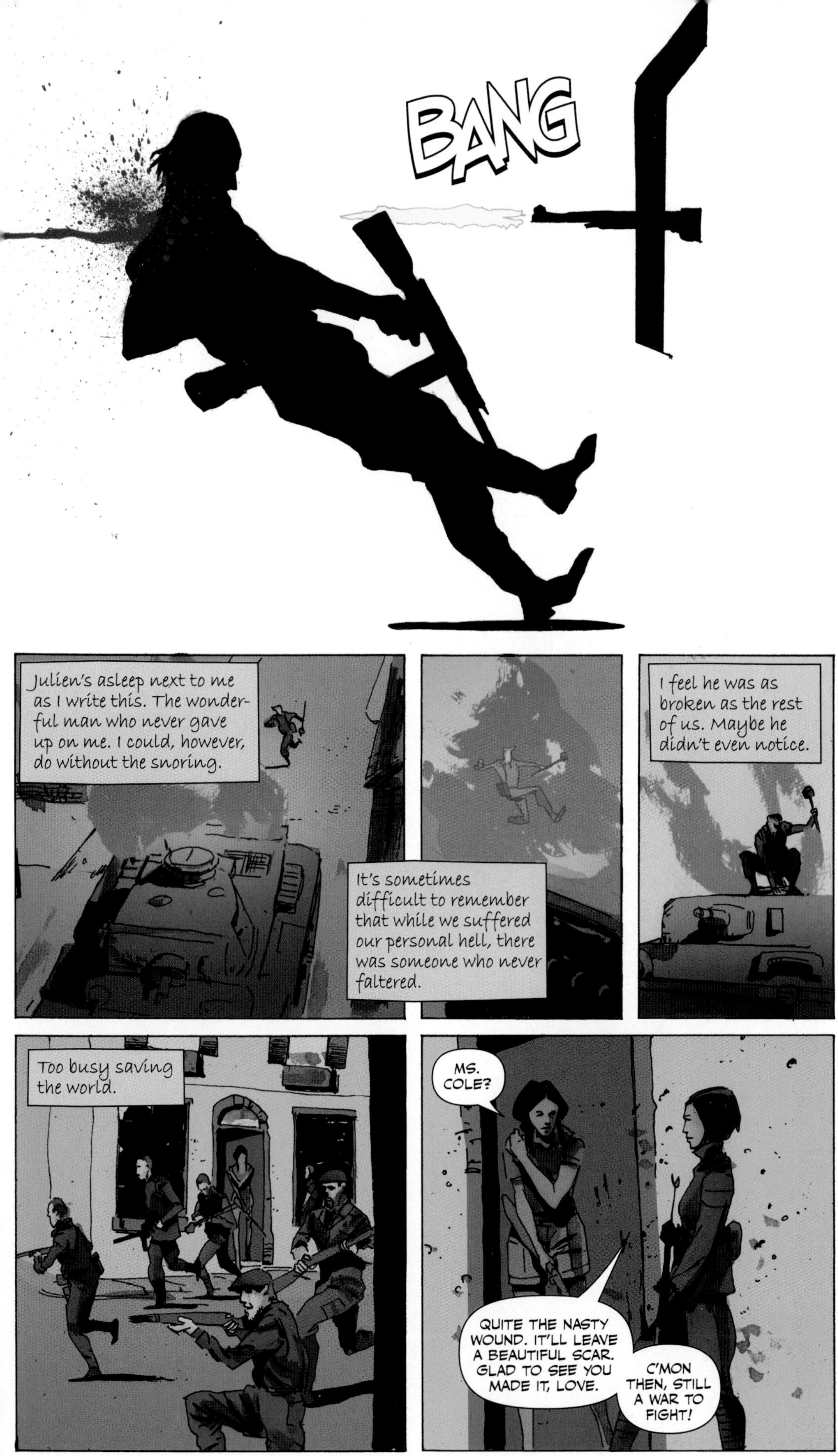
BANG
Julien's asleep next to me as I write this. The wonderful man who never gave up on me. I could, however, do without the snoring.
It's sometimes difficult to remember that while we suffered our personal hell, there was someone who never faltered.
I feel he was as broken as the rest of us. Maybe he didn't even notice.
Too busy saving the world.
MS. COLE?
QUITE THE NASTY WOUND. IT'LL LEAVE A BEAUTIFUL SCAR. GLAD TO SEE YOU MADE IT, LOVE.
C'MON THEN, STILL A WAR TO FIGHT!

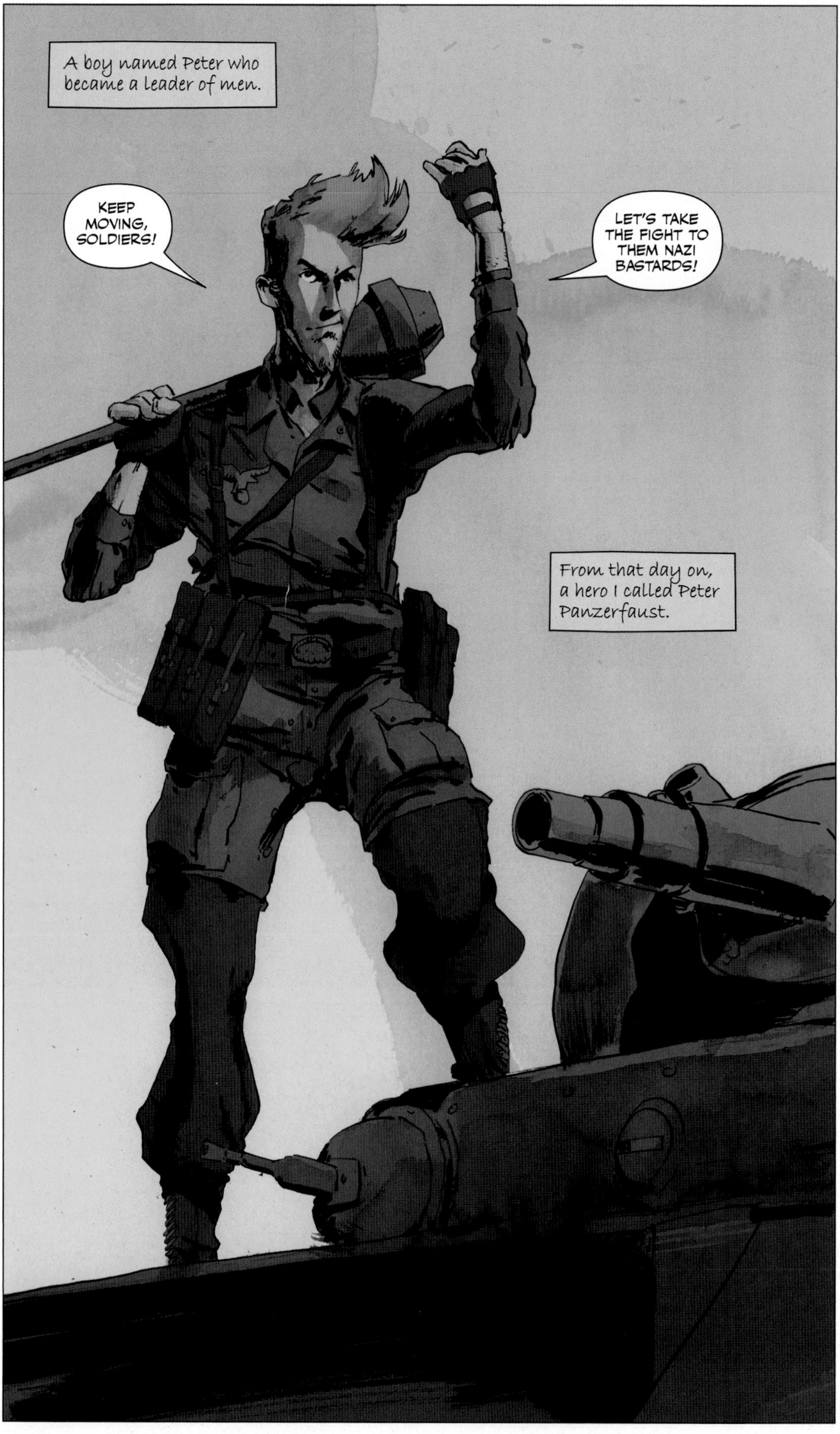
A boy named Peter who became a leader of men.
KEEP MOVING, SOLDIERS!
LET'S TAKE THE FIGHT TO THEM NAZI BASTARDS!
From that day on, a hero I called Peter Panzerfaust.

CHAPTER TWENTY

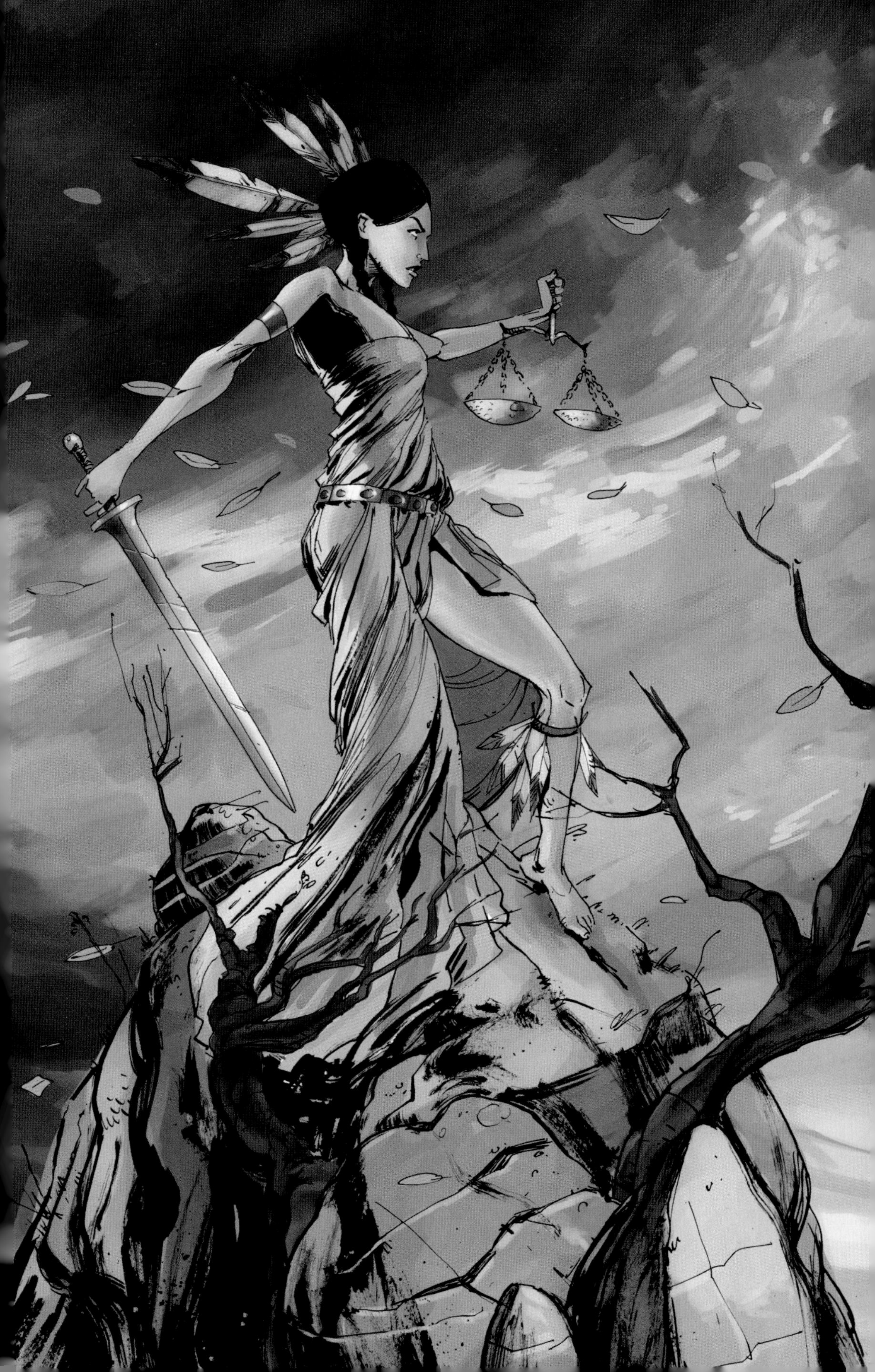

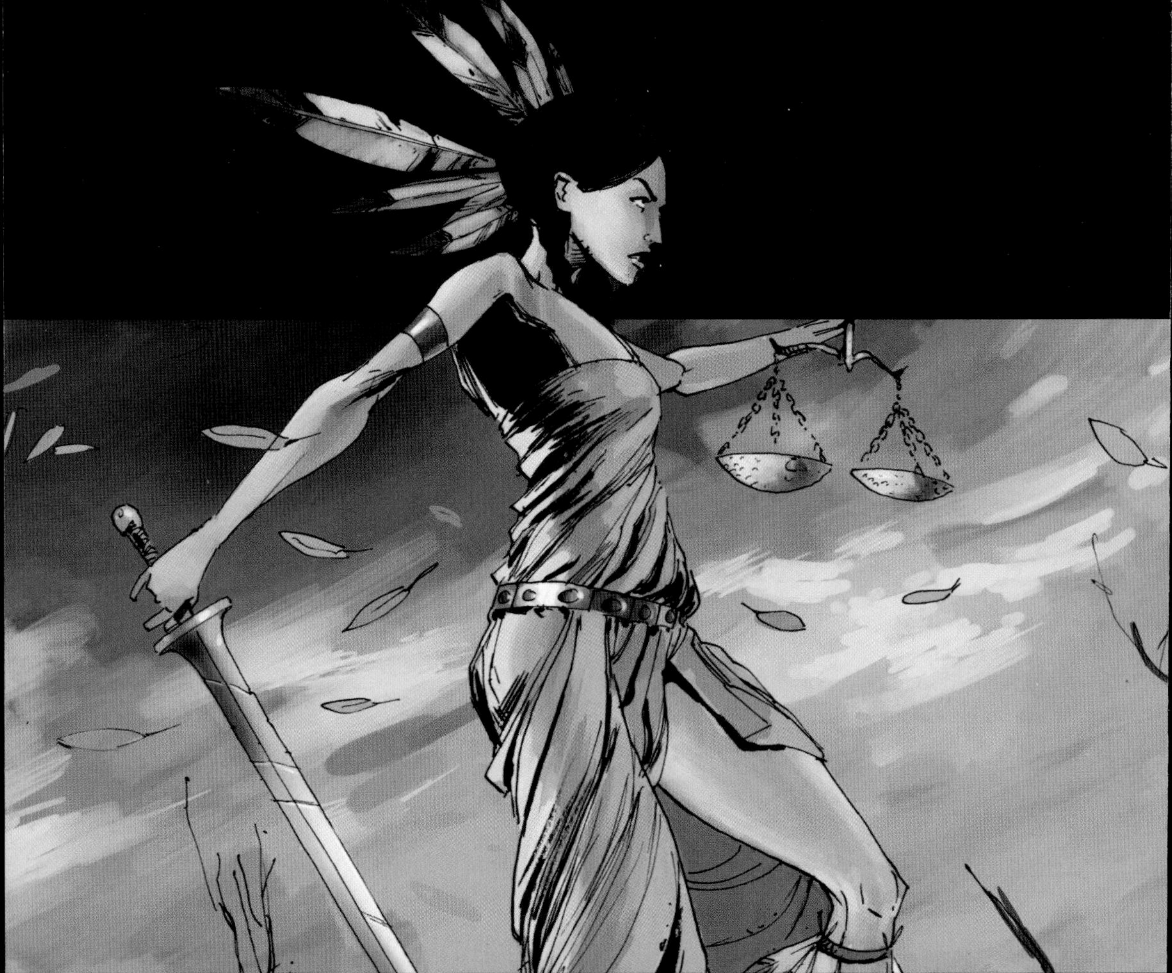

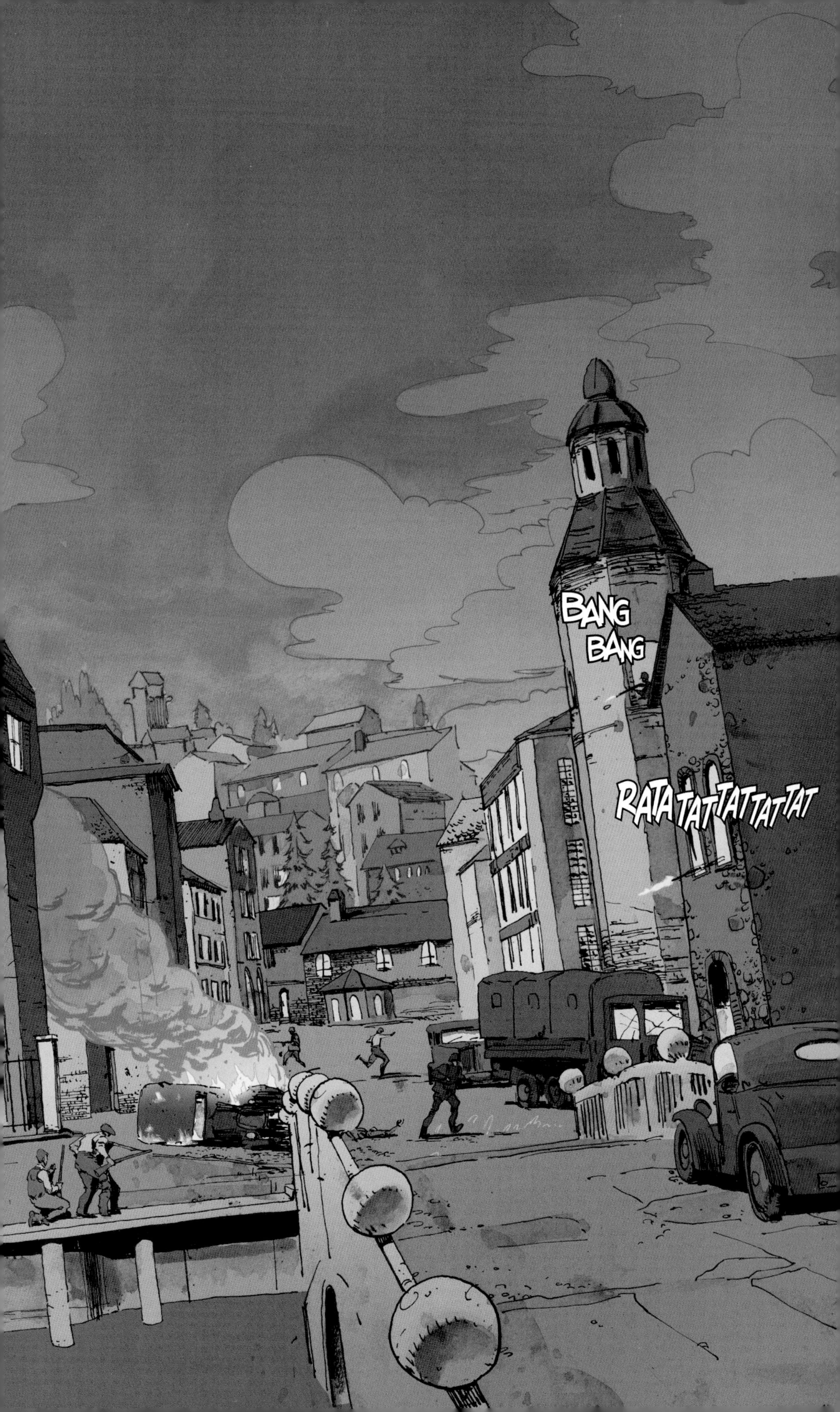
BANG
BANG
RATA TAT TAT TAT TAT

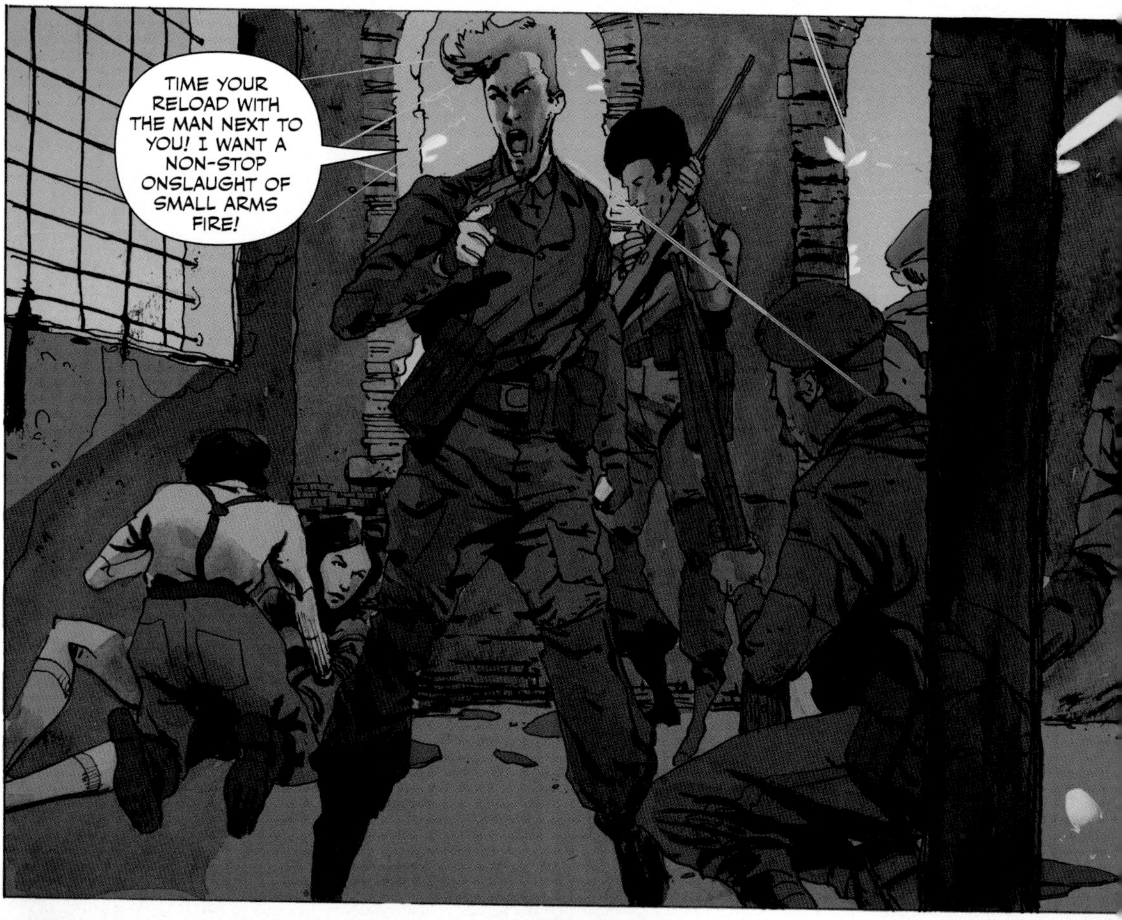
TIME YOUR RELOAD WITH THE MAN NEXT TO YOU! I WANT A NON-STOP ONSLAUGHT OF SMALL ARMS FIRE!

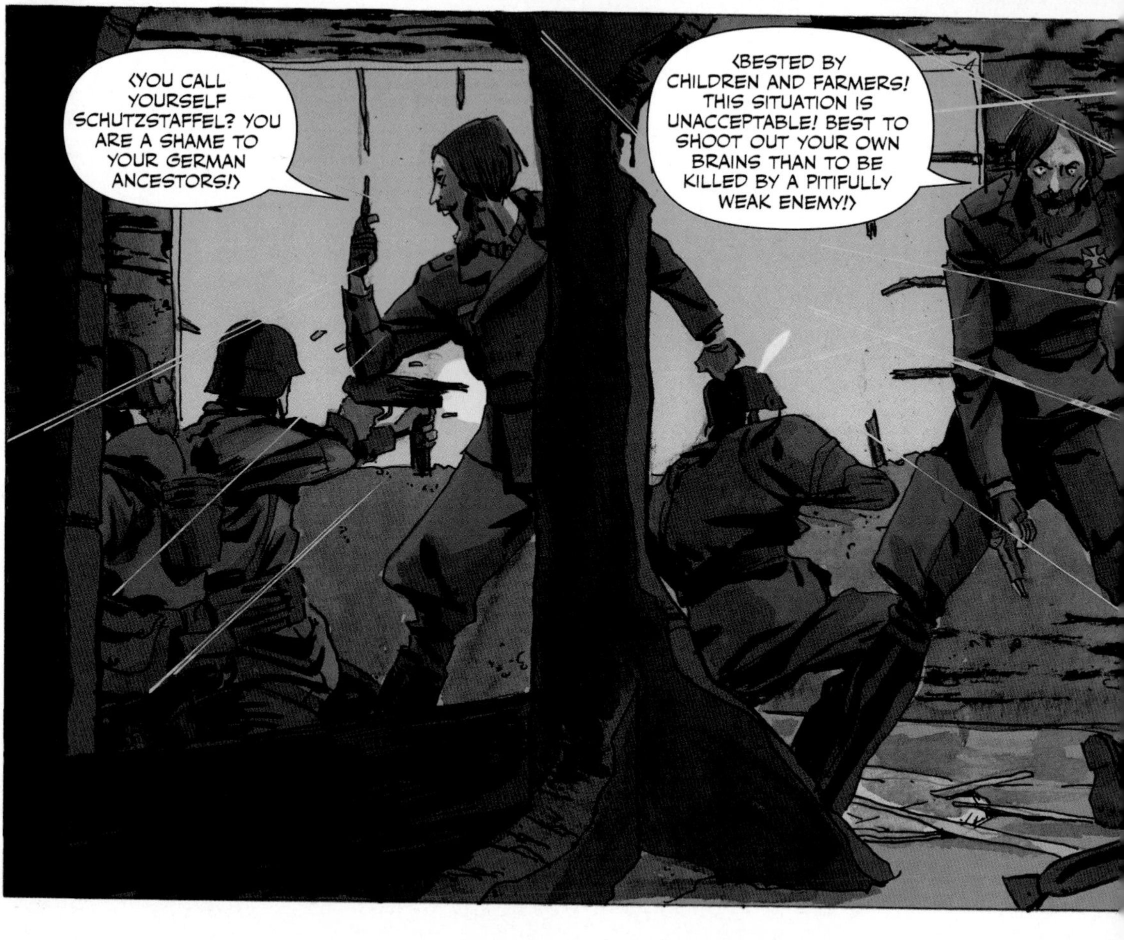
<YOU CALL YOURSELF SCHUTZSTAFFEL? YOU ARE A SHAME TO YOUR GERMAN ANCESTORS!>
<BESTED BY CHILDREN AND FARMERS! THIS SITUATION IS UNACCEPTABLE! BEST TO SHOOT OUT YOUR OWN BRAINS THAN TO BE KILLED BY A PITIFULLY WEAK ENEMY!>

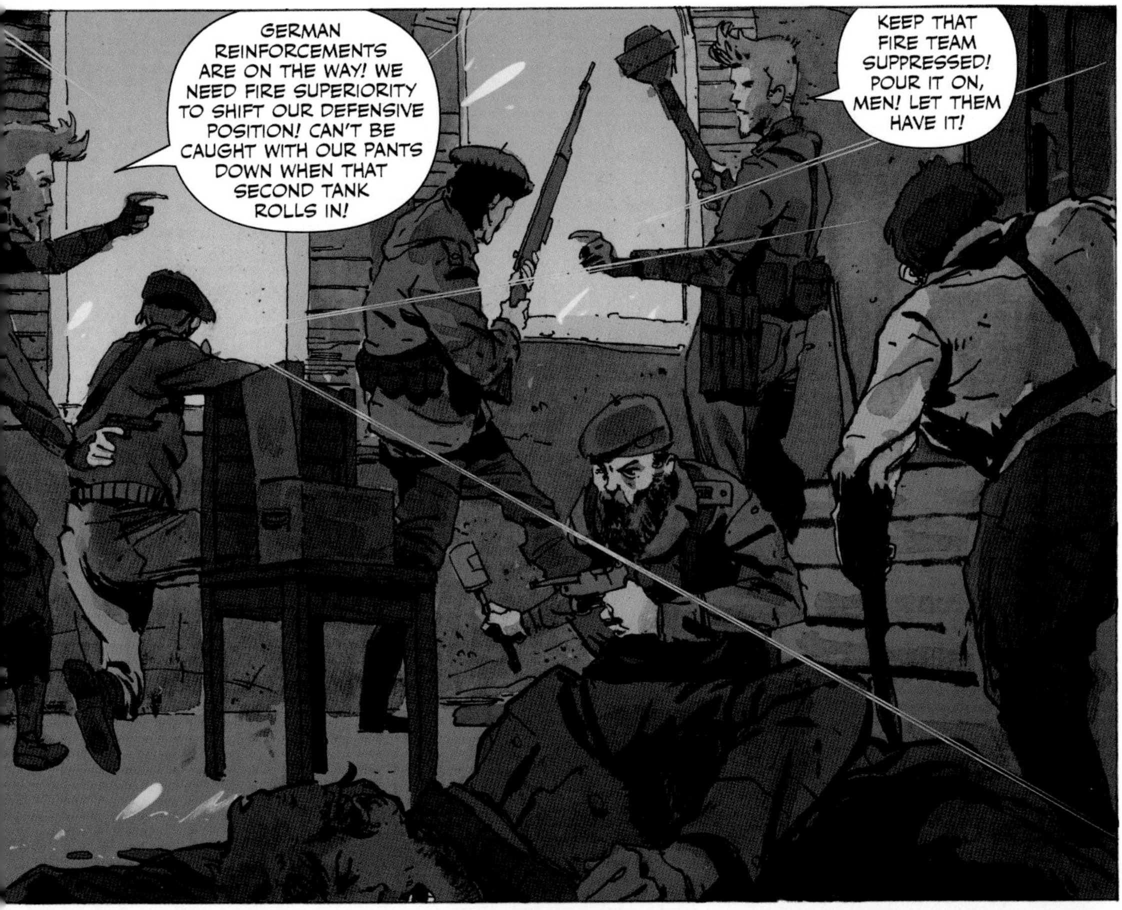
GERMAN REINFORCEMENTS ARE ON THE WAY! WE NEED FIRE SUPERIORITY TO SHIFT OUR DEFENSIVE POSITION! CAN'T BE CAUGHT WITH OUR PANTS DOWN WHEN THAT SECOND TANK ROLLS IN!
KEEP THAT FIRE TEAM SUPPRESSED! POUR IT ON, MEN! LET THEM HAVE IT!

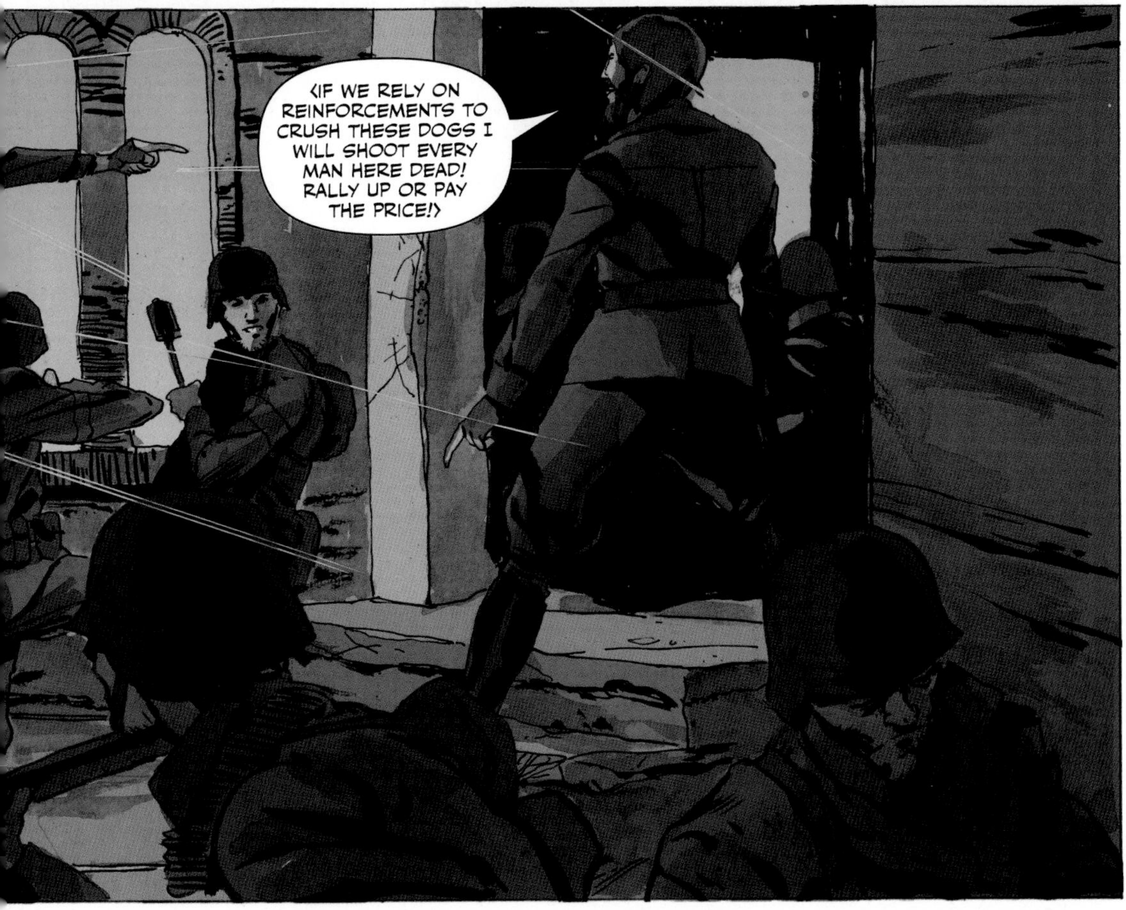
<IF WE RELY ON REINFORCEMENTS TO CRUSH THESE DOGS I WILL SHOOT EVERY MAN HERE DEAD! RALLY UP OR PAY THE PRICE!>

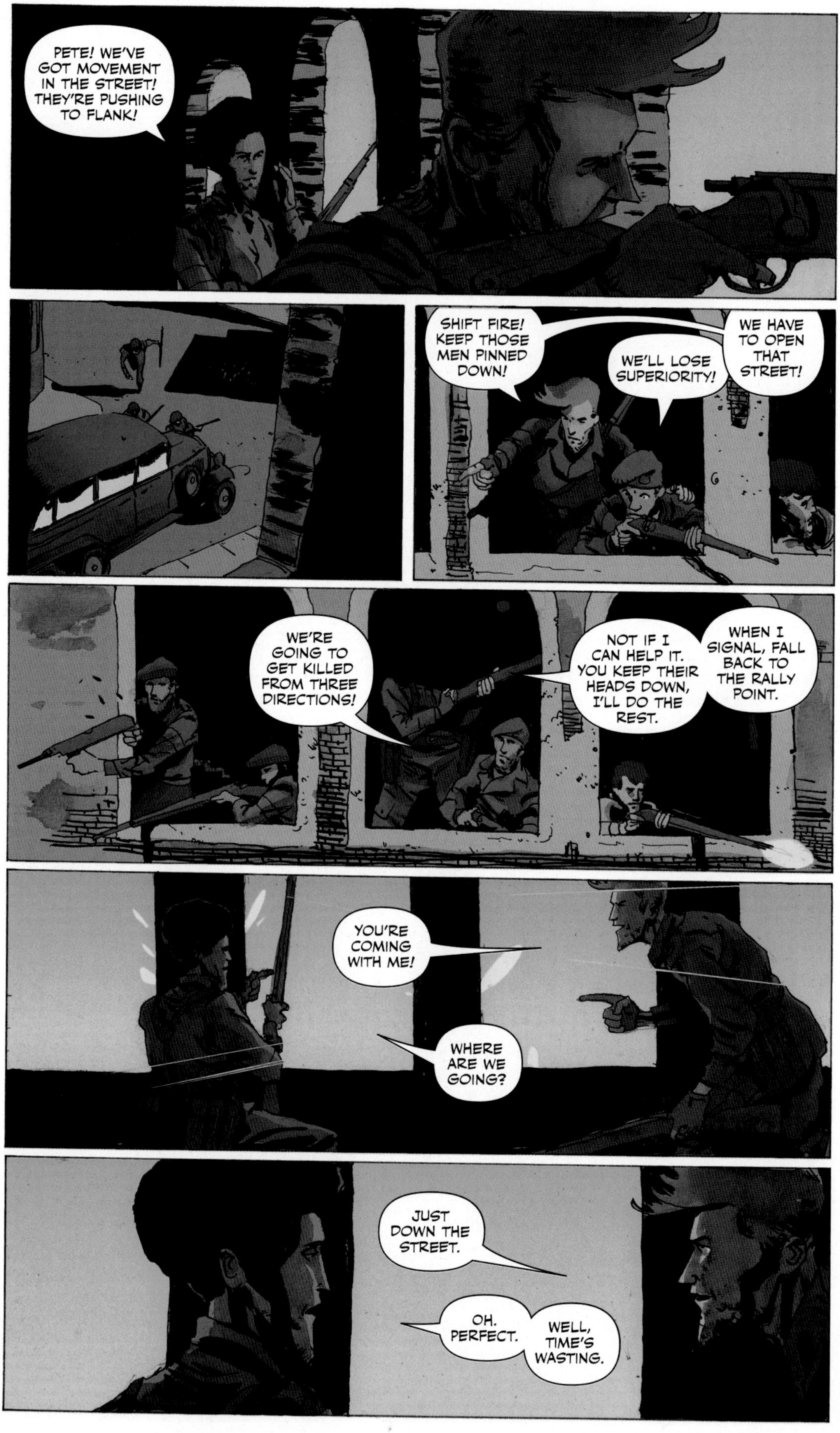
PETE! WE'VE GOT MOVEMENT IN THE STREET! THEY'RE PUSHING TO FLANK!
SHIFT FIRE! KEEP THOSE MEN PINNED DOWN!
WE HAVE TO OPEN THAT STREET!
WE'LL LOSE SUPERIORITY!
WE'RE GOING TO GET KILLED FROM THREE DIRECTIONS!
NOT IF I CAN HELP IT. YOU KEEP THEIR HEADS DOWN, I'LL DO THE REST.
WHEN I SIGNAL, FALL BACK TO THE RALLY POINT.
YOU'RE COMING WITH ME!
WHERE ARE WE GOING?
JUST DOWN THE STREET.
OH. PERFECT.
WELL, TIME'S WASTING.

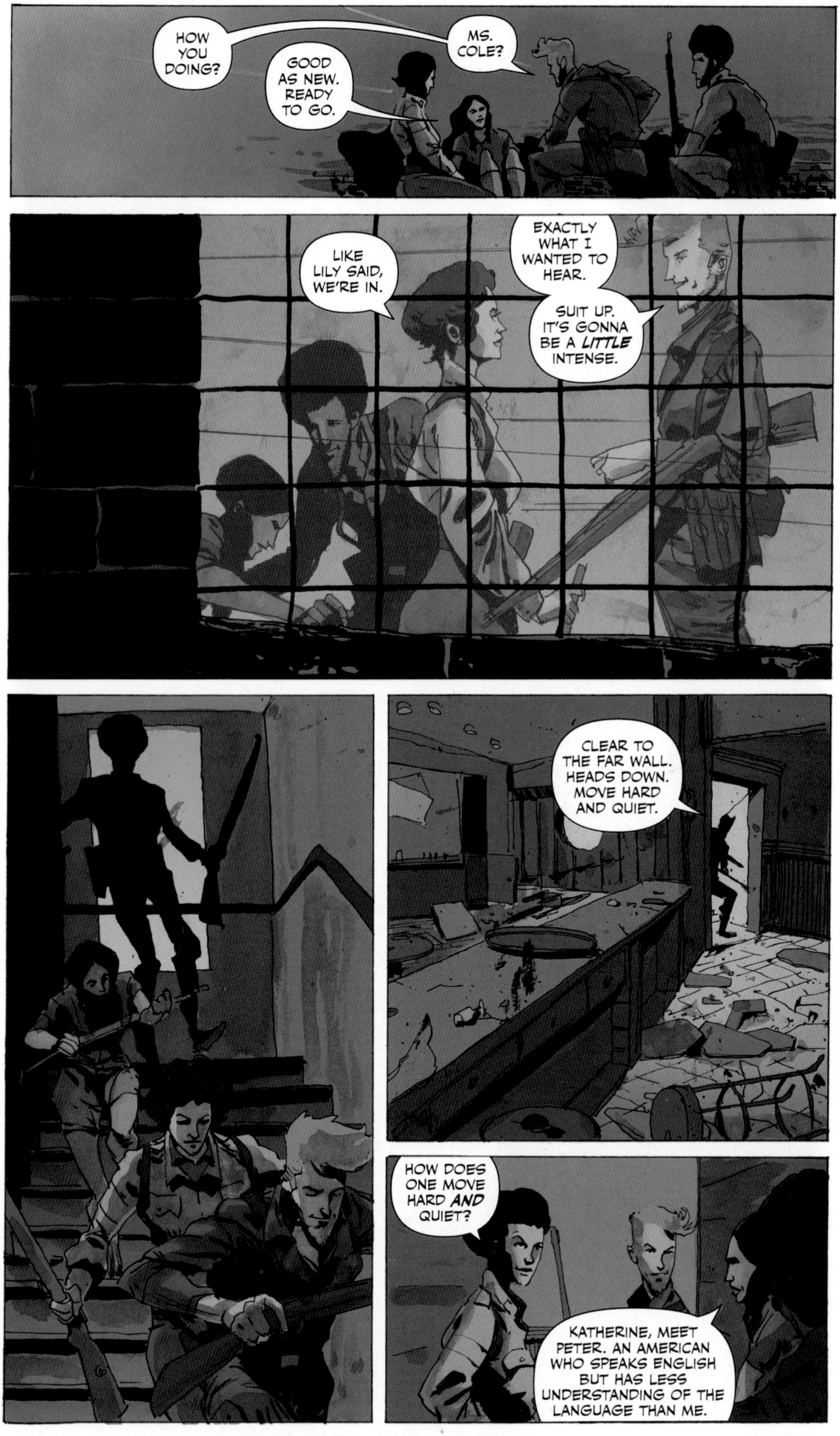
HOW YOU DOING?
MS. COLE?
GOOD AS NEW. READY TO GO.
LIKE LILY SAID, WE'RE IN.
EXACTLY WHAT I WANTED TO HEAR.
SUIT UP. IT'S GONNA BE A *LITTLE* INTENSE.
CLEAR TO THE FAR WALL. HEADS DOWN. MOVE HARD AND QUIET.
HOW DOES ONE MOVE HARD *AND* QUIET?
KATHERINE, MEET PETER. AN AMERICAN WHO SPEAKS ENGLISH BUT HAS LESS UNDERSTANDING OF THE LANGUAGE THAN ME.

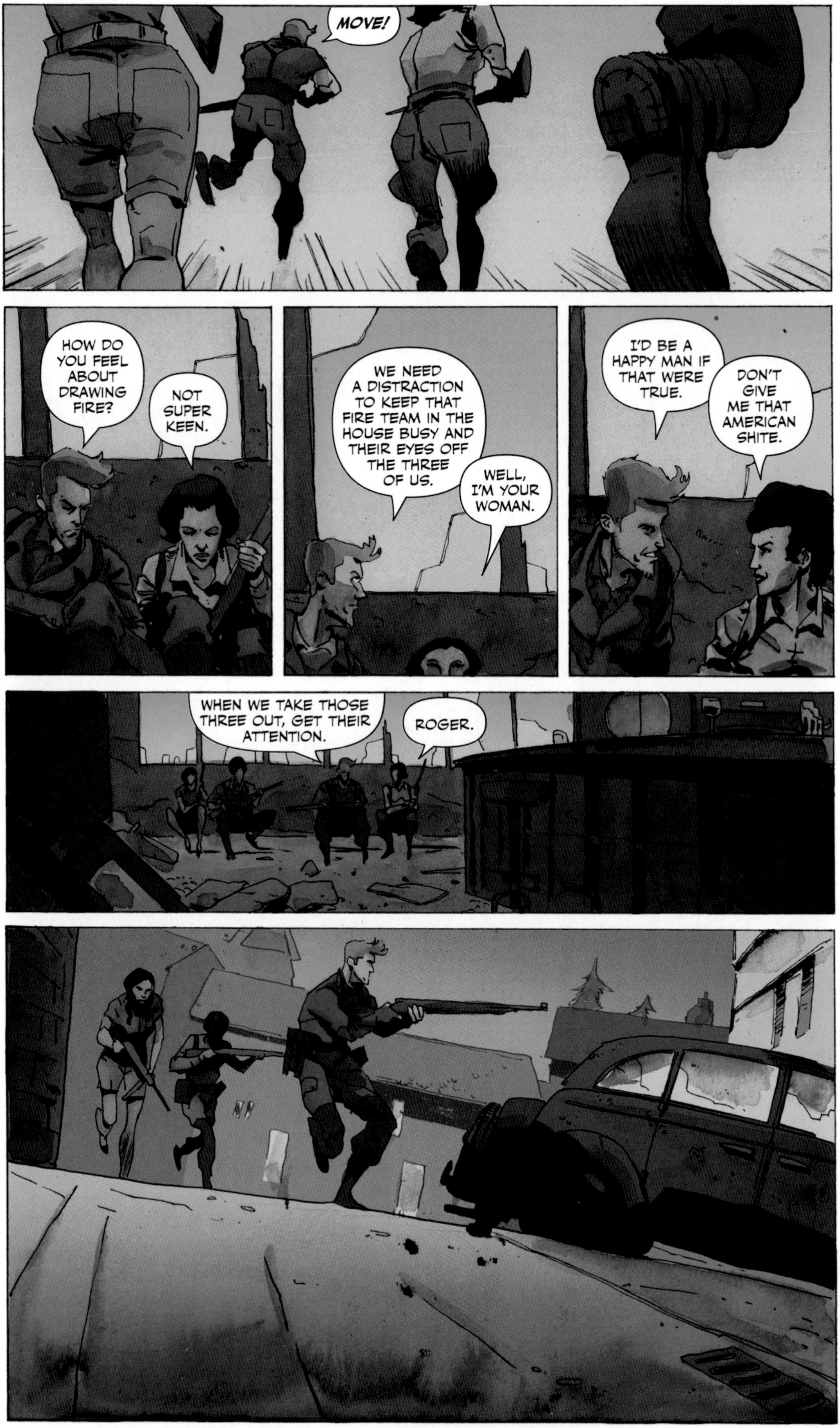
MOVE!
HOW DO YOU FEEL ABOUT DRAWING FIRE?
NOT SUPER KEEN.
WE NEED A DISTRACTION TO KEEP THAT FIRE TEAM IN THE HOUSE BUSY AND THEIR EYES OFF THE THREE OF US.
WELL, I'M YOUR WOMAN.
I'D BE A HAPPY MAN IF THAT WERE TRUE.
DON'T GIVE ME THAT AMERICAN SHITE.
WHEN WE TAKE THOSE THREE OUT, GET THEIR ATTENTION.
ROGER.

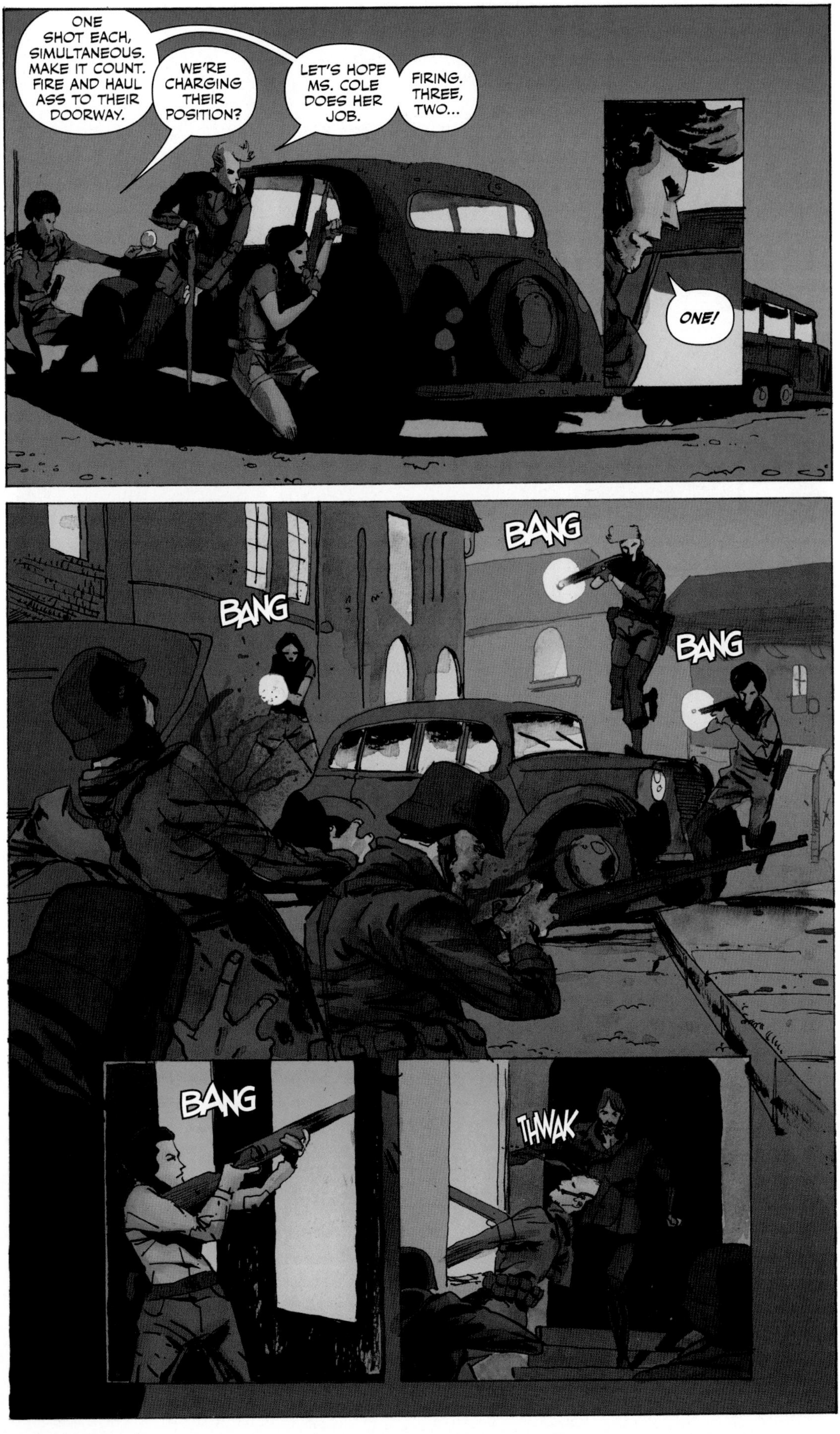
ONE SHOT EACH, SIMULTANEOUS. MAKE IT COUNT. FIRE AND HAUL ASS TO THEIR DOORWAY.
WE'RE CHARGING THEIR POSITION?
LET'S HOPE MS. COLE DOES HER JOB.
FIRING. THREE, TWO...
ONE!
BANG
BANG
BANG
BANG
THWAK

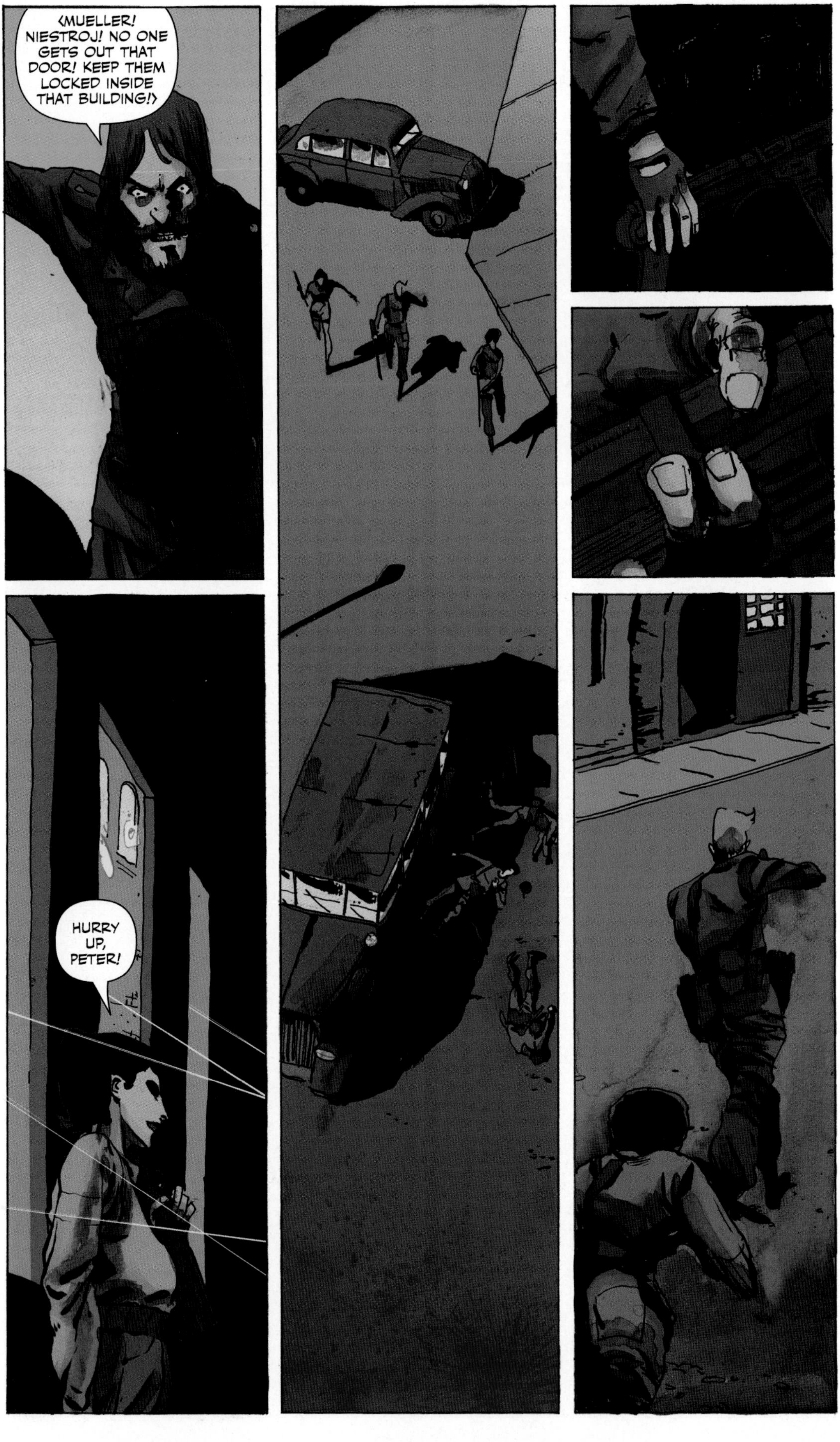
<MUELLER! NIESTROJ! NO ONE GETS OUT THAT DOOR! KEEP THEM LOCKED INSIDE THAT BUILDING!>
HURRY UP, PETER!

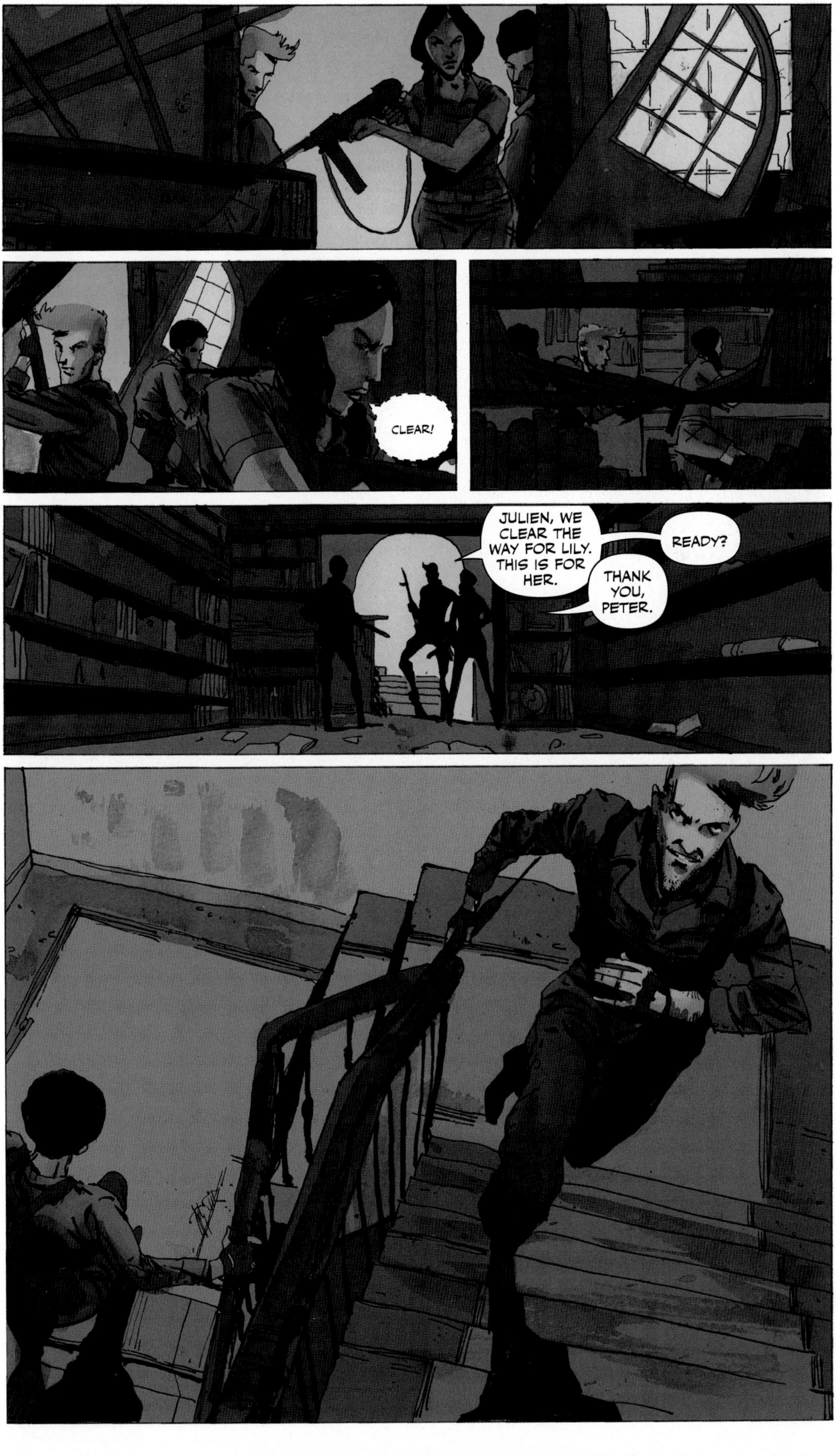
CLEAR!
JULIEN, WE CLEAR THE WAY FOR LILY. THIS IS FOR HER.
READY?
THANK YOU, PETER.

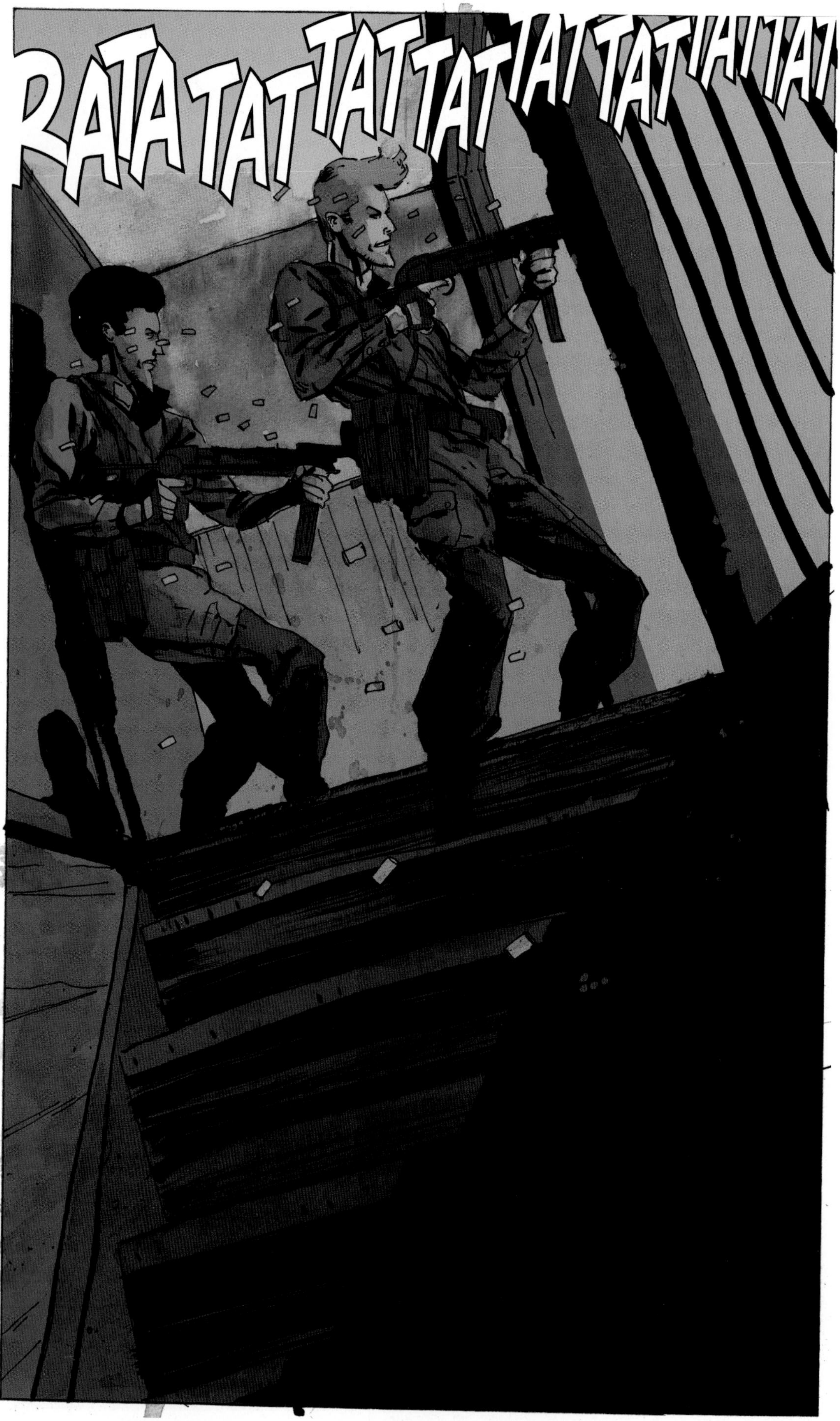
RATA TAT TAT TAT TAT TAT TAT TAT

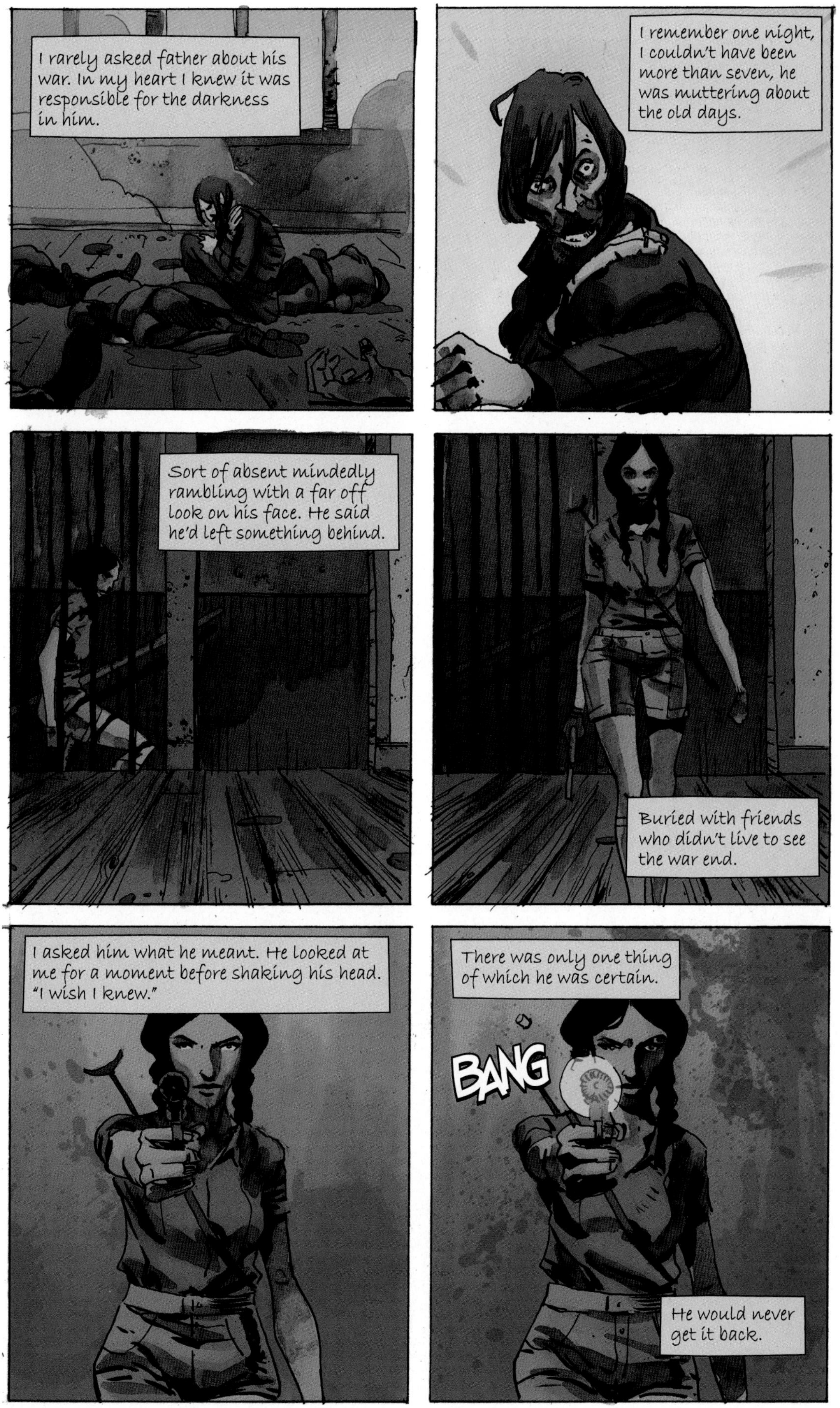
I rarely asked father about his war. In my heart I knew it was responsible for the darkness in him.
I remember one night, I couldn't have been more than seven, he was muttering about the old days.
Sort of absent mindedly rambling with a far off look on his face. He said he'd left something behind.
Buried with friends who didn't live to see the war end.
I asked him what he meant. He looked at me for a moment before shaking his head. "I wish I knew."
There was only one thing of which he was certain.
BANG
He would never get it back.

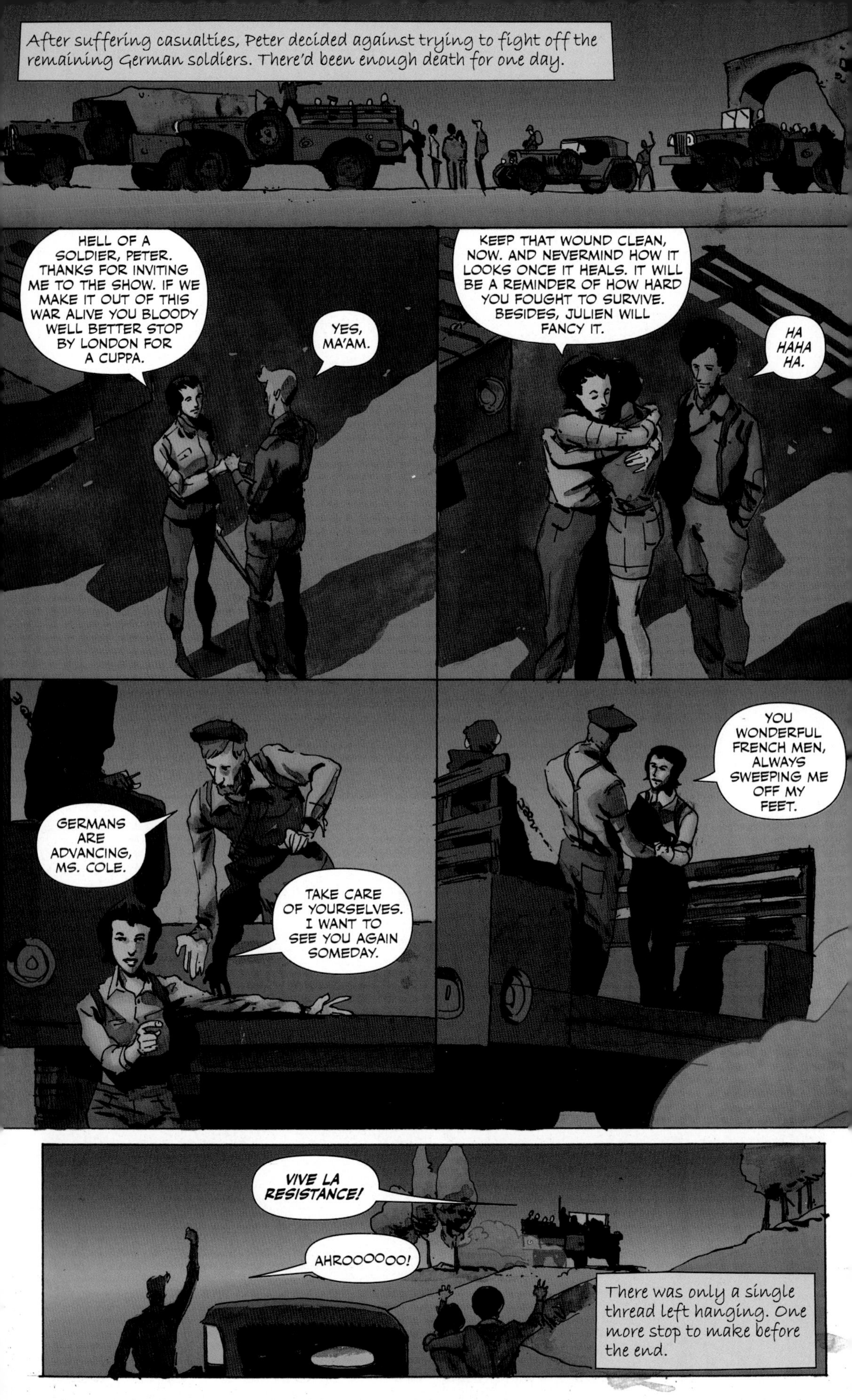
After suffering casualties, Peter decided against trying to fight off the remaining German soldiers. There'd been enough death for one day.
HELL OF A SOLDIER, PETER. THANKS FOR INVITING ME TO THE SHOW. IF WE MAKE IT OUT OF THIS WAR ALIVE YOU BLOODY WELL BETTER STOP BY LONDON FOR A CUPPA.
YES, MA'AM.
KEEP THAT WOUND CLEAN, NOW. AND NEVERMIND HOW IT LOOKS ONCE IT HEALS. IT WILL BE A REMINDER OF HOW HARD YOU FOUGHT TO SURVIVE. BESIDES, JULIEN WILL FANCY IT.
HA HAHA HA.
GERMANS ARE ADVANCING, MS. COLE.
TAKE CARE OF YOURSELVES. I WANT TO SEE YOU AGAIN SOMEDAY.
YOU WONDERFUL FRENCH MEN, ALWAYS SWEEPING ME OFF MY FEET.
VIVE LA RESISTANCE!
AHROOOOOO!
There was only a single thread left hanging. One more stop to make before the end.

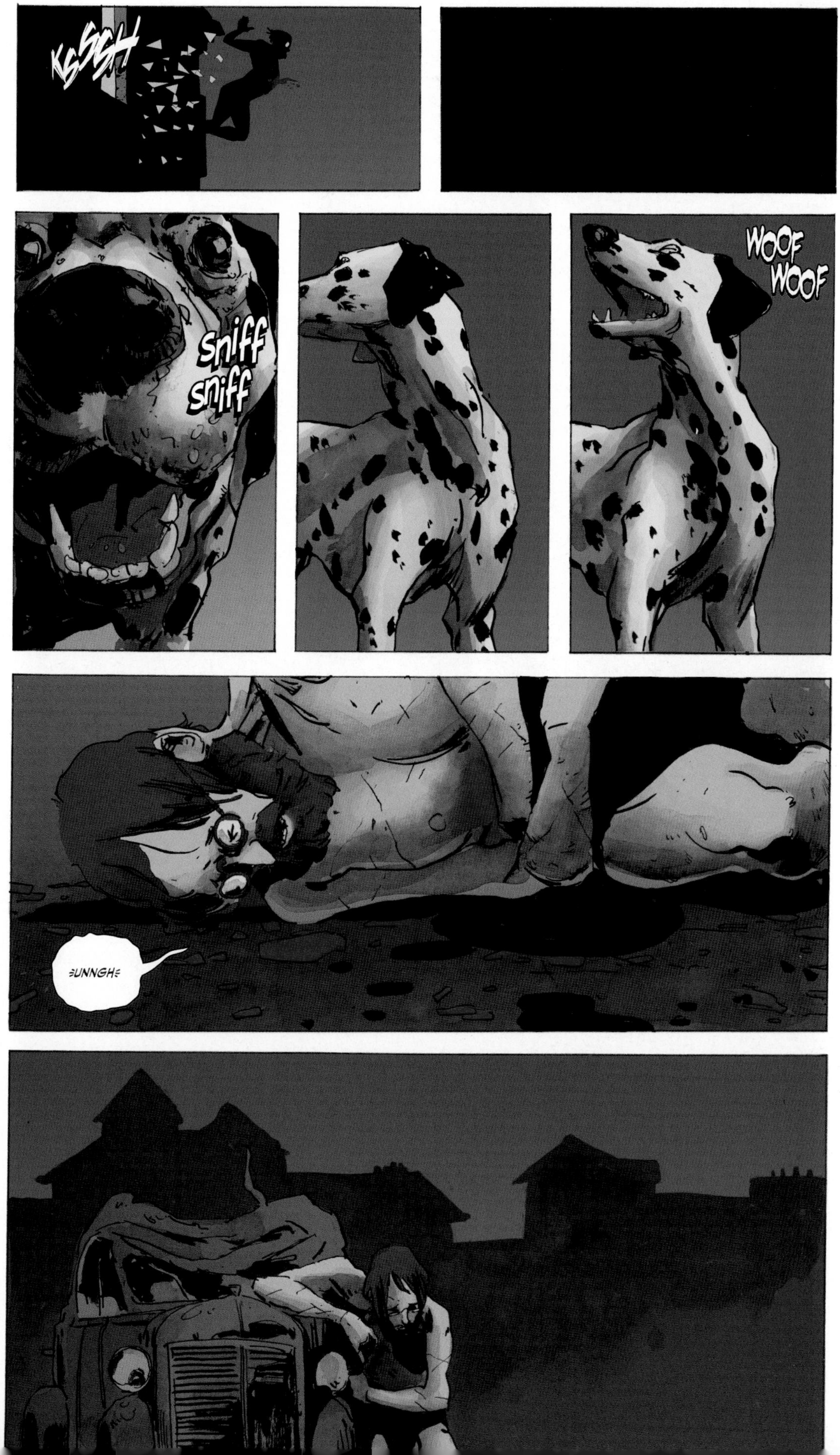
KSSSH
sniff sniff
WOOF WOOF
UNNGH

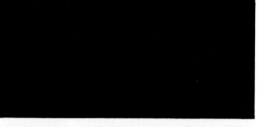

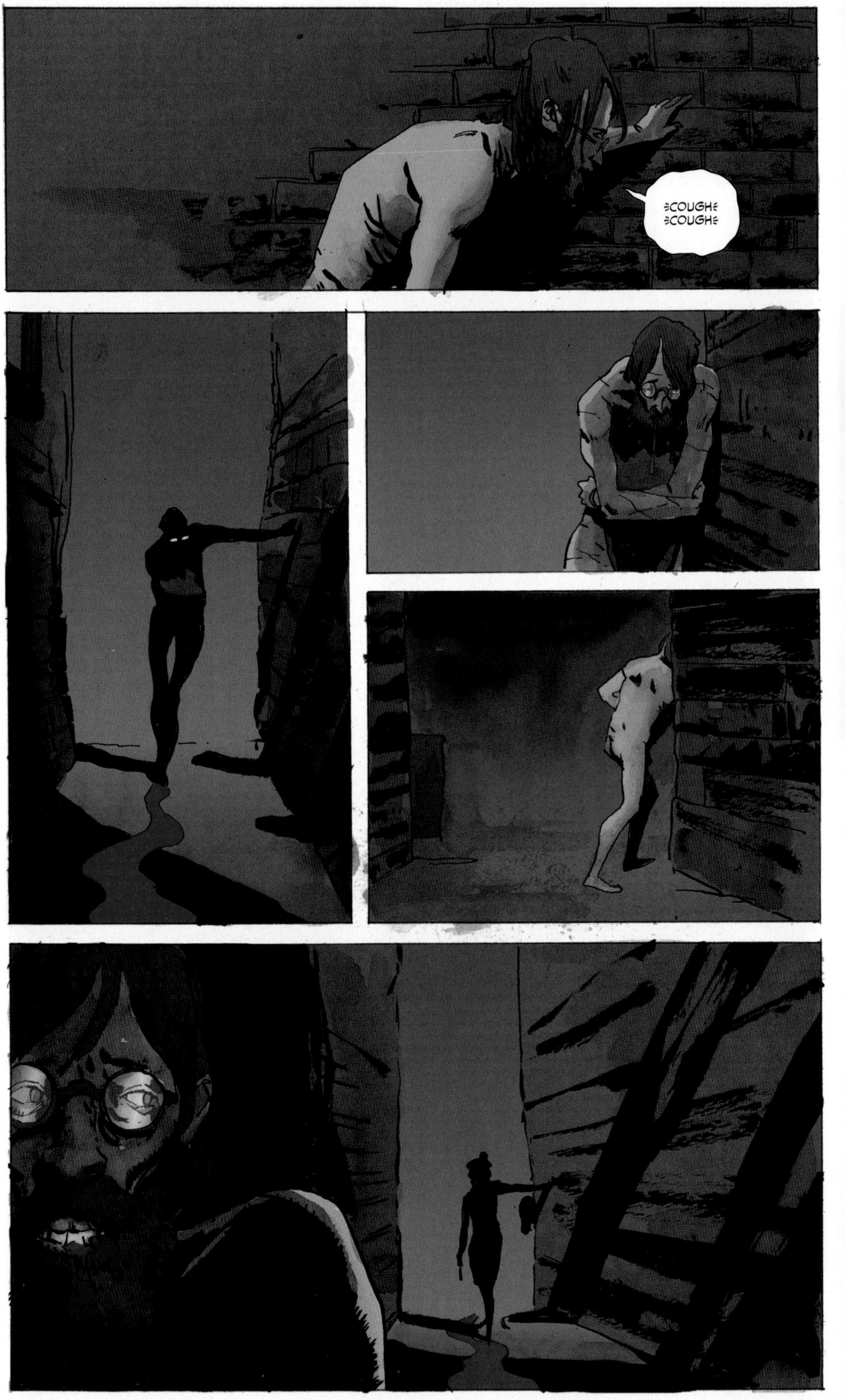

COUGH
COUGH

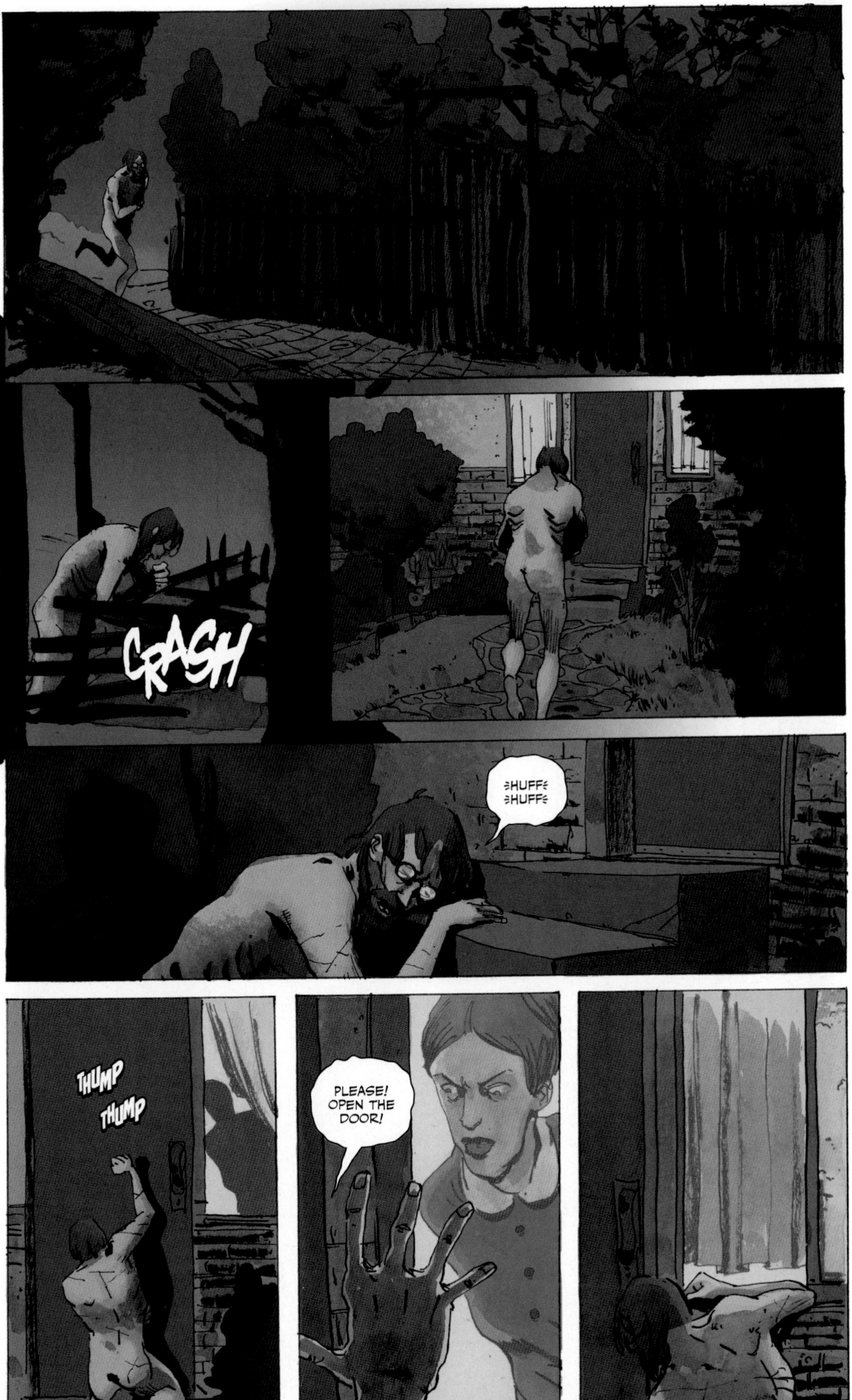
CRASH
HUFF HUFF
THUMP
THUMP
PLEASE! OPEN THE DOOR!

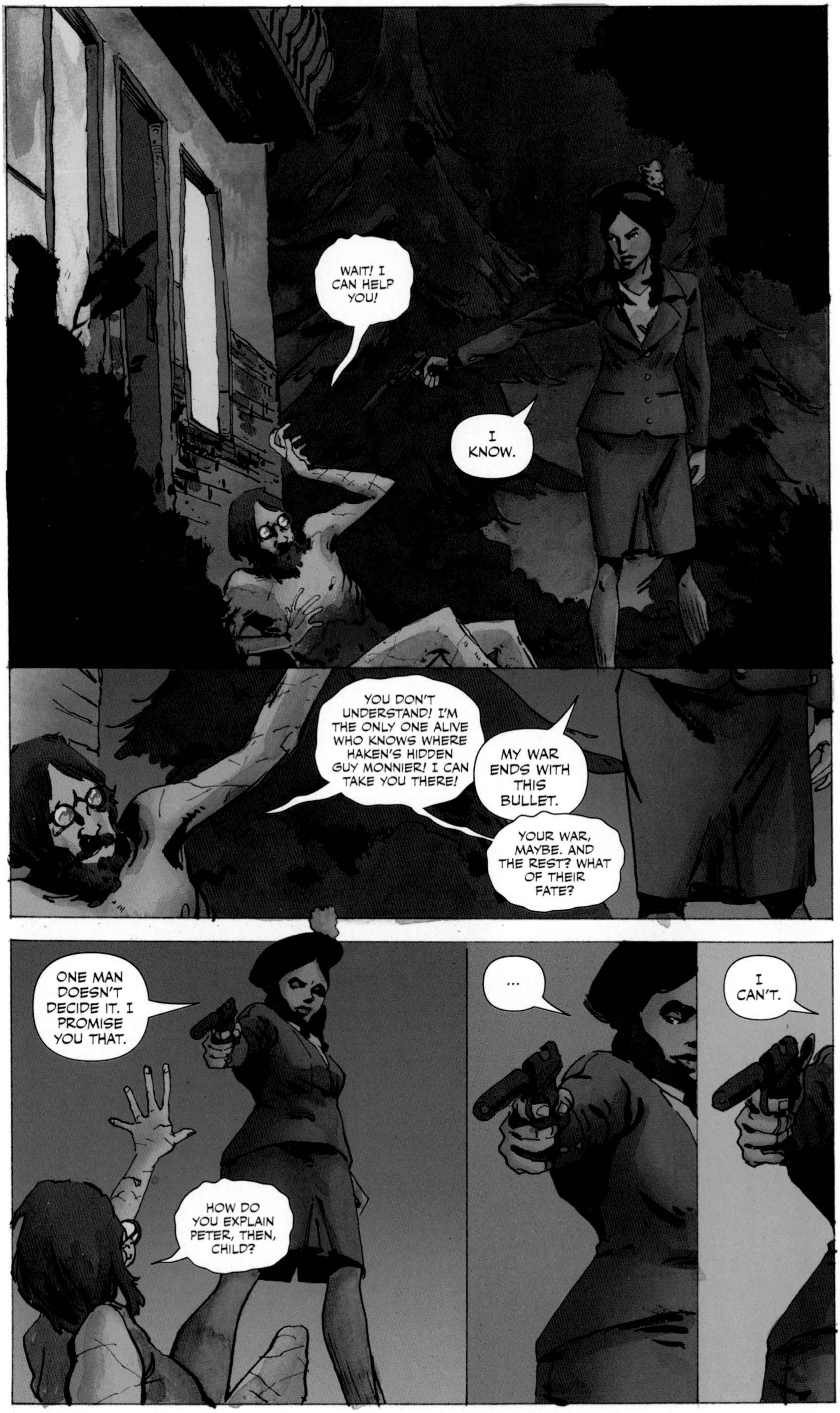
WAIT! I CAN HELP YOU!
I KNOW.
YOU DON'T UNDERSTAND! I'M THE ONLY ONE ALIVE WHO KNOWS WHERE HAKEN'S HIDDEN GUY MONNIER! I CAN TAKE YOU THERE!
MY WAR ENDS WITH THIS BULLET.
YOUR WAR, MAYBE. AND THE REST? WHAT OF THEIR FATE?
ONE MAN DOESN'T DECIDE IT. I PROMISE YOU THAT.
HOW DO YOU EXPLAIN PETER, THEN, CHILD?
...
I CAN'T.

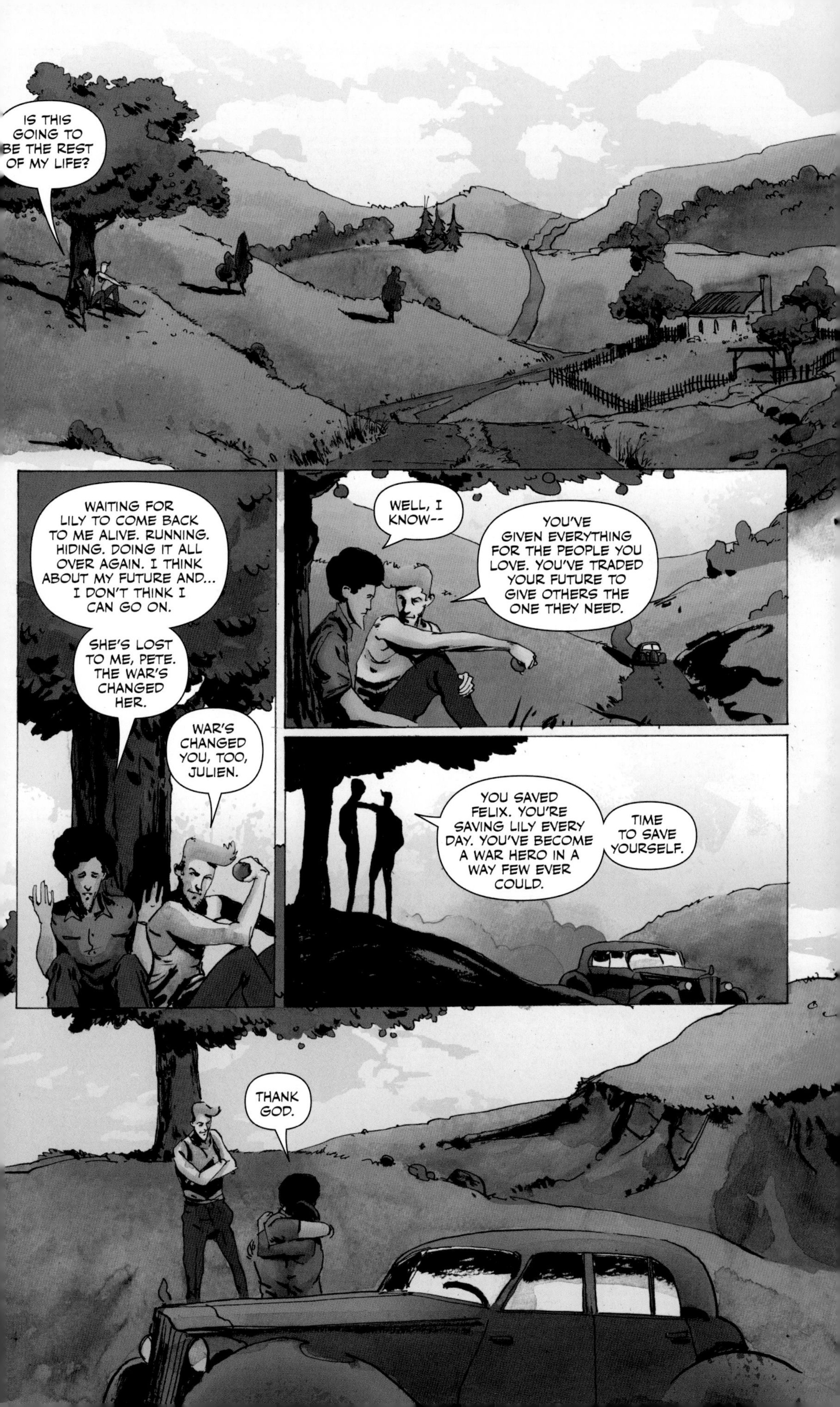
IS THIS GOING TO BE THE REST OF MY LIFE?
WAITING FOR LILY TO COME BACK TO ME ALIVE. RUNNING. HIDING. DOING IT ALL OVER AGAIN. I THINK ABOUT MY FUTURE AND... I DON'T THINK I CAN GO ON.
SHE'S LOST TO ME, PETE. THE WAR'S CHANGED HER.
WAR'S CHANGED YOU, TOO, JULIEN.
WELL, I KNOW--
YOU'VE GIVEN EVERYTHING FOR THE PEOPLE YOU LOVE. YOU'VE TRADED YOUR FUTURE TO GIVE OTHERS THE ONE THEY NEED.
YOU SAVED FELIX. YOU'RE SAVING LILY EVERY DAY. YOU'VE BECOME A WAR HERO IN A WAY FEW EVER COULD.
TIME TO SAVE YOURSELF.
THANK GOD.

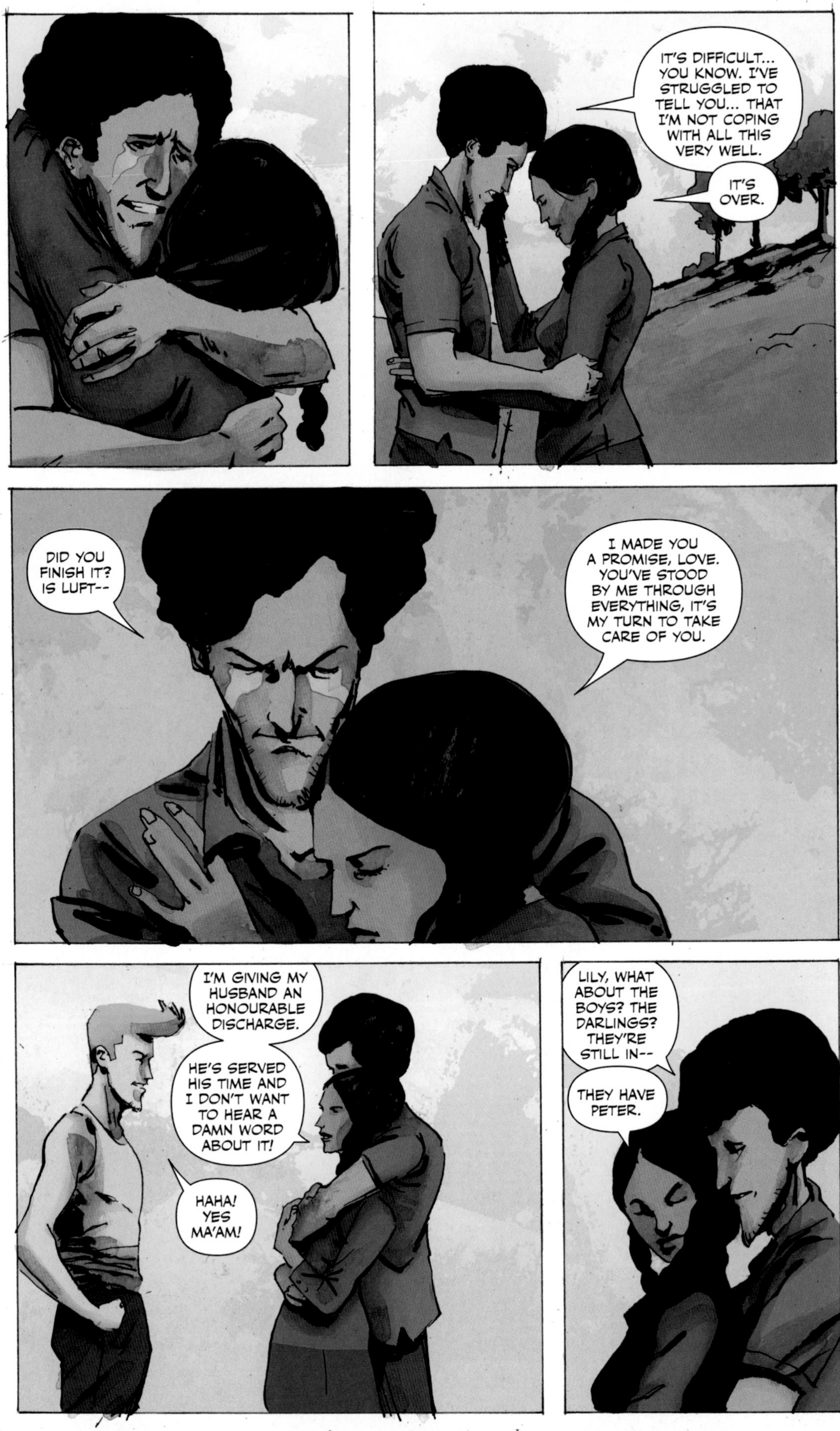
IT'S DIFFICULT... YOU KNOW. I'VE STRUGGLED TO TELL YOU... THAT I'M NOT COPING WITH ALL THIS VERY WELL.
IT'S OVER.
DID YOU FINISH IT? IS LUFT--
I MADE YOU A PROMISE, LOVE. YOU'VE STOOD BY ME THROUGH EVERYTHING, IT'S MY TURN TO TAKE CARE OF YOU.
I'M GIVING MY HUSBAND AN HONOURABLE DISCHARGE.
HE'S SERVED HIS TIME AND I DON'T WANT TO HEAR A DAMN WORD ABOUT IT!
HAHA! YES MA'AM!
LILY, WHAT ABOUT THE BOYS? THE DARLINGS? THEY'RE STILL IN--
THEY HAVE PETER.

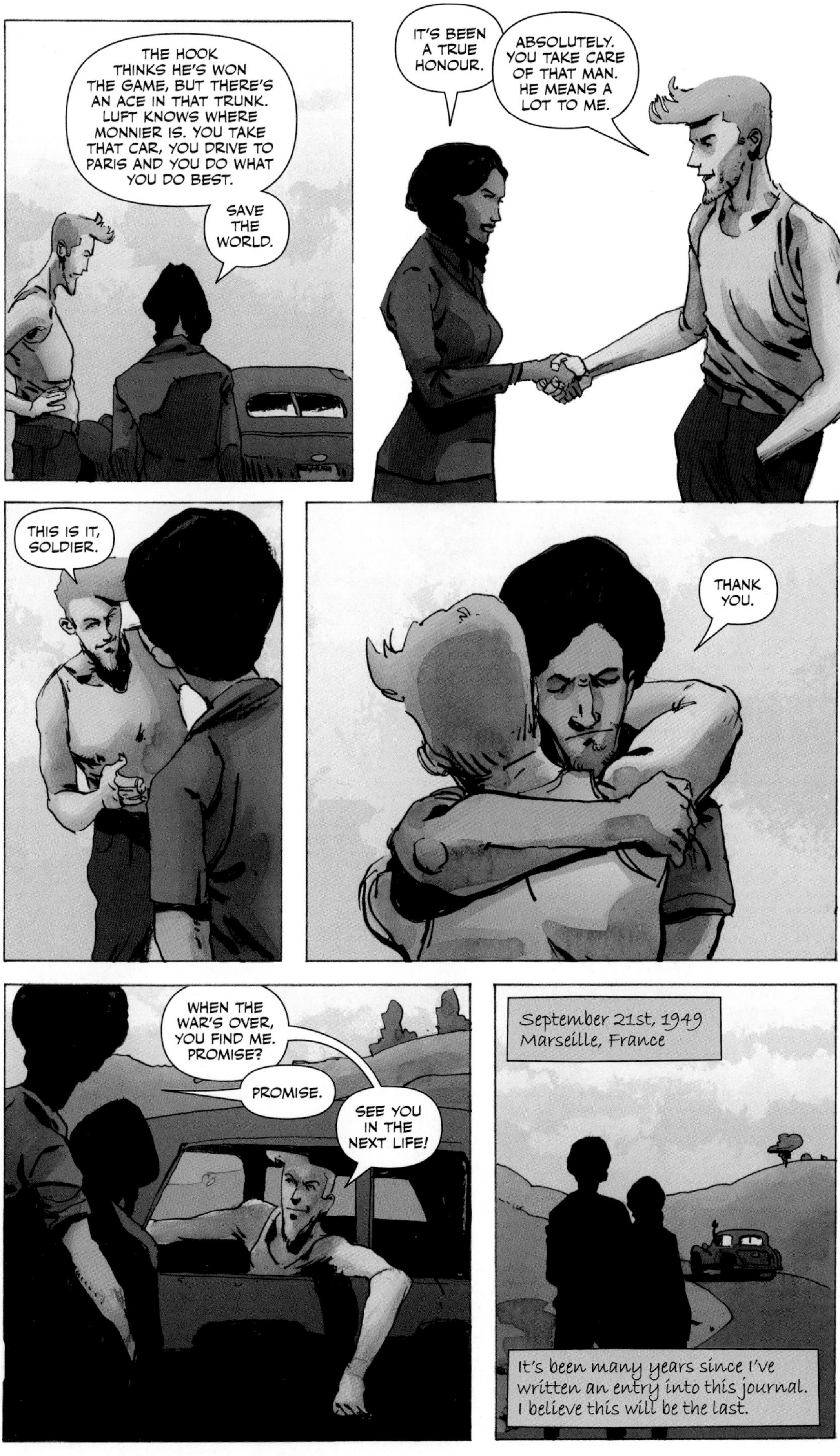
THE HOOK THINKS HE'S WON THE GAME, BUT THERE'S AN ACE IN THAT TRUNK. LUFT KNOWS WHERE MONNIER IS. YOU TAKE THAT CAR, YOU DRIVE TO PARIS AND YOU DO WHAT YOU DO BEST.
SAVE THE WORLD.
IT'S BEEN A TRUE HONOUR.
ABSOLUTELY. YOU TAKE CARE OF THAT MAN. HE MEANS A LOT TO ME.
THIS IS IT, SOLDIER.
THANK YOU.
WHEN THE WAR'S OVER, YOU FIND ME. PROMISE?
PROMISE.
SEE YOU IN THE NEXT LIFE!
September 21st, 1949
Marseille, France
It's been many years since I've written an entry into this journal. I believe this will be the last.

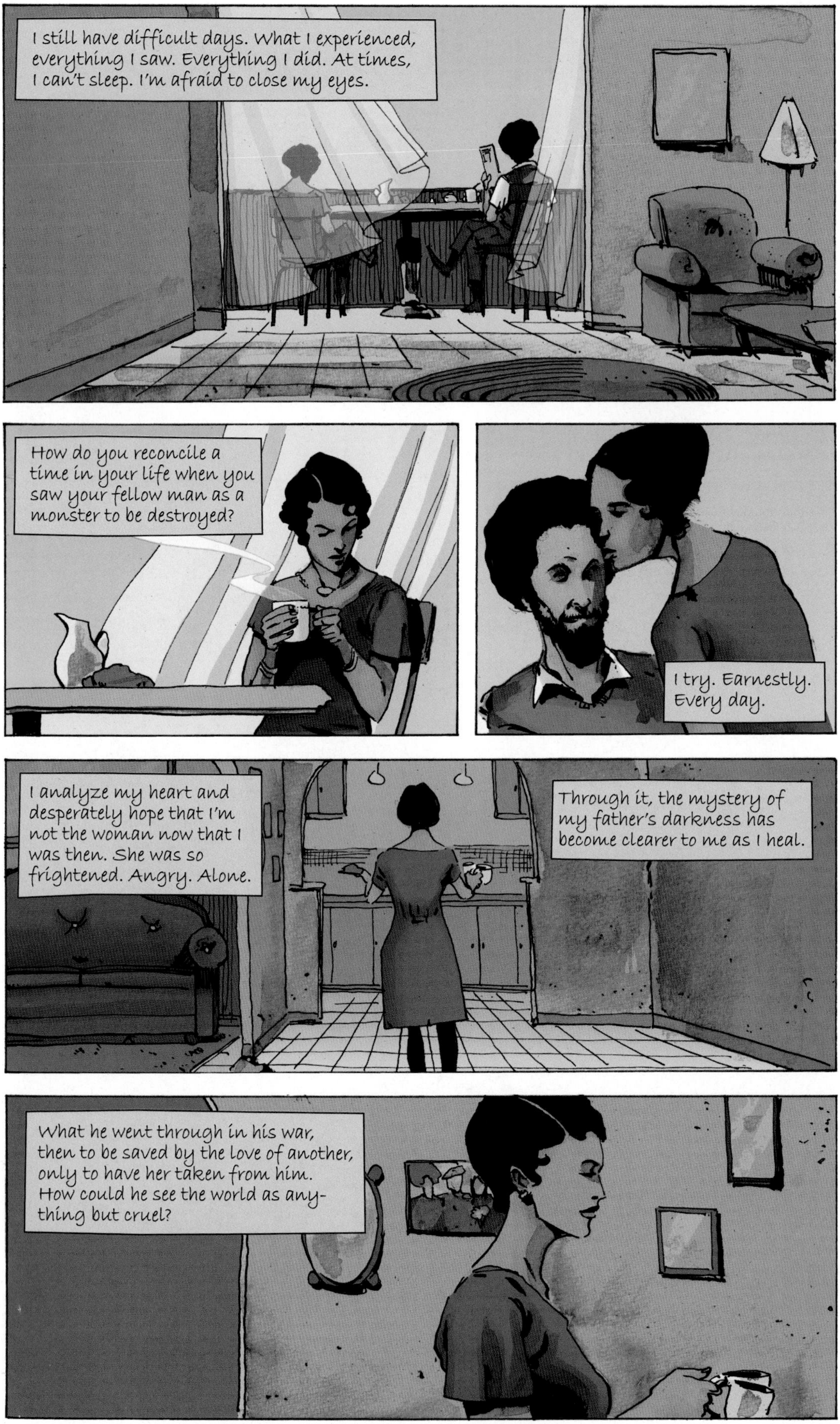
I still have difficult days. What I experienced, everything I saw. Everything I did. At times, I can't sleep. I'm afraid to close my eyes.
How do you reconcile a time in your life when you saw your fellow man as a monster to be destroyed?
I try. Earnestly. Every day.
I analyze my heart and desperately hope that I'm not the woman now that I was then. She was so frightened. Angry. Alone.
Through it, the mystery of my father's darkness has become clearer to me as I heal.
What he went through in his war, then to be saved by the love of another, only to have her taken from him. How could he see the world as any-thing but cruel?

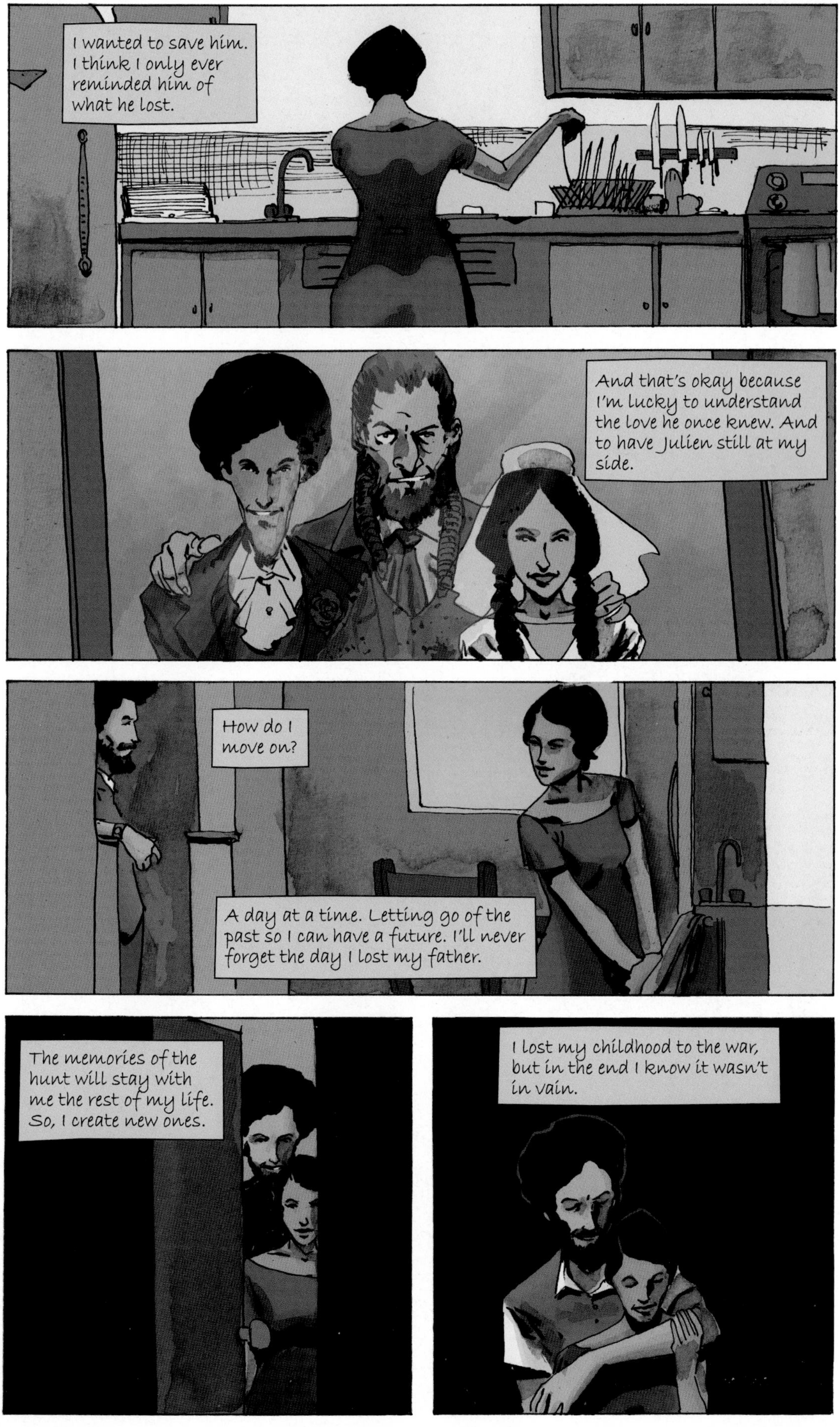
I wanted to save him. I think I only ever reminded him of what he lost.
And that's okay because I'm lucky to understand the love he once knew. And to have Julien still at my side.
How do I move on?
A day at a time. Letting go of the past so I can have a future. I'll never forget the day I lost my father.
The memories of the hunt will stay with me the rest of my life. So, I create new ones.
I lost my childhood to the war, but in the end I know it wasn't in vain.

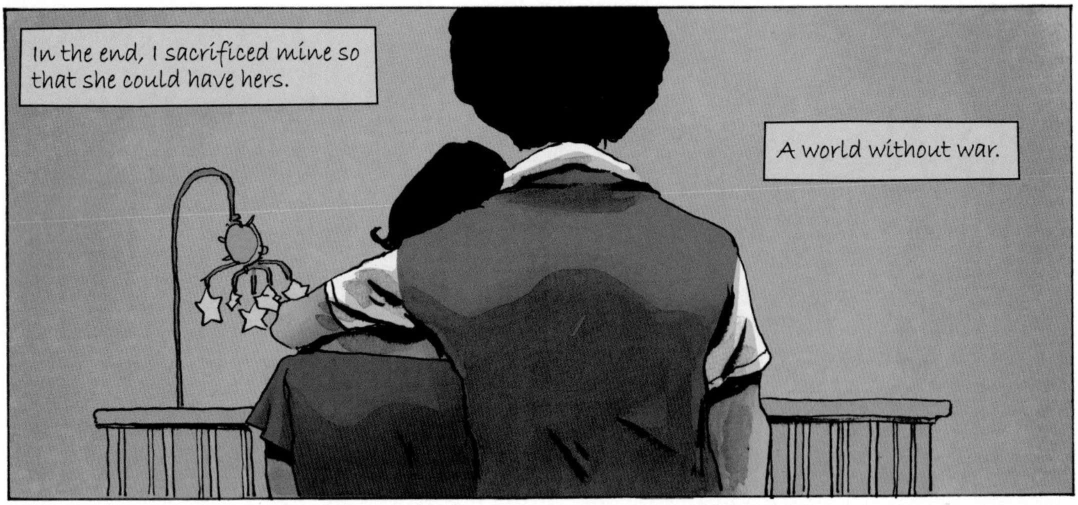
In the end, I sacrificed mine so that she could have hers.
A world without war.

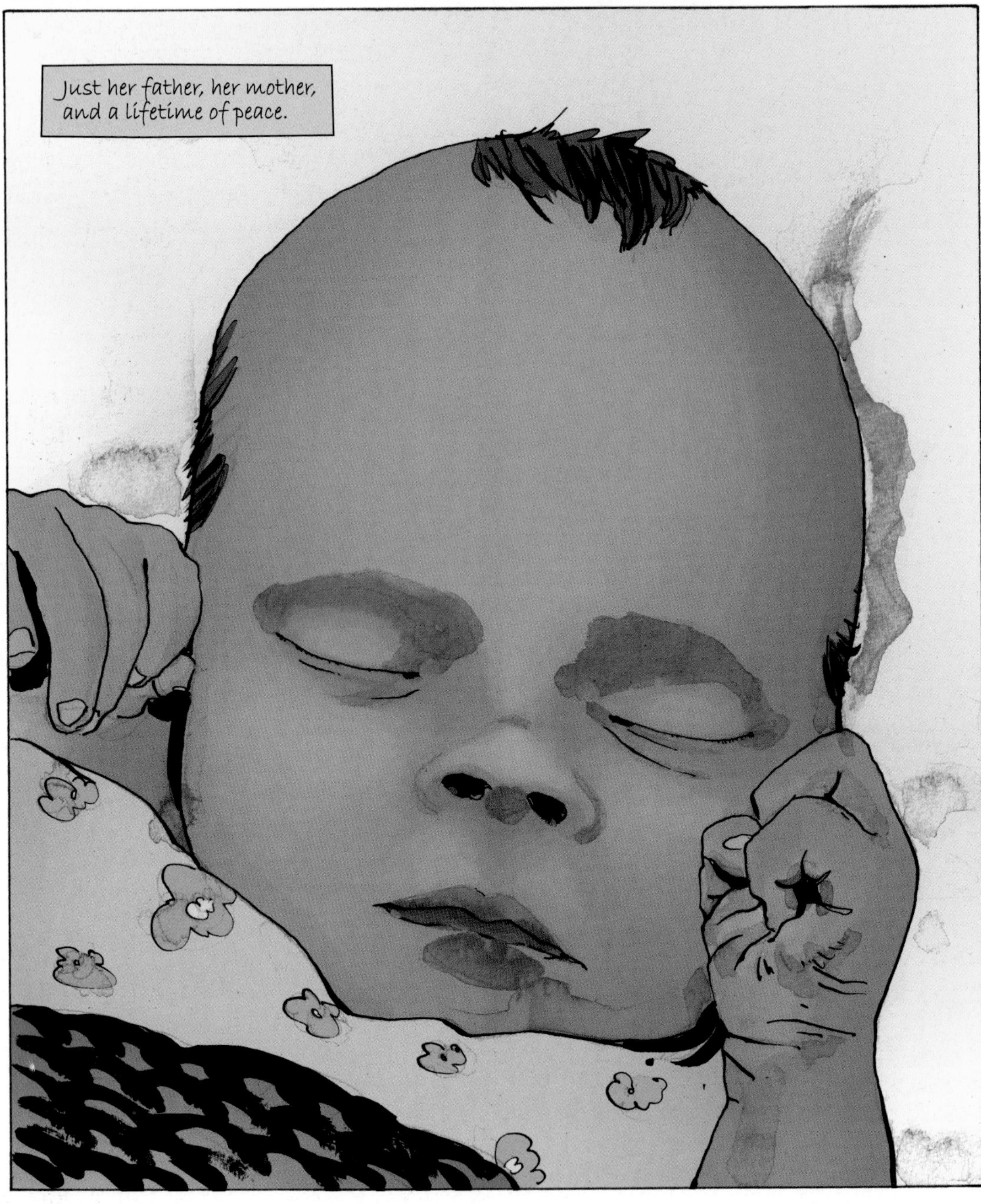
Just her father, her mother, and a lifetime of peace.

omplete your PETER PANZERFAUST library...

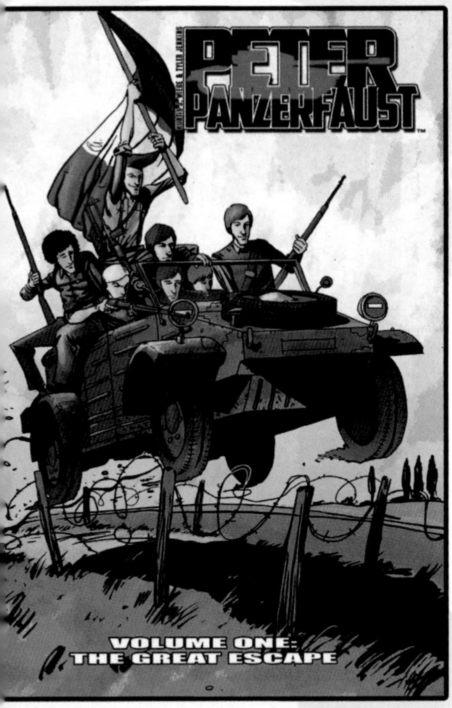
PETER PANZERFAUST
VOLUME ONE:
THE GREAT ESCAPE

OLUME ONE: THE GREAT ESCAPE
ollects Issues 1-5 with Special Features
ISBN: 978-1-60706-582-1

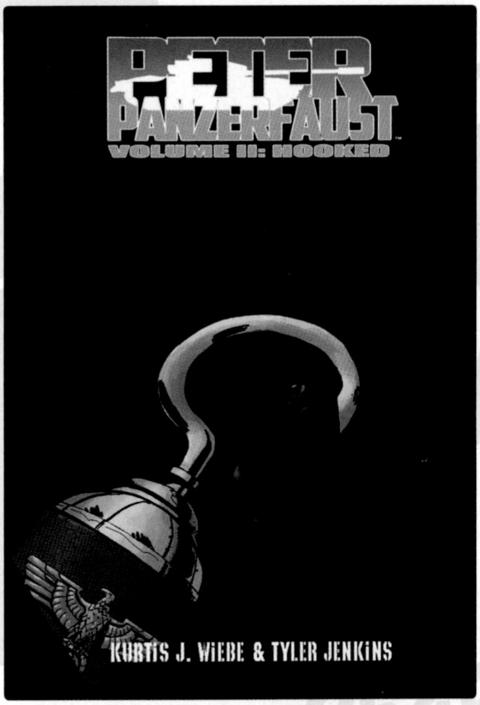
PETER PANZERFAUST
VOLUME II: HOOKED
KURTIS J. WIEBE & TYLER JENKINS

VOLUME TWO: HOOKED
Collects Issues 6-10 with Special Features
ISBN: 978-1-60706-728-3

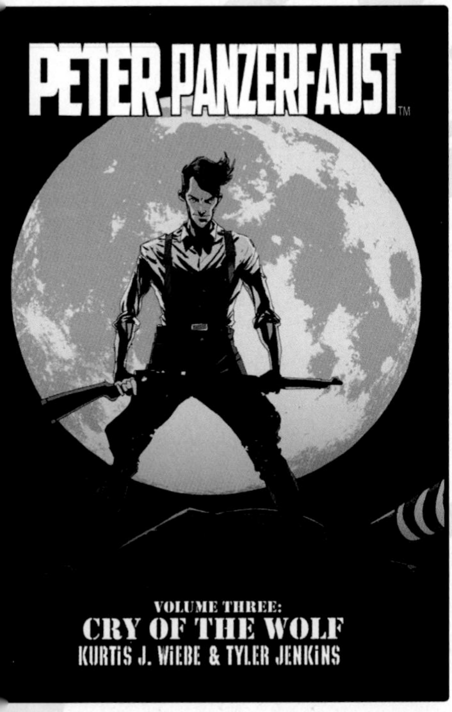
PETER PANZERFAUST
VOLUME THREE:
CRY OF THE WOLF
KURTIS J. WIEBE & TYLER JENKINS

LUME THREE: CRY OF THE WOLF
llects Issues 11-15 with Special Features
ISBN: 978-1-60706-864-8

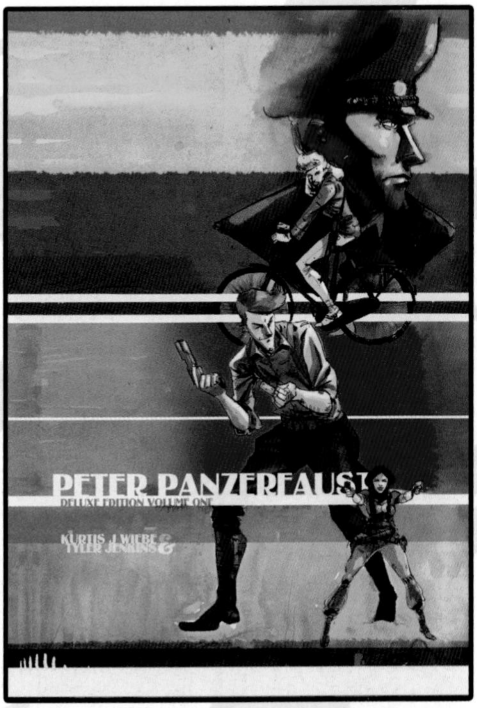
PETER PANZERFAUST
DELUXE EDITION VOLUME ONE
KURTIS J. WIEBE & TYLER JENKINS

DELUXE EDITION VOLUME ONE
Collects Issues 1-10 in a deluxe oversized hardcover. **ISBN:** 978-1-60706-968-3

n sale at finer comic stores everywhere!

THIS is diversity! Graphic Novels For the Discriminating Read

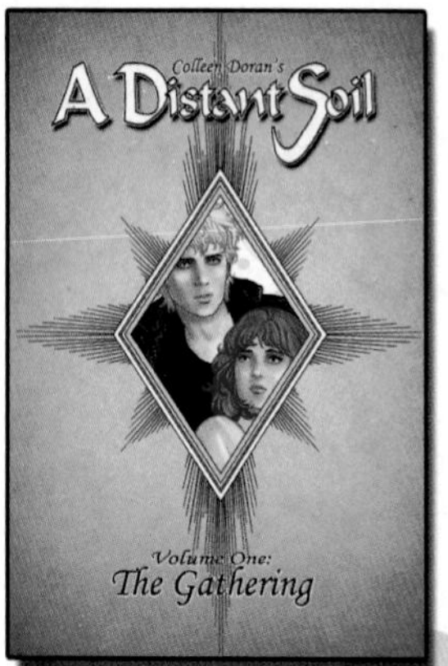
Colleen Doran's
A Distant Soil
Volume One:
The Gathering

A DISTANT SOIL

Colleen Doran's legendary magnum opus completely remastered and re-edited with beautiful new die-cut covers. Five volumes.

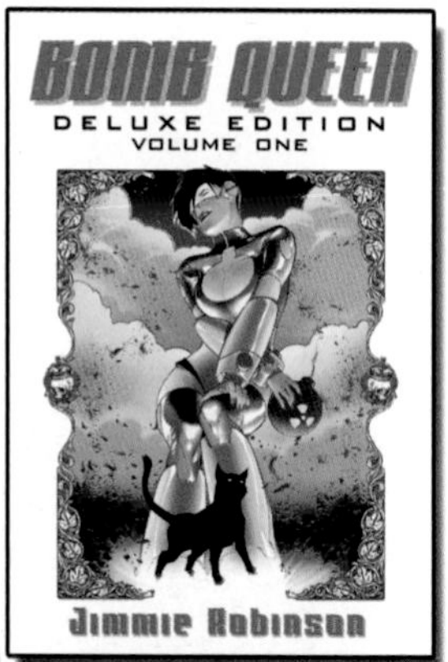
BOMB QUEEN
DELUXE EDITION
VOLUME ONE
Jimmie Robinson

BOMB QUEEN DELUXE

Jimmie Robinson's adults only satire of politics, sex and social mores. Not for the easily offended! Four Over-size hardcover volumes.

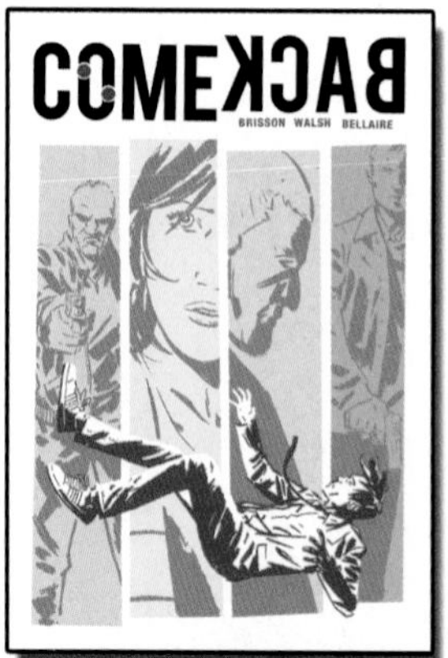
COMEBACK
BRISSON WALSH BELLAIRE

COMEBACK

Comeback is more than a company--we will bring your loved ones back moments before their untimely deaths...for a price.

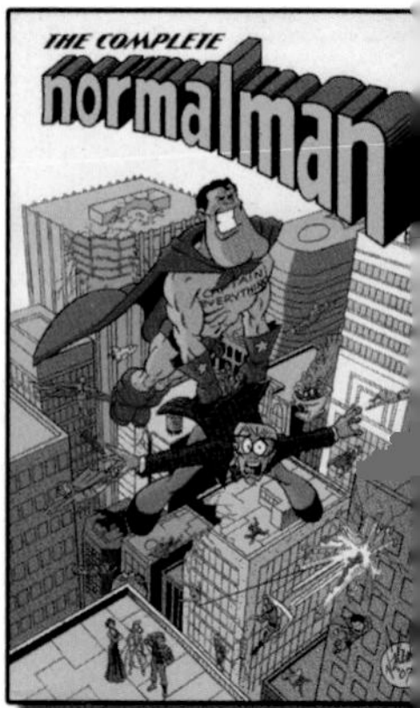
THE COMPLETE
normalman

COMPLETE normalman

The legendary classic parc series collected in c gigantic volume for the f time!

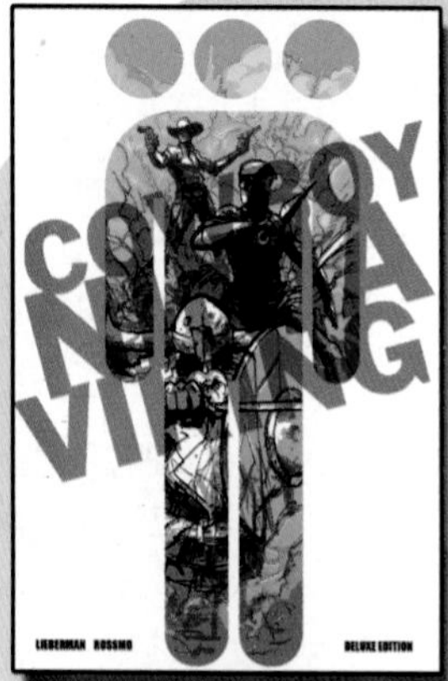
LIEBERMAN ROSSMO
DELUXE EDITION

COWBOY NINJA VIKING

Now in a Deluxe Oversize hardcover edition! Duncan has three distinct personalities...of course he's a government agent.

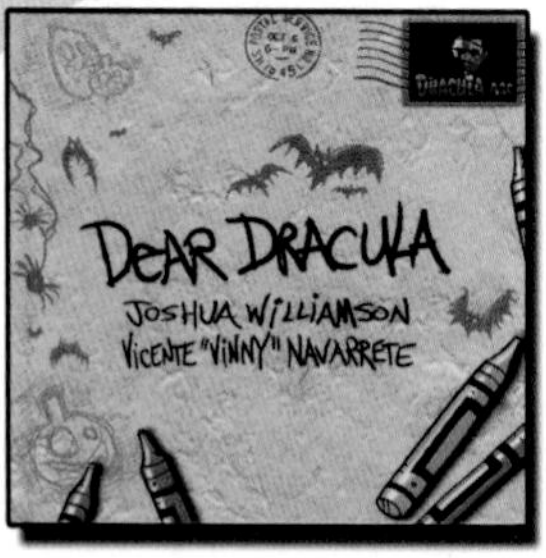
DEAR DRACULA
JOSHUA WILLIAMSON
VICENTE "VINNY" NAVARRETE

DEAR DRACULA

All Sam wants this Halloween is to become a real vampire! So he writes a letter to his hero, Count Dracula...who pays him a visit!

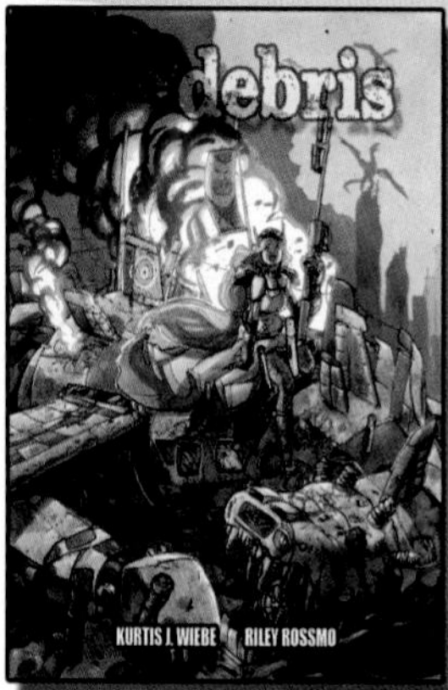
debris
KURTIS J. WIEBE
RILEY ROSSMO

DEBRIS

Maya must find a source of pure water to save the world before the garbage monsters bring it all to an end.

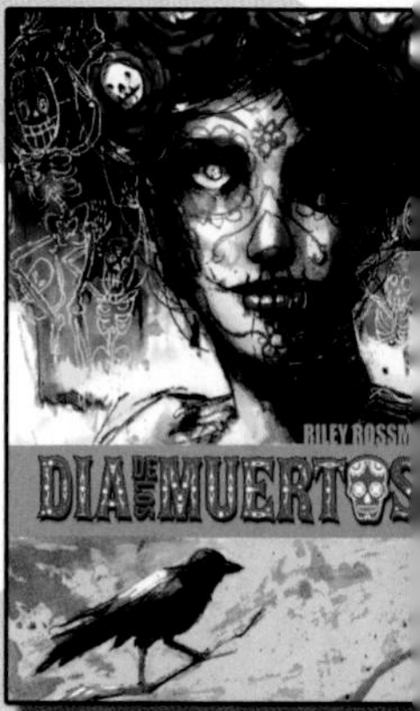

DIA DE LOS MUERTOS

Nine acclaimed writers a one amazing artist, Ri Rossmo, tell tales from Mexican Day of the Dead.

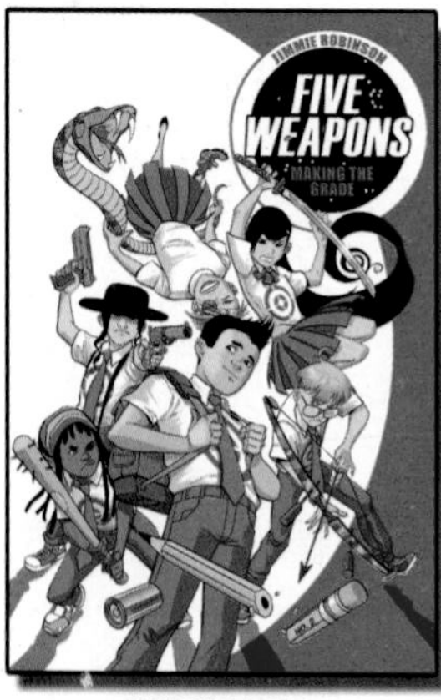
JIMMIE ROBINSON
FIVE WEAPONS
MAKING THE GRADE

FIVE WEAPONS

In a school for assassins, Tyler has the greatest of them all going for him...his mind! Jimmie Robinson's latest epic makes the grade.

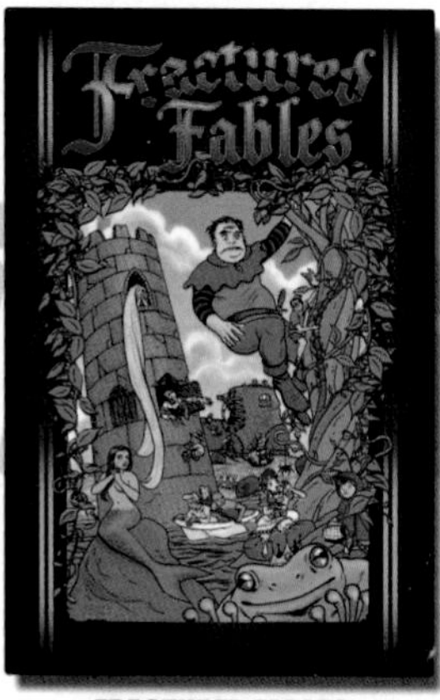
Fractured Fables

FRACTURED FABLES

Award winning cartoonists put a wicked but hilarious spin on well worn Fairy tales in this not-to-be-missed anthology.

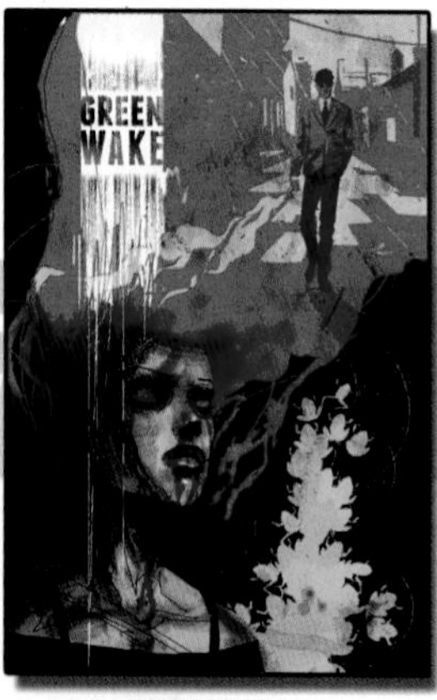
GREEN WAKE

GREEN WAKE

A riveting tale of loss and horror that blends mystery and otherworldly eccentricity in two unforgettable, critically acclaimed volumes.

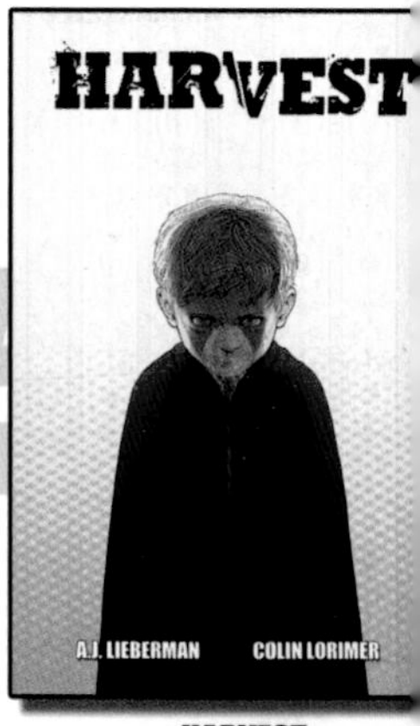
HARVEST
A.J. LIEBERMAN
COLIN LORIMER

HARVEST

Welcome to Dr. Benja Dane's nightmare. His o way out is to bring down man who set him harvesting organs.